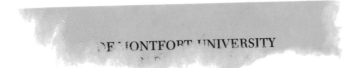

POWER AND PRIVATIZATION

Also by Joel D. Wolfe

THE POLITICS OF ECONOMIC ADJUSTMENT: Pluralism, Corporatism and Privatization (*co-editor with Richard Foglesong*)

WORKERS, PARTICIPATION AND DEMOCRACY

Power and Privatization

Choice and Competition in the Remaking of British Democracy

Joel D. Wolfe
Associate Professor of Political Science
University of Cincinnati, Ohio

First published in Great Britain 1996 by
MACMILLAN PRESS LTD
Houndmills, Basingstoke, Hampshire RG21 6XS
and London
Companies and representatives
throughout the world

A catalogue record for this book is available
from the British Library.

ISBN 0–333–63734–8

First published in the United States of America 1996 by
ST. MARTIN'S PRESS, INC.,
Scholarly and Reference Division,
175 Fifth Avenue,
New York, N.Y. 10010

ISBN 0–312–15952–8

Library of Congress Cataloging-in-Publication Data
Wolfe, Joel D.
Power and privatization : choice and competition in the remaking
of British democracy / Joel D. Wolfe.
p. cm.
Includes bibliographical references and index.
ISBN 0–312–15952–8 (cloth)
1. Privatization—Great Britain.   2. Industrial policy—Great
Britain.   I. Title.
HD4148.W658   1996
338.941—dc20   95–52540
                                                                CIP

---

10   9   8   7   6   5   4   3   2   1
05 04 03 02 01 00 99 98 97 96

Printed and bound in Great Britain by
Antony Rowe Ltd, Chippenham, Wiltshire

To
my family

Maureen Ann Wolfe
and
Conrad Patrick Wolfe

Contents

List of Tables

Acknowledgements

I am grateful to the William Taft Foundation at the University of Cincinnati for providing travel grants in the summers of 1986 and 1989 and a sabbatical grant in 1993.

In addition, I am indebted to numerous libraries and individuals. The staff at the Langsam Library at the University of Cincinnati has been helpful throughout. The British Library of Political and Economic Science, the TUC Library, the OFTEL Library and the now defunct Royal Institute of Public Administration Library provided access to a wide range of publications. In addition, I learned much from conversations with specialists in British politics, in particular Alan Beattie, Patrick Dunleavy, Desmond King, Julian Le Grand, Stephen Glaister, David Thomas, Geoff Whitty and Kenneth Wiltshire. I appreciate the comments of Jill Hills and Jack Hayward on earlier parts of this project.

In the final stages, I am much obliged to Gerard Braunthal, who commented on the entire manuscript in detail. Henry Winkler made valuable comments on Chapter 2. For Chapter 7, Chris Howell provided helpful comments and research materials. Luis Lobos-Fernandes commented insightfully on several chapters. Also, I am grateful to Michael Margolis, whose administrative and moral support, helped sustain my effort.

Finally, I thank my wife, Maureen, who gave help and encouragement and my son, Conrad, who as a toddler provided both distraction and renewal. Responsibility for any remaining errors is mine.

JOEL D. WOLFE

Abbreviations

ACAS	Advisory, Conciliation and Arbitration Service
AEU	Amalgamated Engineering Union (formerly AUEW)
APEX	Association of Professional, Executive, Clerical and Computer Staffs
ASTMS	Association of Scientific, Technical and Managerial Staff
AUEW	Amalgamated Union of Engineering Workers
BA	British Airways
BAe	British Aerospace
BAA	British Airports Authority
BIFU	Banking, Insurance and Finance Union
BG	British Gas
BL	British Leyland
BT	British Telecommunications
BTUC	British Telecommunications Union Committee
BP	British Petroleum
BR	British Rail
CAA	Civil Aviation Authority
C&W	Cable and Wireless
CBI	Confederation of British Industry
CCT	Compulsory Competitive Tendering
CEGB	Central Electricity Generating Board
COHSE	Confederation of Health Service Employees
CPS	Centre for Policy Studies
CWU	Communication Workers' Union
DES	Department of Education and Science
DG	Director General
DGT	Director General of Telecommunications
DHSS	Department of Health and Social Security
DLO	Direct labour (public sector) organization
DTI	Department of Trade and Industry
EC	European Community
EEC	European Economic Community
EETPU	Electrical, Electronic, Telecommunications and Plumbing Union
ERA	Education Reform Act 1988
ERM	Exchange Rate Mechanism

ESI	Electricity Supply Industry
EU	European Union
GCHQ	Government Communications Headquarters (Cheltenham)
GDP	Gross Domestic Product
GEC	General Electric Co
GMB	General, Municipal, Boilermakers and Allied Trades Union
IEA	Institute for Economic Affairs
IMF	International Monetary Fund
KIO	Kuwaiti Investment Organization
LEA	Local Education Authority
LSE	London School of Economics
MCL	Mercury Communications Ltd.
MMC	Monopoly and Mergers Commission
MP	Members of Parliament
MSF	Manufacturing, Science and Finance Union
MTFS	Medium Term Financial Strategy
NALGO	National and Local Government Officers' Association
NCU	National Communications Union
NEB	National Enterprise Board
NEDC	National Economic Development Council
NFC	National Freight Consortium
NGA	National Graphical Association
NHS	National Health Service
NPIB	National Prices and Incomes Board
NUM	National Union of Mineworkers
NUPE	National Union of Public Employees
NUR	National Union of Railwaymen
NUS	National Union of Seafarers
OFTEL	Office of Telecommunications
OFGAS	Office of Gas Supply
OFWAT	Office of Water Services
OFFER	Office of Electricity Regulation
OFT	Office of Fair Trading
PABX	Private automatic branch exchanges
PMR	Private mobile radio
PNCs	Personal communication networks
POEU	Post Office Engineering Union
PTE	Passenger Transport Executives
RMT	National Union of Rail, Maritime and Transport Workers
RPI-X	Retail Price Index minus X
PSBR	Public Sector Borrowing Requirement

SOGAT	Society of Graphical and Allied Trades
STE	Society of Telecom Executives
TASS	Technical Administrative and Supervisory Section of the AUEW
TGWU	Transport and General Workers Union
TSB	Trustees Savings Bank
TUC	Trades Union Congress
TURERA	Trade Union Reform and Employment Rights Act 1993
UCATT	Union of Construction, Allied Trades and Technicians
UCW	Union of Communications Workers
VANS	Value-added network services
WAA	Water Authorities Association

Introduction

Since the 1970s the growth of ideas about the virtues of choice, competition, and efficiency has changed the way public policy is conceived and made. The focus on monetarism gave way in the early 1980s to a more significant programme of privatization and deregulation. In turning to privatization, the governments of Margaret Thatcher installed the market as a medium of policy-making. Building on success in one sector after another private commercial processes came to encompass an ever wider variety of ways of deciding and implementing public sector ends. Her successor, John Major, pressed this Thatcherite or neoliberal agenda forward.

During the 1980s and the 1990s privatization grew into a major global movement. Reaping £60 billion since 1980, the privatization programme in Britain succeeded in significantly reshaping the balance in the relationship between state and society. Similar but more limited measures followed in numerous advanced and developing nations. The United States, though moving slowly to sell-off public assets, experienced a significant shift toward deregulation. France implemented major sell-offs of state assets in the late 1980s and early 1990s. In the former Communist countries large-scale privatization programmes are taking place. In terms of value, sales in Latin America have been proportionately higher than in any other region. Overall returns from sales of public assets since 1985 total $328 billion; plans for future privatizations would double that figure. In pioneering states like Britain, New Zealand, Chile and France, privatization has been more ideologically motivated and more encompassing; elsewhere it has been a more limited response to pragmatic needs. However, the huge financial returns on the sale of state assets obscures the political motives, scope, and effects of privatization.

The popularity of privatization among governments of both left and right reflects an ideological convergence on how to deal with budgetary and other economic problems. The *Economist* (August 21, 1993) recently summed up reasons for selling public assets: 'One [motive] is to shrink the state, in pursuit of greater economic efficiency; the other is to raise cash'. Private ownership and the threat of bankruptcy purportedly compel managers to make choices that improve value for money (efficiency), facilitate making government regulation of private firms more overt and specific, and motivate higher productivity and responsiveness to consumer demands. Stimulating economic growth and efficiency by reducing state

1

interference and using the yields on public assets sales to finance tax cuts dominate political debates and the headlines.

Moreover, advocates argue that an even more fundamental benefit of privatization is to enlarge individual choice and freedom. In the words of proponent Cento Veljanovski, 'The link between private property, markets and liberty is a strong one and is the primary defence of privatisation' (1987, p. 206). For Margaret Thatcher, privatization 'was one of the central means of reversing the corrosive and corrupting effects of socialism...[and] is at the centre of any programme of reclaiming territory for freedom' (1993, p. 676). In short, by reducing state control privatization purportedly increases individual choice or freedom and enhances democracy (cf. Almond, 1991).

In examining the political effects of privatization, most journalists and academic economists simply confirm the virtues of economic competition and its contribution to democracy. Cento Veljanovski's *Selling the State* (1987), Vickers and Yarrow's *Privatization* (1988), and C.D. Foster's *Privatization, Public Ownership and the Regulation of Natural Monopoly* (1992) are important examples of economists thinking from the British literature. Political analysts like Shirley Letwin in *The Anatomy of Thatcherism* (1992) take a similar view. Many political scientists and commentators, however, view privatization as one aspect of political leadership imbued with powerful ideas. There are many useful and fascinating books in this group, for example, Peter Jenkins' and Hugo Young's biographies of Thatcher, Peter Riddell's survey of the Thatcher years, Dennis Kavanagh's more scholarly *Thatcherism and British Politics* (1990), and Jeremy Moon's *Innovative Leadership in Democracy: Policy Change Under Thatcher* (1993).

These writers reveal the implicit, though occasionally conscious, use of a commonly accepted concept of power. Focusing on the impact of public opinion, the institutional power of Prime Ministerial government, the personal leadership of Margaret Thatcher or John Major, or the way groups comprising policy communities respond to policy failure rely on notions of sovereign agents asserting forces or pressures on other sovereign agents. Economists' thinking assumes autonomous agents voluntarily and freely making mutually advantageous exchanges. Their idealization of pure market exchange conceptually fixes freedom as mutually agreed trade-off between equal economic agents. Because privatization promotes such market exchange relations, it advances individual autonomy and freedom. This set of analysts of privatization rely on what political scientists call agency models of power, overt contests of strength between agents in which one uses his or her resources to get the other to do what he or she otherwise would not.

A second set of analysts explains the political effects of privatization by invoking objective mechanisms and processes as force-bearing entities. These more abstract explanations utilize what political scientists call structural models. They include public choice, state-centric, and marxist analyses. Public choice models explain how offering individuals advantageous trade-offs promote private sector activity. In his *Micropolitics*, Madsen Pirie (1988a) uses a public choice approach to show how political leaders can restructure the public sector by changing individuals' material incentives. The state-centric analyses focus on how the organizational structure of the state and other institutions like political parties, capital, and labour explain political capacity. Peter Hall's (1986) suggestion that the organization of state, capital, and labour in Britain would retard radical policy-making exemplifies this approach. Finally, marxists argue that a crisis in capitalist class relations enables a government to assume a near authoritarian posture toward society. Freed of domination by class power, the state imposes free markets, compelling workers in turn to accept lower wages and to increase their productivity, and centralizes policy-making in other areas. Andrew Gamble's *The Free Economy and the Strong State* (1988), Stuart Hall's and Martin Jacques' *The Politics of Thatcherism* (1983), and Bob Jessop's *et al.*, *Thatcherism* (1988) illustrate the use of a marxist perspective to connect privatization to state power.

Each produces a distinctive picture of neoliberal politics, whether through agent causality or institutional capacity. What is common, however, is a reliance on assumptions that depict power as coercion, imposition, or conquest. Power is the external, objective, and direct application of force. Yet, a focus on direct power restricts explanation. It focuses attention on how privatization serves the ends of one force in opposition to others. Different analyses identify different victors; they include the capitalist and financial elites, the Conservative party, the state, the person of Margaret Thatcher, and the mass public. In short, models of direct power visualize who prevails in imposing their will and who benefits from it by the way they predetermine encounters between victor and vanquished.

Challenging the neoliberal contention that privatization increases freedom and democracy, then, requires more than conceptually reshuffling combatants. Thomas Kuhn argued in *The Structure of Scientific Revolutions* (1970) that scientific paradigms represented the triumph of a worldview and could not be refuted by simple empirical falsification. What did lead to shifts in paradigms was a growing uncertainty in a paradigm's ability to solve problems and the development of alternatives aspiring to be more emotionally as well as intellectually satisfying. A new paradigm asked different questions, while giving new perspective to old ones. Similarly, challenging neoliberalism requires undermining the reigning certitude about the virtues of the free market. This means seeing privatization and its consequences from a new perspective. Only a different paradigm, an alternative approach to politics, can offer this possibility.

Drawing on the pragmatist thought of John Dewey, I present an analysis of power that advances beyond the agency model of pluralist thinking and the structuralist models developed by public choice, state-centric, or marxists scholars. This pragmatist approach distinguishes between *direct power* involving sovereign agents who externally impose behaviour and *indirect or internally motivated control* where activity-defining situations regulate particular behaviour. Further, the pragmatist approach suggests a framework for analyzing the form or structure of power relations. As will be seen, ideas are central to shaping power relations or the control of collective doings, providing the connections that constitute forms of power. Agents use ideas as tools to provide the grounds warranting action, to identify the possibilities for initiatives, and to define the criteria for making judgments. Analyzing how privatization reflects variations in relationships between the types and forms of power makes it possible to clarify relations of control.

From this viewpoint, privatization poses two sets of questions. The first concerns types of power. Can privatization operate as a type of power? Can privatization itself constitute a response to a problem of governance or political control? How did privatization operate to facilitate the reforms of Thatcher and Major governments when previous governments were immobilized by the collectivist policy process and how does it work to sustain them?

Reconceptualizing privatization as a response to a problem of governance directs attention to how privatization itself advances governments' ability to control their environments. In this book, I show how state authorities found in privatization a way to use market-driven decision-making processes to shape the way interests are represented and public choices made. Control through markets is not just as a substitute or surrogate for government decision-making; it does not function as another, albeit nonpolitical, form of coercion. The market rather adds to the blunt, public, and costly use of direct force a more efficient, flexible, and individualized form of control. This indirect control facilitates the extension of state power into new domains.

The argument that the market functions as an indirect type of state control has two components. First, market-driven control is indirect, deriving from the participation of individuals in market situations. Market situations engage actors in calculations about possible rewards and losses and games about advantageous trade-offs. These situations define the ends and standards of behaviour, while being dynamic, open-ended, and totalizing. This is evident in the law of comparative advantage, which explains the generation and regeneration of the specialization in the division of labor and the consequent shifts in wealth and poverty. Most important, commercial transactions establish a regimen that guides participation, drawing on agents' internal motives, skills in economic transactions, and knowledge of prevailing external market circumstances. Second, while government officials cannot directly control market actors or activities, they can institute, monitor, participate in, and redirect its behaviour. The state changes the rules and shape of the playing field, monitors behaviour for violations of acceptable practices, and even acts as a player in market activities. Occasionally, the government directly intervenes to impose penalties, settle conflicts, or to impose a certain market pattern. In short, the market itself becomes a self-operating and indirect medium of state control, overseen and guided by direct political power.

Second, the pragmatist standpoint questions how privatization affects the form of power. What are the consequences of this type of control for the form or distribution of effective power relations? How does privatization affect which values predominate, who initiates actions, and what method decides outcomes. How do marketizing reforms change representation, participation, and choice in democracy?

Privatizing policy-making diminished freedom and thereby democracy in three ways. First, by ending inclusive representation and political consensus, privatization narrowed political debate and prohibited the posing of alternative values. The basic or dominant values – those of market logic, economic institutions, and managerial elites – marginalized other, non-economic perspectives. As a mode of indirect control, economic practices rely on the givens of economic thinking to warrant action and justify outcomes. In becoming a faith, neoliberalism also squashed intelligent discussion about alternative visions of politics.

Second, privatization strengthened the state's capacity because it enlarged its ability to shape the agenda and to determine which interests had priority. In turning to market types of decision-making, the government established the agenda and gave initiative to those with commercial skills and resources. Commercializing decision-making succeeded because the Thatcherites employed private transactions to engage key actors in the process of reform and post-reform policy-making. In so doing, markets drew on the energies of key individuals and institutions and directed them into productive, self-driven activities. In using business aims and practices to set the agenda and decide outcomes, political leaders largely marginalized non-economic interests, effectively excluding them from decision-making. In drawing on agents' own inner motivation and capability for utilizing economic resources, thus, market-driven decision-making takes advantage of and benefits those with market skills, confidence and resources, facilitating and rewarding risk-taking.

Third, utilizing the single criterion of optimizing returns in the making of decisions elevates instrumental rationality or the efficiency of means into the predominant and substantive value. Efficiency triumphs over all other values and demands greater productivity in the use of resources and labour. Markets assign everything its price and subject it to potential trade-offs. Efficiency does propel economic growth; however, absolute aggregate gains coincide with increasing gaps in relative standing among participants. Contrary to the way it has been presented by recent Conservative governments and sympathetic commentators, the result of these 'economic' practices limit participation to business and government, while marginalizing or excluding the interests and worldviews of workers, the unemployed, and consumers. Market participation and choice, in sum, replaces popular political participation and representative democracy.

Chapter 1 develops a pragmatist analysis of power and derives hypotheses explaining how the market can function as a form of indirect state power, enhancing its control of the political environment. The study then turns to a detailed analysis of power and privatization in Mrs Thatcher's and in some cases Mr Major's Britain, testing hypotheses about the indirect model of state control. Chapter 2 examines the crisis of governability that gave rise to ideological change. Chapter 3 details the way in which the ideology and strategy of privatization prescribes reforms to enhance state power. Chapter 4 presents an analysis of the policy process involved in the programme of selling-off state assets, showing the important role of ideas and intelligent problem-solving in the development of a reform programme utilizing market transactions to institute a politics based of indirect controls. The sale of British Telecom (BT) is a major focus. Chapter 5 examines how market-based indirect controls operate in post-privatized regulated monopoly sectors, with particular reference to the telecommunications sector. It looks at the process of competitive tendering and contracting out to private sector providers by public sector authorities. Chapter 6 studies cases of deregulation, in which commercial practices become the driving force of public policy making. Cases focus on bus deregulation and the role of markets in education. Chapter 7 examines the marketizing of trade union associational activity, making organization membership depend on individual choices about the return on individual expenditure. Finally, Chapter 8 develops the image of 'privatized democracy' and asks about the future of democracy in Britain.

1 Explaining the Politics of Privatization

The neoliberal programme of the Thatcher and Major administrations in Britain provides a clear and well-developed case for examining the role of New Right ideas in policy-making. Described by journalist Peter Jenkins as 'The Thatcher Revolution', the Conservative governments after 1979 broke the Keynesian social democratic mold that had dominated British politics after WWII. Britain offers the leading case of privatization, where privatization started and has gone the farthest and is most clearly theorized as a governing ideology and analyzed by a wide range of scholars.

Privatization proved a fertile design, applicable to a wide range of problems. Christopher Johnson neatly summarizes the scope and pace of the programme:

> Privatization was not part of the Thatcherite vocabulary during the years of Conservative Opposition. It subsequently came to cover a wide range of policies affecting different parts of the economy. First there was the right of sitting tenants to buy their homes from councils. Then there was the contracting out of central and local government services to private sub-contractors. Most central, but slowest to emerge, was the sale to the private sector of state shareholdings, nationalized industries and other public corporations. Finally, and most hesitantly, there were attempts to boost the small private component in largely public services such as education, health and social services.   (1991, pp. 144–5)

During the Thatcher years, then, while the core institutions of cabinet government remained largely unchanged, significant changes took place in the relationship between state and society, within the organization of the state itself, and means by which public policy operated (Fry, 1988; Jones, 1989; Atkinson, 1990). Since 1979 the British Conservative party has privatized most of the state industries and introduced market discipline into many areas of social provision. According to Madsen Pirie, 'Taken together the privatization programme in Britain probably marked the largest transfer of power and property since the dissolution of the monasteries under Henry VIII' (1988b, p. 4). The sell-off of state industry cut the industrial public sector in half, moving over 650,000 workers to the

7

private sector, trebling the proportion of share-owners to about 20 per cent, and shifting owner-occupation from 57 per cent in 1979 to 68 per cent in 1989 (Grimstone, 1990, p. 3; Marsh and Rhodes, 1992a, p. 35; Marsh, 1991, pp. 463–4). Furthermore, privatization in Britain inspired a movement that now affects over 100 countries around the world (see Letwin, 1988).

State organization and interest group power also changed. Thatcherites reduced the responsibilities of and financial authority of local governments. Ironically, the weakening local government autonomy, the increases in spending on law and order, the diminishment of the civil service, and the rejection of open government were the manifestations and not causes of central state autonomy (Dunleavy, 1989, p. 415; Peele, 1988; King, 1987). And Government reestablished its authority over trades unions (Marsh and Rhodes, 1992, p. 41).

Yet, how privatization was achieved and how it affects democracy remains controversial. Did these changes involve a new way of governing or a change in democratic power relations? Two types of answer have been provided: those utilizing an agency model of power and those applying a structuralist or objectivist model. The agency model pictures sovereign agents such as individual leaders vying for influence, their success depending on their total resources. The structuralist models portray power in terms of objective forces, such as capital or the state shaping the behaviour of individual agents, either constraining action or transforming agents into bearers of institutional interests and dispositions.

AGENCY AND STRUCTURALIST MODELS OF POWER

One agency model explanation, the theory of party democracy, pictures voters as main agents influencing policy. Yet, as Ivor Crewe and Donald Searing (1988) have shown, the changes in policy introduced by Thatcher governments did not follow the electorate nor did they make public opinion supportive of further measures. Similarly, Ian McAllister and Donley Studlar (1989) demonstrate that privatization policies resulted from elite-initiatives rather than demands from the electorate. And Nigel Lawson, as Financial Secretary at the Treasury, Energy Secretary, and then Chancellor of the Exchequer, acknowledged that in the case of privatization government policy disregarded public opinion: 'In advance of every significant privatization, public opinion was invariably hostile to the idea, and there was no way it could be won round except by the Government going ahead and doing it' (1992, p. 201). More generally, in reference to Thatcher's success Robert Skidelsky insightfully concludes, 'The voters were not imbued with her cause, but they realized that the old regime was bankrupt and that something new had to be tried' (Skidelsky, 1988, p. 2). If public opinion did not lead, the electoral outcome did give the new Thatcher government space within which to try implementing a new method of democratic government. If the British electorate, then, did not demand the break with postwar Keynesian social democracy, what other explanations have been offered?

A second agency model answer is the institutional framework of cabinet government, that the British parliamentary system fosters an elective dictatorship. From this viewpoint, the British party, parliamentary and unitary structures provide the government, and especially the Prime Minister, with a concentration of power unparalleled in constitutional systems based on the separation of powers, permitting a radical Prime Minister the privilege of imposing a new order. Yet this argument fails. Thatcher's immediate predecessors, as concerned about and determined to reverse Britain's political debilitation and economic decline as she, did not find that the British constitutional order gave them automatic autonomy in a 'differentiated polity' (Budge and McKay, 1993). Conservative Prime Minister Edward Heath, in robust fashion, first tried free market and then corporatist strategies in an effort to gain control over inflation and unemployment, only to find his policies checked by organized labour. Labour Prime Ministers Harold Wilson and James Callaghan strove to no avail to enlist the union movement's commitment to cooperative pro- grammes (social contracts) designed to legitimate public policy and reverse national economic decline.

A third type of agency model account of power, the pluralist, portrays numerous pressures on British governments and partly autonomous networks of key policy-makers in various sectors. The result has been described as one of fragmentation and weakness (Budge and McKay, 1993; Punnett, 1988). Important pluralist analyses of privatization in Britain are found in the work of Jeremy Richardson and his associates, although the range of pluralist analyses of Thatcherism is much broader (Marsh and Rhodes, 1992b). Utilizing concepts of 'policy community', 'issue networks,' and 'internalized policy-making', Richardson, Maloney and Rudig (1992, pp. 157–75) show in a detailed study of water privatiz- ation the break-up of a stable policy community of functional interests with shared attitudes and exclusive participation. The Conservative gov- ernments' plans to privatize water, encouraged in part by leading members of the water industry's management, provoked changes in the way policy was made. Proposed legislation politicized the sector, enlarging the participants into what the authors call an issue network. At a critical moment Nicholas Ridley, then Secretary of State for Environment, insisted that industry privatize supply, sewerage, and sewage disposal under the authority of an industrial regulator and accept a separate regulator for the environmental aspects of the water industry. This reestablished the basis for the regeneration of a slightly different policy community, operating in the privatized industry.

The pluralist model of power emphasizes representation of multiple and functionally crucial agents, revealing a focus on observed interests, continuity in routines, bargaining and compromise. Richardson, Maloney, and Rudig summarize:

> It is in the possible re-constitution of a new policy community that previous 'outsiders' may see their chance to influence decisions. But our evidence also points to the limits of influence: once a new consensus is established between the main client industry and the government, the policy area becomes relatively 'closed' again and the old patterns of interaction appear to re-establish themselves, albeit in the context of new institutions and new regulatory regimes. (1992, p. 173; also see Maloney and Richardson, 1992, pp. 14–20)

Looking at a 'policy community' suggests that change under Thatcher was limited at best, varying with policy areas and factors other than government policy (Marsh and Rhodes 1992a, p. 47). Thus, the pluralist concern to focus on specific processes leads to a perception of continuity. The focus of multiple actors and complexity most likely overemphasizes sameness.

A fourth agency model answer focuses on the agency of Thatcher's personality, vision, and will, as the factor which enabled her to achieve fundamental reforms. Kavanagh refers to her as exhibiting a mobilizing style of leadership. He writes: 'The very forcefulness with which Mrs Thatcher has projected her views and style, separate from those of her Cabinet, has also established a model of premiership. It is one which, whether measured in terms of winning elections or carrying through policies, has been remarkably successful' (1990, p. 275). Her cunning use of her patronage powers as Prime Minister, a populist appeal, fortuitous events, and divided opposition facilitated her domination of cabinet government. Combining style with policies and her peculiar relations with institutions, the Thatcher personality becomes the source of power and force for change (Moon, 1993). Unfortunately, this explanation puts too much weight on the individual person, neglecting the context as a source of support and constraint and failing to explain the substance or acceptance of her leadership and policies.

Finally, a fifth agency model theory is the liberal or economic model of power, exemplifying what Norman Barry (1990, p. 30) calls the 'potency of ideas school'. Economists, advancing various reasons for privatizing and classifying the forms or types of privatization, assume that ideas are agents with their own force in creating change. Covering the vast bulk of the privatization literature, the liberal model encompasses a variety of goals that can be applied at different times or receive different emphasis with particular privatizations, while remaining true to the liberal perspective that recognition of economic truth will lead to its triumph (Veljanovski, 1987, pp. 7–8; Wiltshire, 1987, pp. ix and 29).

Vickers and Wright (1989, pp. 4–9), for example, offer an inclusive summary of the liberal reasons for privatization. They cite ideological motives (based on anti-state attitudes, preference for consumer sovereignty to prevail, and the desire to build a 'property owning democracy'), economic motives (a means to further liberalization, efficiency, labour discipline, an enterprise culture, and the rationalization of assets), managerial motives (breakup public sector empires), party political motives (creating a conservative, anti-socialist electorate), and financial motives (reducing the Public Sector Borrowing Requirement [PSBR], giving firms access to capital markets, fostering stock exchange growth, ending costly state rescue operations, and raising money for the state treasury).

Similarly, Marsh's literature review identifies the following motives: reducing government involvement in industry, improving efficiency, reducing the PSBR, weakening public sector unions, widening share ownership, encouraging employees' share-owning; and gaining political advantages (Marsh 1991, pp. 463–77; see also Wiltshire, 1987, pp. 20–9; Veljanovski, 1987, p. 8; Vickers and Yarrow, 1988, ch. 12). On the side of practitioners, British Conservative Party leaders offered four main arguments: enhancing economic freedom, increasing efficiency, easing public-sector pay problems, and reducing public sector borrowing (Steel and Heald, 1982). Further, according to Shirley Letwin (1992, esp. pp. 101 and 104–5), the effects of the market style of accountability are moral and political, freeing individuals from dependency, families from decay, and Britain from weakness. The transfer of ownership assets motivates individual autonomy and ignites energy and creative activities. From the liberal perspective, privatization is an economic programme that furthers freedom and democracy.

Discussion of the forms and definitions of privatization also reflect the liberal perspective of free agents voluntarily making mutually advantageous exchanges. Privatization commonly refers to a whole variety of ways in which the market is used in place of direct state administration. David Heald (1983, ch. 13) identifies four separate components of privatization: 1) private financing of services still provided by the public sector (reducing subsidies and increasing charges); 2) private production of services continuing to be financed by the public sector (contracting out); 3) denationalization (selling public assets to private sector owners) and load-shedding (transferring state functions to the private sector); and 4) liberalization (increasing competition). Others (Young, 1986; Heald, 1983; Wiltshire, 1987; Vickers and Yarrow, 1988, 156) add the sale of public sector housing. And Young (1986) mentions investment projects encouraging private sector involvement in deprived areas and the extension of private sector practices into public sector organizations, aiming for commercial returns on assets.

The liberal literature shows the link between analysis and prescription, how assuming the virtues of markets entails an imperative to promote competition and increase efficiency. Yet, the liberal model fails to provide a strategy for change. It ignores institutions, personality, and groups in the making of policy. More particularly, without a means, the potency of ideas assumes that ideas do their own work.

Turning to structuralist models of power explaining privatization, public choice theory provides a structural consequentialist analysis. Analyzing how rational actors behave in different circumstances, the analyst's conceptualization of context becomes fundamental to explanation. Dunleavy (1986 and 1991), developing his radical reconstruction of rational choice analysis that differentiates among bureaucrats' structural location, explains privatization as a trend that reflects the self-serving attempt of upper level state managers to enhance their power and privilege, to increase their control of policy and decrease their responsibilities for day-to-day operations. More generally, Ellen Pint (1990) uses a public choice approach that separates the political from the economic to argue that political motives better explain privatization than economic efficiency interests. Mariusz Dobek (1993a, 1993b) similarly argues from a public choice perspective that politicians use privatization as a means for enhancing their own political benefits.

Yet, Madsen Pirie's (1988a) post hoc reconstruction of Thatcherite policy-making in his theory of micropolitics most clearly reveals the new right's appropriation of this model of power. Micropolitics shows how to use the public choice theory model of power to calculate how conditions can be changed to achieve desired consequences. In plotting reforms that undermine the public sector, Pirie's micropolitics contends that policy

makers strategize how to use public choice theory to analyze the benefits
enjoyed and the influence and support traded by unitary actors (individuals
and groups) (Pirie, 1988b, pp. 125-6). Micropolitics proposes that the
structuralist aspects of the model of power developed in public choice
analysis give politicians the instrument (incentives) to reform and control
conduct, proposing that the rational actor model can be used to calculate
how to motivate trade-offs leading to desired consequences. With external
or structural factors determining individual action, Pirie pictures how
elites can shape trade-offs and their collective consequences, making all
participants winners (Grimstone, 1990, p. 13). Pirie's thesis is interesting
because it blends the agency and structuralist models, arguing that elites
can manipulate circumstances in order to motivate responses.

While shifting attention to means and arguing that this type of strategy
was fundamental to the success of privatization, Pirie's account fails
because it contains elements of both agency and structuralist models of
power. His analysis pictures politicians exercising power by manipulating
incentives through changing the circumstances determining an actor's role
and outlook. First, Pirie uses circumstances or incentives as the cause or
motive force in the same way that agency theory used personality or
public opinion. This means that the exercise of power must constantly be
renewed, that rewarding circumstances constantly be kept in place or
changed to maintain the desired behaviour. Moreover, Pirie fails to
appreciate that circumstances as defining situations depend on interpretation. In motivating participation, some actors are more predisposed, more
capable, or more practiced than others. The effects of changes in incentives like the incentives themselves are not equal. The responsiveness to
incentives thus varies. Some players will join enthusiastically, others
cautiously, and still others will resist.

Peter Hall's institutionalist analysis of the Thatcher experiment
exemplifies a second type of structural explanation of privatization (1986,
ch. 5). The state under Thatcher became a decisive and determined actor,
committed to enhancing state power by weakening the trade unions and
breaking up opposition through the application of markets and direct
assaults. The Thatcher government, while not clearly successful, relied on
monetarist ideas as 'a weapon and a screen' to break the hold of interests
on public policy. As Hall argues: 'A coherent and technically plausible
set of ideas, commanding the support of some body of experts, can confer
a degree of independence on the state' (1986, p. 128). Monetarism, thus,
enabled the Thatcher government to deny representation, to force business
to face the challenges of international competition alone, and to justify
rising unemployment. Yet, according to Hall, the Thatcher revolution is

not really genuine: 'Recent increases in the power of the state relative to society depend heavily on conjunctural factors; and there is a potential contradiction in the Government's strategy' (1986, p. 130). With organizational changes to the state being of little significance for enhancing state capacity to direct industrial reorganization and with deregulation even weakening its leverage, the success of Thatcher's monetarism depended on market pressures to force firms into becoming more competitive (p. 131). A deep recession with skyrocketing unemployment might enhance state autonomy in the short-term by weakening trade unions and industry. But, there can be little hope of long-term success since free market strategies have already proved to be historically unfruitful.

Another version of the new institutionalist approach is Jim Bulpitt's (1986) interpretation of Thatcherism. Focusing on the Conservative Party as an institution, Bulpitt develops a concept of statecraft as its main objective. Statecraft is 'the art of winning elections and achieving some necessary degree of governing competence in office' (1986, p. 21). It involves party management, a winning electoral strategy, a hegemony in setting the political agenda, and establishing a governing competence. The statecraft concept presupposes that the Conservative party (and the British state) is an actor in its own right, is preoccupied with gaining power and advantage, and will achieve centre autonomy to the extent that a Conservative government can act in its own interests rather than those of any societal force (1986, pp. 27–8). Like Hall, Bulpitt emphasizes the important functional role of monetarist ideas in prescribing an automatic pilot that could depoliticize economic management. But ideas are secondary to the primacy of organizational interests and goals. Party, industry, and trade union institutions constrain action or reduce individuals to bearers of their collective interests.

A third structuralist approach is marxism. Stuart Hall interpreted Thatcherism as an 'authoritarian populism', constituting a consolidation of popular discontent with social democracy around a rightwing and authoritarian programme (1983 and 1988). Following Antonio Gramsci, Hall focuses on hegemonic strategies involved in changing the 'balance of forces' when a deep crisis of class rule has emerged. Criticizing Hall, Bob Jessop *et al.* (1988) develop a more institutional or statist approach. They argue that Thatcherism represents not just an ideological triumph but a dual state crisis (between parliament and functional modes of representation) and is built on and reflects a divisive 'Two Nations' strategy. Joel Krieger (1986) also contends that a crisis of social democracy, generating a stalemate in the balances of class forces, resulted in an enhanced state autonomy in Britain and America, leading to a 'de-integrative' strategy creating greater social division.

Andrew Gamble (1988 and 1989) offers a marxist explanation of privatization as consistent with his observation that Thatcherism as a strategy combined a strong state and a free economy. The new right strategy emerged out of a global recession generated by an exhaustion of a Fordist regime of accumulation and a collapse of the hegemonic position of the United States in the international economic system, leading to a crisis of social democracy with its characteristics of universal citizenship, corporatism, and economic management or planning (1988, ch. 1). In response the new right set about '...stripping from the state the extended roles and additional functions which have been placed upon it during the social democratic era in order to restore its authority and make the state strong again' (1989, p. 5). The key was to roll back the state, reducing the range of decisions subject to the political process. This project, according to Gamble, required a strong state, capable of forcefully breaking the hold of social democracy on the economy, policing the market order, making the economy more efficient, and defending the social order (1988, p. 32).

POWER AS DIRECT AND INDIRECT CONTROL

The inadequacy of these accounts derives from their use of agency and structural models of power to explain privatization. The models exemplify a conception of power as causation by physical force and coercion. Agents, like billiard balls in the metaphor of Galilean mechanics, move against one another with causal effect when projected by internal motivations, variously called wants, preferences, appetites, desires, or interests, or external barriers like the organization of industry. The causal effect of agent A is then measured by the response of agent B (Clegg, 1989, ch. 3; Lukes, 1974; Dahl, 1984, ch. 3). Deriving from a Hobbesian tradition, they emphasize mechanistic metaphors of causal relations, particular prime movers, and moral grounding for submission to authority (Clegg, 1989, p. 34). In examining causal relations, agency theories point to empirical regularities while structural theories identify processes and mechanisms that entail capacities and dispositions. Yet, these models are incomplete, picturing power as monolithic, blunt and inefficient causation.

In contrast, Michel Foucault's theory of disciplinary power provides an important alternative. It focuses on efficiency of means, while linking the contingent and strategic character of power to discursive practices. Disciplinary power works not by coercive force or violence but by detailed supervision, not at the level of sovereign societal or individual agents but at the level of specific choices, and not by constraining but by generating actions (Foucault, 1979; Mitchell, 1991; Clegg, 1989, ch. 7). Disciplinary power introduces efficiency at the level of detailed activities, uses external surveillance and procedural standards to generate economy and order. Yet, such power is objective, referring to the way the organization of discipline and production regulates agents' interests and capacities for action. The routines of observations, examinations, and standardizing assessments constitute disciplined subjects by means of real objective processes, with desires, thoughts, and energies becoming epiphenomenal. Disciplinary power decentres human agents, picturing power as a product of objective relations that, while eliminating individual sovereignty, enlarge societal capacities.

Pragmatism develops a more adequate picture of power focusing on individual human beings and their use of energy and intelligence in cooperative and purposive activity. John Dewey and George Herbert Mead frame an analysis of power in which acts of direct control are continuous with participation in indirect control. Dewey writes:

> Adults are naturally most conscious of directing the conduct of others when they are immediately aiming so to do. As a rule, they have such an aim consciously when they find themselves resisted; when others are doing things they do not wish them to do. But the more permanent and influential modes of control are those which operate from moment to moment continuously without much deliberate intention on our part. (Dewey, 1916a, p. 31)

Coercive force, violence, and law are forms of direct power, while social processes of all sorts exemplify indirect power. Thus, this analysis is more comprehensive than either the agency model which focuses on the power of sovereign agents, or the disciplinary model, which subjugates the agent through modes of objectification.

The notion of indirect or internal control, while similar in its facilitating and detailed working to Foucault's objectivist concept of disciplinary power, relies on ideas to establish control and efficiency in working, identifying control in purposive activity. Dewey writes, 'the activities in which all participate are the chief carrier of control' (1938, p. 35). Indirect control operates through whole situations involving participating individuals, sharing in participation and coordination among interacting parts. Indirect control is more productive and more efficient. Dewey explains, 'Nevertheless force is efficient socially not when imposed upon a scene from without, but when it is an organization of the forces *in* the scene' (1916b, p. 212; cf. 1916c, p. 251).

Power lies in the ability to direct the way force translates into consequences, either by directly imposing an outcome or indirectly by shaping the situations molding participation and experience. Indirect control, the most pervasive mode of power, depends on the ability to control the internal and external conditions defining situations in which persons take part. Behaviour depends on the way a person defines his or her situation. According to Shibutani, 'What a man does, then, is not so much a response to the natural environment as to his interpretation of a part of it' (1961, p. 195). Moreover, definitions are in the process of constant reconstruction, involving successive and serial adjustments to changing circumstances.

Adjustments depend on self-control, which in turn involves social control. Self-control relies on the development and use of self-images through perception and thinking to control plans of action. Social control depends on the person assuming the standpoint of the groups or audience as part of their deliberations. As a result, external circumstances are dealt with, made use of, or experienced in accordance with internal directions or use of ideas. External control, in other words, presupposes internal control. Restating Mead's notion of social self, 'The planning and direction of overt behaviour become possible because men are able to respond to themselves in their imagination; they can chart their course in such imaginative rehearsals by pre-testing various plans of action' (Shibutani, 1961, p. 198).

Normally overt behaviour draws on 'habits', the term used by Dewey to refer to repeatable cohesively organized programmes of activity which function to satisfy actors' conscious aims. Habits are learned, organized, coordinated, and projective (Dewey, 1922, p. 31). Changing the situation that defines patterns of engagement and experience changes an actor's internal and external conditions. Thereby it reorganizes the patterns of action or habits controlling behaviour.

Since the habits involved in indirect control are learned meanings, they depend on ideas. Ideas realize a human capacity for inference by signifying connections between actions and effects and between present occurrences and future events. As a result, individuals use ideas in participating in cooperative activity, using ideas about how they are to be accountable for what they do and what they are going to do to plan and sequence their involvement (Dewey, 1916a, p. 38 and 1922, p. 217). The use of ideas means that conduct is voluntary, constructed in response to a changing environment. While responses are theoretically unlimited, in practice ideas about the obligations involved in participating in cooperative activities limit and direct behaviour.

ANALYZING FORMS OF POWER

Having distinguished types of power, the question of identifying the structure of power arises. Dewey's pragmatism suggests a framework for
examining power by distinguishing the main categories for analyzing
experience. A first theme in Dewey's work questions first principles, foundational concepts, fixed truths. This anti-foundationalism questions philosophical dualism, the conceptual separation into mind and body, nature
and nurture, objective and subjective and emphasizes the importance of
consequences in accepting justification. Second, Dewey's pragmatism
emphasizes the insurgent or creative character of human action.
Experience involves projection into circumstances not fully known; it is
experimentation for the purpose of connecting with the future. As human
actors undergo a situation they simultaneously attempt to control it.
Finally, Dewey develops an analysis of thinking, focusing on the making
of inferences, judgements or decisions as resolutions to problematic
situations.

   These major themes in Dewey's pragmatism provide categories for analyzing relations of control. These elements of a pragmatist analysis of
power identify values that motivate action, agency relations between
actors, and the method of linking conditions to valued consequences. The
first concerns the justification, values, or grounds of activity. As men-
tioned above, Dewey's pragmatism rejects philosophical dualism and
foundationalism. Dewey challenges theories authorizing experience by
invoking separate and distinct givens such as mind and body or state and
society. Instead he favours locating the basis of action through empirical
and intellectual scrutiny of experience. In his exposition of the pragmatist
approach in 'The Need for a Recovery of Philosophy', Dewey (1917)
acknowledges that experience is a matter of the relationship between a
living being and its environment. He holds that, rather than being purely
subjective or reflective of an independent reality, experience involves the
way the objective world affects human action and is in turn modified by it.
Thus, pragmatism conceptualizes knowledge as valuation, as knowledge
for the sake of realizing desirable and intended events or states, and
assigns intelligence the role of clarifying and devising connections
between conditions and consequences. More broadly, Dewey's focus on
consequences rather than fixed principles as the starting point in thinking
and action poses the need to examine the origins and character of
justifications used by political actors.

   The second element of power is the analysis of the striving for control,
of agency, or initiative. Dewey's pragmatism emphasizes the projective,

plural, dynamic and experimental nature of human experience, while rejecting simple and mechanical causal relations between independent units. Captured in the notion that individuals are 'live creatures', never totally passive, experience refers to the 'simultaneous doings and sufferings' of human activity. As Dewey writes, 'Our undergoings are experiments in varying the course of events; our active tryings are trials and tests of ourselves' (1917, p. 9). In Dewey's words, 'The most patient patient is more than a receptor. He is also an agent–a reactor, one trying experiments, one concerned with undergoing in a way which may influence what is still to happen' (1917, p. 8). This central concern with experience highlights the issue of the locus of initiative in power relations.

The third element of power is the criterion of inference or judgement, transforming the objective and external by means of internal standards that link conditions to effects. Attempting to make use of the environment for future success requires thinking and inference. Pragmatism proposes that reality is remade or transformed through judgement, functioning through experience in accordance with the test of consequences and for the purpose of 'readjusting and expanding the means and ends of life' (Dewey, 1903, p. 296). Thinking provides for control by projecting consequences from interpretation of events. As Dewey puts it, 'A being which can use given and finished facts as signs of things to come; which can take given things as evidences of absent things, can, in that degree, forecast the future; it can form reasonable expectations' (1917, p. 15–16). In so doing, thinking creates a conjecture or rule of operation which serves as the criterion determining conduct.

These three elements of power distinguish the complexity and flow of power relations. Actors use ideas to develop and adjust these basic elements which classify forms of direct and indirect effective power. Thought and ideas define situations and so regulate human behaviour in relation to an environment. These elements reveal the way ideas serve agents in interacting with their environment and the way the internal influences the external for its own ends. They distinguish particular patterns of control or power, direct or indirect. Values or grounds define the quality of experience or goals, initiatives the relationship between external and internal in determining an agent's autonomy for mobilizing actions that have influence among actors, and judgements operationalize values by connecting condition to effects. The interplay of these elements define power relations and distinguish how various patterns of collective control and coordination within formal-legal institutions have different consequences.

This suggests that changing the representation or picture agents use to hold themselves accountable for their behaviour involves redefining

agents' understandings about the foundations of action, relations of
agency, and standards of decision-making. Ideas are crucial in shaping
power relations among actors. They guide the design of interactions and
rules of play in the form of expectations imputed to other participants.
These expectations amount to the rules of accountability that define habits
of interaction with an agent's environment.

STATE POWER THROUGH INDIRECT CONTROL

The concepts of the type and form of control facilitate understanding
how choice and competition operate to enhance state control. Instead of
relying on acts of direct power based on parliamentary institutions, personal charisma, class domination, or pressure group interactions, government politicians used New Right ideas to design and implement
policies that redefined the patterns of indirect or social control. While
the state maintained and even enhanced its direct powers expressed
through its right to legislate, tax, control information and coerce, neoliberal policies did not succeed by force. Rather their effectiveness
resulted from the way neoliberal strategies remolded expectations regulating individual accountability and so activities defining and controlling
participation. Neoliberal reforms changed the way actors held each other
and themselves accountable, defining both new rules of internal control,
which guided participation in cooperative activities, and new external
circumstances. With these market controls monitored by the state, public
policy-making itself can be described as privatized, since policy-making
by market processes and disciplines replaced the political controls exercised by pressure groups that had become so prominent after the late
1960s. Policy-making becomes self-driven as market transactions guide
the interplay among participants. State agencies either participate in the
new situations as market actors or occasionally intervene to impose an
outcome.

The New Right's use of economic or rational actor models of power as
standards of accountability in policy-making changed the prevalent
methods of decision-making. According to Shirley Letwin's sympathetic
exposition of the essentials of New Right politics under Thatcher, privatization as the 'textbook' case of Thatcherite policy is important because it
provided an alternative mode of decision-making. She writes perceptively
that privatization '...is not merely a policy but a means of changing how
policy is conceived and executed – a means of changing expectations
about the nature of government and the nature of politics' (1992, p. 107).

According to a pragmatist analysis, methods of decision-making connect conditions to effects, which by regulating patterns of experience and the interaction between objective and subjective aspects of experience admit certain values and exclude others. Thus, without agreeing with Letwin's assertion that property ownership promotes freedom and entrepreneurial virtues, this analysis suggests that Letwin correctly points out that privatization involves a change in policy-making.

Politicians freed themselves from the obligations and costs of collectivism by establishing in practice a neoliberal mode of indirect control. It provided them with a strategy for handling the detailed processes of implementing privatization. The New Right model of power offered a method of operating by locating control in actors' participation in private commercial transactions. This shifted the substance of internal controls from political to market criteria, redefining the justification for and the course of action taken in terms of individual self-interest, locating agency in individual effort, and stipulating the maximizing of self-interest as the final criterion for deciding and acting. The model enabled politicians to redesign patterns of accountability in terms of a direct and transparent linkage between individual choice, effort or input, and consequent rewards or losses. In short, while direct power remains in reserve and is used on occasion, neoliberalism provided a model of indirect or internal power that could be put to work. It was a strategy enabling governing elites to establish self-governing arenas of policy-making.

PRIVATIZATION AS FORMS OF INDIRECT STATE POWER

In order to be successful, though, New Right ideas had to open up opportunities by turning hindrances into means. Instead of state power using concentrated force to overcome overt resistance, New Right ideas proposed noncoercive strategies of action. These economic strategies redrew connections between the government and society. They reorganized the activity that defined the relationship and established new definitions of accountability by separating individuals from the social, means from ends, and subjective and objective interests. These strategies displaced state dependence on direct control of social groups by instituting courses of private commercial behaviour which, by having nothing to do with overt state autonomy, helped achieve the politicians' desire for greater power.

The means, the how to, or the 'what next' involved in introducing and expanding the rules of business practices into new spheres of decision-making replaced the conscious use of direct state power. John Dewey

argued that understanding the relationship of goals to change requires
abandoning the dualism of ends and means.

> The 'end' is the last act thought of; the means are the acts to be
> performed prior to it in time. To *reach* an end we must take our mind
> off from it and attend to the act which is next to be performed. We must
> make that the end...But when the proposed end involves any deviation
> from usual action, or any rectification of it – as in the case of standing
> straight – then the main thing is to find some act which is different from
> the usual one... Otherwise we shall simply do the old thing over again,
> no matter what is our conscious command. The only way of
> accomplishing this discovery is through a flank movement. (Dewey,
> 1922, p. 27)

New Right ideas proposed just such a 'flank movement', a series of
actions that became both the means and ends of reform.

Once in office, Thatcherites introduced market mechanisms through a
strategy of incentives, using individual choice and accountability backed by
the direct force of the law. As the Thatcherite Nicholas Ridley summed up
the New Right strategy in a *Guardian* (July 1, 1986) interview, 'I think
everything can be done by making it in people's interests to do it, or against
the law. You work with the grain'. Privatization, which changed the situations defining who participated and the manner of participation,
augmented the direct force of the state. Thereby, privatizing decision-
making undermined the privileged influence of various state and traditional
institutions, such as the trade unions, the media, the civil service, and the
universities, by discouraging collective organization and participation.

New Right ideas, then, served Thatcherite interests in enhancing state
autonomy because they prescribed and justified a new method of indirect
internal control. They transformed the media of social controls typical of
collectivism into forms of market accountability. New Right ideas enabled
Thatcherites to engage the interest and support of key participants required
to make reforms successful while eliminating alternative options. They
enabled the Thatcherite core to set and develop the privatization scheme,
and facilitated their control of the key players in the reform process. The
economic model of market accountability prescribed an alternative method
of governance that Conservative government officials used to enhance
their capacity for reform and at the same time to institute new rules of
democracy.

Changing the norms and practices of social control occasions the use of
direct power in the form of overt acts of state imposition and coercion.

However, the main method of change involved altering the situation defining the motivation and activity of the participants themselves and engaging participation in the regimen of markets. Neoliberal ideas enabled the government to recast decision-making process as private commercial transactions formalized by the law. How privatization expanded the state's capacity for control can be characterized by the three elements of power outlined above.

1) Core Thatcherite politicians used New Right ideas as tools to ground and justify market accountability. These ideas helped determine the quality of experience, the interpretation of future experiences, and the objective conditions under which further experiences are to take place. Neoliberal ideas about individual material betterment provided an alternative method of making decisions that offered a working solution to the failings of the postwar consensus on democratic policy-making.

Privatization attained the status of a theology, envisioning a different kind of policy, disregarding empirical tests as capable of disproof, and rejecting all notions of accountability except those based on the market (Heald and Thomas, 1985, pp. 7–8). The framework of economic consequentualism, individual action premised on calculations of self-reward and self-improvement, reduced the capacity of opponents to make their support or participation conditional on particular substantive outcomes of politicians' actions. Because privatization policies institute the self-contained and self-monitoring standard of rewarding self-interest, leaders could weaken opposition built on non-material solidarities, bargain effectively with those groups threatened with a loss of benefit, and gain wider support by encouraging participation in share-ownership. Officials gained political power by justifying the market mechanism as the only medium for expressing individual self-interest and dismissing traditional democratic modes of public accountability, where, in the words of Heald and Thomas, 'there are different parties espousing different interests, and often articulating different values systems which have to be reconciled through the political process' (1985, p. 16).

2) Thatcherite politicians took initiatives that set in motion and made use of individual market-oriented initiatives and involvement. They drew out support and enlisted the energies of actors whose predispositions already favoured market accountability, built on early successes, and isolated actors holding alternative ideas. Thatcherite politicians, by drawing groups into the private sector, could claim that participants had themselves benefited and constituted a new and self-sustaining market-oriented interest group, while removing themselves from positions of direct accountability. By setting new ground rules, the Thatcherites succeeded through

the initiatives of those participating in the new commercial transactions determining policy.

3) Market accountability separates ends from means and defines instrumental interests as the criterion for making decisions. Therefore, it reinforces authorities' capacity to control process and criterion determining final decisions. Although direct pressures like legislation, threats to revoke privileges, or outright attacks on vested interests did occur, the government reorganized the energies of the actors into the reforming process itself. Privatization provided for turning means (market methods of decision-making) into ends; it was the business (the how to) of arranging for and concluding business practices. Standard of evaluation determined participation and procedures or processes. Officials used the routines of market accountability to redefine the policy-making regime, by equating the method (market practices) and the end (private sector accountability). They turned political decision-making into rewarding trade-offs.

Applying the elements of power to the privatization programme leads to three propositions summarizing how indirect control enlarged the power of state authorities: one, market thinking became the chief grounds for policy; two, initiating market processes drew out the preexisting support and self-interest of key players; and, three, market rationality provided the criterion for choice, the meaning of the desirable. Officials in the Thatcher governments used neoliberal ideas to fashion a medium of control that was self-organizing and relatively independent of the need for direct state intervention. Constituting a regime of control, market decision-making regulated the internal and objective situations that controlled actors' behaviour.

FORMS OF POWER AND THE SCOPE OF PRIVATIZATION

The capacity to introduce indirect power varied with the way politicians could use market grounds, the proclivity of individuals to engage in market activities, and economic rationality to reorganize policy-making processes. The ability to control the objective and internal conditions of choice and so change behaviour explains the developing scope and pace of the policy in addition to what appears as contradictions in the privatization process. Privatization soon gained a momentum of its own and stood at the centre of government policy in the 1980s. It translated the consequentialist model of economic analysis, namely, making the return of resource expenditure transparent and direct, into policy options. Four subtypes of economic accountability became prominent: 1) accountability deriving from

the ownership and tradeability of property; 2) accountability through principals using private sector means to control public service providing
agents (in which a public function is sub-contracted to the lowest priced
private or public sector provider or operated by public sector agents
according to business standards and practices); 3) accountability through
the contestability of competition in service or product markets; and 4)
accountability based on linking the acquisition or purchase of a good or
service to a payment for it. Each of these modes operates to limit the
formation of interests and pressures that create demands for pushing up
public spending or lead to overt conflicts between government and group.
Diffusion of privatization as a form of indirect power involved different
policy patterns in different circumstances.

In this effort, politicians utilized both direct and indirect forms of
control, with indirect power being both a means and end of a reform
process that continues to evolve. The government used commercial strategies to redefine actor's subjective interests and to change the objective
conditions of decision-making in order to draw key participants into these
reform processes. The utility of market practices as instruments for engaging participation in market-based policy-making grew over time and
varied with policy areas. Implementation also depended on closing off
substantive criticism and constructing political support through the control
of the privatization process.

The introduction of privatization occurred most easily where the
resources for the use of business standards and disciplines seemed most
ready-made and natural. This is why privatization started in areas that
drew on a pre-existing interest in ownership, as in housing or the sale of
state-owned firms in competitive product markets. Where the ground was
less fertile for market accountability, that is, where internal predispositions and objective conditions were hostile, and allies were less forthcoming or even nonexistent, the introduction of market accountability was
slower. It was more likely to combine various forms of market accountability and to be more directly imposed. This accounts for the slower pace
of privatization in the form of liberalization and in making the welfare
state assimilate private sector practices (cf. Peacock, 1984, pp. 18–19).

The pace and scope of privatization became more radical over time.
From 1979 to 1983 initiatives were limited and tentative, covering housing
sales, tendering, liberalization in telecommunication and energy, and the
beginning of a decade long process of the marketization of internal union
politics. Next, the main drive in asset sales gained pace. From 1979
private asset sales started, but after 1983 the larger public utility sales
became the chief targets. Finally, after 1987 the programme expanded to

include mandatory tendering and the application of market accountability to the health service, education, housing, community care, local government finance. John Major advanced privatization further, though in a more reconciliatory style (Kavanagh, 1994).

The elaboration of privatization initiatives gained momentum as politicians learned how to implement programmes and gained confidence from previous successes. The government rejected frontal assaults on opposing interest groups in favour of strategies that assured the political success of its ideological goals because other groups joined in the transaction. As in Madsen Pirie's characterization of government strategy, political pay-offs depended on the ability of policy to 'satisfy the various groups involved in public enterprises, and to offer them trade-offs for their benefits which they would willingly accept' (Pirie, 1988a, p. 174; Self, 1990, p. 25).

Pirie expresses and captures the strategic nature of the Thatcherite programme. Yet, such trade-offs had to be grounded and behaviour redirected, with individual initiative and continued participation necessary for success. The regimen of the market was more important than the material benefit. Individuals conceptualized themselves as insurgent yet accountable agents in a complex economic system. They became personally responsible for rewards or losses as a result of the way the expectations that they themselves imputed to other market participants and to market signals played out. In enabling politicians to reorganize the situations defining indirect controls, New Right ideas succeeded, creating self-organizing economic regime which distanced state officials from a need for continuous direct involvement.

CONCLUSION

Contrary to the popular view that neoliberal policies advance choice and competition, I argue that these policies effectively expanded state control over the formation of political demands in Britain. Thatcher and a few of her leading associates achieved this by using market practices as a form of indirect power – a medium of self-generating social control – rather than by relying on direct force. The Thatcher governments ended collectivist policy processes that gave wide access, protected vested interests and encouraged new claims. They were able to narrow the range and mute the extent of popular claims while promoting a more efficient use of resources without regard to wider concerns of social justice in many arenas of public decision-making. This increased inequality and diminished the influence for many traditional groups. Thus, privatization diminishes democracy.

2 The Collapse of Social Democracy

From the end of WWII until 1973 Britain's economy grew, with an absolute rise in living standards, while simultaneously experiencing relative economic and geopolitical decline. Political success coincided with economic success as prosperity promoted political stability until the late 1960s. The 1950s produced the paradigmatic type of two-party parliamentary government. But by the 1970s British governments saw events move beyond their control. How a collectivist consensus or governing strategy brought autonomy to the British state and then came apart forms the backdrop to understanding the emergence and impact of privatization on British democracy.

Affluence and a new individualism, unleashing a wider and often incompatible range of values, in an emerging era of increased economic competitiveness undermined the effectiveness of the collectivist policy process and consensus. Collectivist processes and policies strengthened group bargaining and facilitated wage and union demands that undermined the community interest in economic stability. Political, bureaucratic, and administrative processes facilitated producer group self-aggrandizement, which in turn, led to the breakdown of the postwar reliance on compromise and consensus in decision-making. This chapter outlines the postwar British collectivist pattern of governing and analyzes the processes that led to its breakdown.

THE POSTWAR COLLECTIVIST PLURALISM

Labour's electoral victory in 1945 shaped the distinctive politics of the collectivist era. According to David Heald, 'Politicians during this period knew what they were doing: sharply increasing the share of national resources taken by the state and allocated on nonmarket criteria' (1983, p. 5). This collectivist process, in which public policy aimed 'toward control over the economic and social order as a whole' (Beer, 1982, p. 10), led to an increase in the growth of public expenditure and public employment. Full employment and the welfare state could only be developed through faster and sustainable economic growth, the dominating question of the postwar years (Jenkins, 1989, p. 5).

27

The evolving postwar settlement or consensus is one of pluralist collectivism. The main features centred on state intervention in economic management, on providing welfare, and in permitting influential interests groups to have an important role in decision-making (Savage and Robins, 1990, pp. 2–4). Colin Crouch, focusing more on industrial relations, views World War II as a turning point in developing the postwar consensus. He lists five main developments: a commitment to full employment, the involvement of trade unions in government policy-making bodies on a wide range of matters, all-party agreement to depoliticize industrial relations, all-party commitment to build the welfare state, and finally the emergence of centralized union leaderships capable of enforcing agreements made with the government on their membership (Crouch, 1979, ch. 1). These developments changed the balance of political influence. Full employment and increased membership strengthened trade union bargaining power; their greater acceptance facilitated their participation in a wider range of public policy-making. Expanding the welfare state and nationalizing inept basic industries pushed in the same direction, increasing employment and personal security. The larger public made for a degree of economic management and reduced the role of the market. (Kavanagh, 1990, pp. 34–5).

The trend toward a quasi-corporatist collectivism changed traditional pressure group politics into a close and continuous interdependence between groups and the state. Samuel Beer characterizes the nature of what he calls the new group politics:

> In the collectivist polity, government undertook not only to lay down the rules under which individuals and groups would pursue their own purposes, but also increasingly to act for the sake of certain specific outcomes, economic and social, which had been adopted as public purposes. In order to achieve these outcomes, government could hardly do without the cooperation of the groups being so used... In this way the managed economy multiplied the syndicalist power of producer groups far beyond what it had been in the liberal economy. (1982, p. 13)

The new group politics grew out of the wartime cooperation between the state and the unions and in the belief that expertise could be applied successfully to solve problems. Social engineering and social policy went together, just as did managerialism, incomes policies, and economic planning. Harold Wilson articulated the mood with his now famous 1963 Labour Party Conference call for applying the 'white heat' of 'the scientific revolution' to modernize Britain.

Keynesian techniques of economic management enabled public authorities to exercise control of the economy without violating the individual
freedoms entailed in physical control, yet strengthened group initiative and
direct power entailed in the new group politics. Providing a means and
justification for government involvement as employer, taxer, and distrib-
utor of services, Keynesian active government proved successful at
increasing the legitimacy of the state, yet made government more dependent on group cooperation (cf. Kavanagh, 1990, p. 43). Demand management and producer incorporation also operated through public ownership
of key industries, where government guarantees and priorities replaced
market failure. Between 1945 and 1951, the Labour Government nationalized the railways and road passenger and freight transport, aviation, iron
and steel, and the coal, electricity, and gas industries. Further but limited
nationalizations followed in the next twenty-five years, including the steel
and shipbuilding industries, British Leyland, British Aerospace, and Rolls-
Royce. By 1979, the public corporations alone contributed 10.5 per cent of
the Gross Domestic Product and employed 8.1 per cent of those in the
labour force (Vickers and Yarrow, 1988, p. 140).

The 1945 Labour Government also directly affected consumption and
developed client group representation by developing welfare provisions.
In 1946 family allowances started, drawing on general taxation. The 1946
the National Insurance Act provided flat-rate benefits for unemployment,
sickness, retirement, and widowhood. A 1948 National Assistance Act
extended coverage to those who had incomplete contributions to the
national insurance scheme. And in 1947 the National Health Service, with
free medical services for all, came into force (Kavanagh, 1990, p. 46).
Following Beveridge's recommendations, in his 1942 review of social
security, these welfare measures were to complement the postwar commitment to full employment. Beer (1969) argues that the new group
politics created new claimants in creating beneficiaries as much as it
represented social grievances.

Demand management and a sharing of public policy-making with functionally critical interest groups produced real economic improvements and
greater political legitimacy that were unmatched anytime earlier in the
twentieth century. Middlemas states, 'At any point before 1956, and
generally until the mid-sixties, commentators could have been forgiven
for concluding that conflict had been institutionalised through a pluralist
system of representation' (Middlemas, 1979, p. 428). Political harmony,
prosperity, and beneficent social change meant that hopes of eliminating
or at least redirecting and containing the class conflict that had riddled
British politics since the First World War became a reality.

The collectivist pluralism or social democratic consensus that became dominant after WWII responded to emergent societal claims for absolute and relative improvement in employment and prosperity, reflecting the impact of wartime practices of successful state intervention. The experiences of the interwar years and the war itself led to a change in the conditions of state power, bringing to the foreground material conditions. If the grounds became remunerative, the class and group claims met with acknowledgement and positive response. State planning engaged group participation and initiative, becoming the mechanism for a wider and fairer distribution of opportunities and benefits. In expanding direct state power to groups, state intervention produced an inclusive, consensual, representative style of policy-making, wherein groups gained direct access and the direct power to influence decisions and implementation in return for promoting legitimacy and stability. Three features clarify this interventionist or collectivist pattern of power.

First, collectivist pluralism aimed to achieve social integration by responding to the claims for a real improvement in the quality of life of those who had suffered prior to the war and who had sacrificed during it. Many felt that the injustices of a class society had to be rectified in order that poverty and unemployment not encourage political instability and promote communism or fascism. The emergent claims represented a change in mass perceptions about what was acceptable, attitudes mobilized or articulated by elites like John Maynard Keynes and William Beveridge. Arthur Marwick records,

> at the end of the war the majority had a clearer idea than ever before of what it was they expected of a modern civilized industrial society: decent living standards, income and health security, a taste of the modest luxuries of life; once the idea was defined it became in itself an agent of further change.   (1968, p. 323)

The new attitudes were reactions to the failures of the past and to new ideas energized by wartime experiences that raised expectations and made progress seem inevitable. The new ideas promised that direct state intervention could produce widespread prosperity and social equality. Even the coalition government acknowledged this need for reform after the war. It instituted a Cabinet Committee on Reconstruction in 1943 that reflected the growing influence of the Labour party. The Government also completed a white paper on postwar employment, passed the 1944 Education Act, the 1945 Family Allowances Act, and promoted some of Beveridge's proposals for social insurance (Kavanagh, 1990, p. 31).

Second, post-WWII collectivism involved government responsiveness to group initiatives in creating a wider and fuller satisfaction of social needs for jobs, health, education and the like. Pluralist representation centred on group initiative and cooperation in public policy decision-making and implementation. State intervention and incorporation of major producer groups grew but remained pluralistic, aiming at winning legitimacy and consent rather than imposing state objectives and constraints. State power and autonomy grew. It led to a period of harmonization of interests and depoliticization of conflict, given cross-party agreement on the collectivist formula. The incorporation of employers and trade unions in economic policy-making meant that they shared in the formation of policy. Public authority the beneficiary for showing the way forward.

More specifically, the war shifted issues of manpower and industrial relations to the forefront. It made manpower the ultimate resource and gave the British labour movement the opportunity to affect the postwar settlement (Middlemas, 1979, p. 271). The postwar collectivist settlement reflected a wartime renegotiation of a political contract, popular sacrifices being exchanged for postwar social reforms. Middlemas argues that the core change was in the area of industrial relations: 'the primary contract in the first, catastrophic war years, when it seemed at least possible that Britain might lose, had to be established in the field of production, between government, employers and the industrial and agricultural labour force, represented by their unions' (1979, p. 274). This rationalization of the polity through representational enlargement enabled Britain to withstand the tribulations of the interwar years, while representing a diminishment of party and parliamentary politics.

Third, the method for policy-making developed an already existing 'corporate bias' (Middlemas, 1979). Interest representation, negotiation, and compromise about relative distributions became the province of a select group of governing institutions, mainly producer groups. Britain's domestic response to World War II boosted this change in ideas about the role and function of the state. The war seemed to prove that state planning and producer group incorporation could be highly effective, leading to the rise of technocratically minded practices and practitioners. This helped Labour win office in 1945, reflecting 'the colossal mood for change engendered by the war, not just among working-class voters, one third of whom, it has been estimated, voted Labour, thus providing the real key to Labour's triumph' (Marwick, 1968, p. 330). The war experience offered proof that state intervention and central planning could effectively serve the national interest gave Labour leaders the self-confidence to respond faithfully to the changed public mood (Marwick, 1968, p. 329).

In making the economy more responsive to societal forces, the politicians elaborated a collectivist pluralism by expanding the network of
groups who along with the government directly controlled public
resources. The state itself changed by facilitating the realization of societal
aspirations. It drew societal agents into a new policy-making relationship.
Groups too underwent changes, in taking advantage of their new privileges. They became more committed to the larger system. Similarly,
individual beneficiaries of full employment, rising real incomes, better
health care, and fuller social benefits lived different kinds of lives, which
in turn changed the expectations even further. As I will argue later, this
pattern of action and transformation had important effects, when combined
with other aspects of the changing environment of individual behaviour,
on class decomposition, party dealignment, the rejection of state intervention, and the subsequent failure of corporatist strategies attempted by
the Labour Party in the 1970s.

THE FAILURE OF COLLECTIVISM

The breakup of the collectivist formula resulted from its success as much
as its inability to adapt to an environment demanding greater competitiveness and flexibility. State interventionism extended the realm of direct
state power to new groups, according groups public status in return for
carrying out public functions. State power expanded as groups became the
direct extension and instruments of government policy. Yet, state intervention gave groups a direct voice in policy formation and implementation, intensifying consciousness of comparisons and making the public
policy process into the province of functional group interests. When the
larger economic and cultural circumstances changed and the government
wanted to impose a new criterion of increasing economic efficiency, governments found overt group resistance and their ability to use direct power
limited by a relative lack of clout and by the damage done in the public's
mind by episodes of overt conflict.

To examine the failure of collectivist pluralism after the 1960s, it is
important to look at the changes in the grounds of power, the relations of
initiatives, and mechanism for decision-making. The proliferation and
diversity of claims reflecting a new individualism combined with and con-
tradicted a new imperative for improving productive efficiency to change
the grounds, breaking down class-based social controls. Further, relations
of agency exacerbated fragmentation. In this context groups with bargaining strength were encouraged to press their claims by the success of

others, without regard to moral justification or to ultimate or wider consequences. The state's efforts to deal with them through the medium of direct power promoted group self-aggrandizement and political controversy rather than obedience and order.

Changing Grounds of Politics

The grounds for policy-making shifted in two major ways in the 1960s. One was the fading away of the historic socialist ambition for equality and social justice that had inspired the collectivist formula. In its place grew the consciousness of the imperative for growth and economic survival in an increasingly interdependent and competitive international capitalism. The other was the flourishing of a new individualism, reflecting a diversity and fragmentation of values. The collectivist postwar settlement yielded affluence and new freedoms that promoted a proliferation of values, material and substantive, changing the justifications for or foundations of public policy.

During the 1960s, it became clear that governments lacked the ability to establish the conditions for sustained economic growth and so was itself contributing to social conflict. In this era, the £ sterling was tied to the US$ at a fixed exchange rate, constraining the amount of spending increases British governments could permit. If spending increased too rapidly, more imports were purchased by this rising demand, creating a deficit in the external balance of trade and weakening the £ sterling (Dunn and Smith, 1990, pp. 24–5). In consequence, British government instituted deflationary economic policies, alternating with expansionary measures (the 'stop-go' problem). Despite this, inflation and unemployment were kept down, though Britain paid the long-term price of persistently lagging behind its major trading partners in competitiveness. Between 1950 and 1955, government economic policy focused on the payments abroad question and price levels at home, as capacity was stretched to the full. But a greater concern for growth developed between 1955–1960, when two years' stagnation were followed by three years of substantial increases in real incomes and continental countries matched Britain in absolute levels of output and income.

A shift away from the postwar settlement began in the early 1960s, marked by Prime Minister Harold Macmillan's programme of planning for economic growth. From 1960–67 growth became the preoccupying concern. The National Economic Development Council (NEDC) was established at the end of 1961 and projected targets of 4 per cent growth rates for the economy. Yet the balance of payments deficit of 1964 led to deflation during the four subsequent years, with the Treasury's concern to defend the financial base of the nation consistently winning out over efforts by the NEDC (and its little neddies) or the Department of Economic Affairs to strengthen the industrial base (Pollard, 1969, pp. 479–81).

Despite this extraordinary sacrifice, the balance of payments deficit drained resources, being financed by short-term debt and interest on it, and revealed the incapacity of collectivist politics to set limits or motivate greater productivity. In late 1967 pressures finally led to the Wilson government capitulating with a devaluation, a turning point for Harold Wilson and the Labour government (Morgan, 1992, ch. 18). This signalled the need for faster growth and underscored Britain's relative economic decline, 'for although its immediate cause was that Britain's prices and costs had been left too high in relation to others by her failure to maintain similar increases in productivity' (Pollard, 1969, p. 481). Devaluation, increased taxes, and incomes policies kept growth in real disposable income at 1 per cent, significantly below the 2.8 per cent of the 1950s (Jenkins, 1989, p. 12). Blame was directed at the lack of investment in industry and poor industrial relations (Dunn and Smith, 1990, p. 25).

The failure of demand management to work from the late 1960s undermined politicians' ability to choose between different levels of inflation and unemployment. The Phillip's curve gave empirical characterization to the Keynesian formula for demand management, 'showing that an increase in the pressure of demand was associated with a rapid rise in prices and employment' (Kavanagh, 1990, p. 125). If unemployment was thought to be too high, politicians could increase public spending to increase output and employment. But if unemployment was already low, increases in public spending would feed inflation. But in the late 1960 and during the 1970s, these trade-off proved unworkable, with rising unemployment having little effect on the rate of increase in money wages and prices. The economic system seemed to have an inner logic that was inflationary. If costs increased in any sector, companies seemed to have the market clout to pass on the costs in the form of higher prices, and as prices went up, trade unions demanded and received further raises in money wages, reinforcing the spiral of inflation. For Keynesians, the main strategy for controlling this process was prices and incomes policy, rejecting as socially and politically unacceptable the severe depression in economic activity that might be necessary otherwise to reign in inflation (Dunn and Smith, 1990, p. 26).

The emergence of stagflation, the combination of slow growth with rising unemployment and inflation, undermined the last vestiges of faith in collectivist pluralism and made establishing the conditions of economic growth primary. The postwar consensus committed government to fighting unemployment, but when demand was stepped up at a rate above the rate of productivity increase it meant higher inflation, leading in turn to the use of incomes policy to control money wage rises and of deflation. The Heath government abandoned its free market policies in 1972 and 1973 in order to maintain its commitment to full employment, countering rising unemployment with reflation and an expanded money supply. As inflation took off, Heath then moved to incomes policies, imposing a statutory policy after efforts to gain a voluntary agreement failed. After the return of Labour in 1974, inflation became more salient, reaching 19 per cent in 1974 and 26.9 per cent in August 1975, while production fell. The event led politicians to abandon the full employment commitment in 1975 with Chancellor Denis Healey's Budget initiating a move toward deficit cutting and in 1976 when Prime Minister James Callaghan explained to the Labour Party conference that it was no longer possible for public spending to counter rising unemployment (Kavanagh, 1990, p. 127). Growth now, it was thought, depended on containing inflation, and this meant abandoning full employment and attacking trade union power.

The second major shift was to a new type of individualist, issue-oriented politics, centering of the rights of subgroups and often defending an absolutist morality. Affluence meant a better quality of life, but also unleashed new claims for liberalization of society and stimulated consciousness of other forms of deprivation, some in the name of absolute values like the sanctity of life and nature, and the superiority of emotion and spontaneity. Roy Jenkins, Labour Home Secretary in 1967, oversaw legislative changes affording greater personal freedoms, by liberalizing the law on abortion, divorce, and homosexuality. During the late 1950s and early 1960s students united in British universities to campaign for a variety of social ideals, often rejecting the instrumental rationality of contemporary society. The Campaign for Nuclear Disarmament of the late 1950s drew on the energy of the middle-class young. The student rebellion and the protest against the American war in Vietnam expressed youthful discontent during the later 1960s. The young protested in part against consumerism and conformism in a world threatened by nuclear war and ecological loss. Youth assertiveness found expression also in the musical revolution of the 1960s started by the Beatles, symbolizing a more permissive society (Morgan, 1988, p. 645). Alan Sillitoe's *Saturday Night and Sunday Morning* (1958) revealed a working-class awareness of the emptiness of the new prosperity.

Other forms of absolute or consummatory values became the centre of attention. Nationalism increased in importance in Scotland and Wales. Demands for employment, housing, and equality of opportunity by the post-1950 immigrants from India, Pakistan, West Africa, and the West Indies emerged during the 1960s (Morgan, 1988, p. 647). A sharp rise in youth crime and a diffusion of popular culture seen in the creation of commercial television evidence a loosening of societal constraints.

The diversification and increased division between instrumental and emotional grounds for action is also evident in the call for modernization of traditional institutions like the civil service and the rise of a new populism based on a 'romantic revolt' (Beer, 1982, ch. 4). Both scientific rationalism in the form of technology and romanticism in the form of populism became exaggerated. The more important, according to Beer, was the emergence of a 'new populism' that rejected technocracy and bureaucratic authority, placing faith in participation, decentralization, and quality of life. A 'political manifestation of the romantic ethos', populism sprung from the foundations of individual subjectivity as the source of the ends and means of conduct. As Beer expresses it, 'The important thing is not the fruit of experience, but experience itself; not utility, but sentiment; not wealth, power, or any external possession, but feeling' (1982, p. 128). The important result for authority is that subjectivity erodes or rejects external groundings, whether inherited from tradition or given by object-ive function. Instead subjectivity grounds authority in cultural values like group identity or community membership. These values break up the solidarity of class that had undergirded the postwar consensus redefining the polity as a mosaic of alternative and competing ways of living.

Affluence meant a complex process in which middle and working classes moved toward a convergence in their life styles and enjoyments. Still, Marwick writes: 'by the late Fifties the British were living in an era of unprecedented material prosperity and were in process of being relieved of much of the remaining apparatus of social control dating from Victorian times' (1968, p. 409). Kenneth Morgan argues that despite emerging con-cerns about economic growth, by the 1960s affluence meant improved lives and security.

> For the British, life seemed now distinctly better. A falling birth-rate meant smaller and more affluent households. Homes were better fur-nished. Families increasingly had cars; they could buy their homes on cheap mortgages; they managed each summer a decent holiday abroad in Spain, France, or Italy. Nor were these growing delights confined to the semi-detached middle class in the suburbs. Working-class people

also enjoyed air-lifted holidays to the sunny Mediterranean coast, and revelled in pubs, clubs, and elsewhere, in the freedom of choice afforded by higher wages and shorter working hours. (Morgan, 1988, p. 644)

More details refine these characterizations. Average real wages increased 20 per cent between 1951 and 1958 and another 30 per cent by 1964 (Marwick, 1968, p. 418). With expenditure on food remaining stable, the extra income went for items like cars, motorcycles, furniture, electrical and other durable goods for household consumption.

Shifting Relations of Agency

The changing character and balance of internal (claims) and external (constraints and benefits) factors of experience affected agency relationships, that is, the initiative of individuals as members and leaders of groups in putting forward their claims and the ability of government officials to lead. Despite macroeconomic failures, rising prosperity and the emergence of substantive claims meant that agents spoke from new and more differentiated platforms. In these conditions individuals and organized groups became more confident, ambitious, and self-interested.

One effect was the upsurge of influence from the shop floor, contributing ultimately to class decomposition. While the 'social contract' and labour legislation of the mid-1970s increased the representative function of the Trades Union Congress (TUC), the General Council increasingly responded to the pressures from below (Middlemas, 1979, p. 451). Middlemas summarizes:

Time and again militant rank and file opinion – of which shop stewards themselves where often only a reflection – stimulated changes in General Council policy, not only because leaders like Jones and Scanlon naturally responded, but because in many areas of industry, particularly the most advanced, technologically and structurally, union officials were being promoted with long experience of shop floor 'unofficial' unionism behind them, men whose political base lay not within the official lay committees of the unions but rather on the shop floor with the rank and file. (1979, p. 448)

Another effect was that as the new group politics evolved, the position of organized labour changed, giving it broader power and new mission. Equality of representation with the Confederation of British Industry

(CBI) on the NEDC or other government bodies was less important than a more general claim, which had been made, granting the TUC the position to speak 'not merely on industrial policy, but on areas which in the past the TUC had recognised as the sphere of government: fiscal policy, investment, monopolies and the location and stature of public and private industry' (Middlemas, 1979, p. 449). Moreover, world events like the Vietnam war, the end of fixed exchange rates, and the OPEC oil embargo and subsequent fuel price increases provided groups with justification and encouragement for assertiveness in making claims and making their influence even greater by placing constraints on the ability of governments to respond.

The greater assertiveness by societal groupings derived from the loosening of the traditional social controls of class society, or, as Beer formulates it, a loss of deference toward authority. Survey evidence from the 1970s revealed a growing distrust and rejection of government, a disgruntlement with government's responsiveness and accessibility, and a tendency to link support for government to its actual performance (Beer, 1982, p. 114). One study even suggested that the British public was increasingly inclined to engage in direct action in contrast to deferring to the government (Norton, 1991, p. 398). A decline in respect for the law, for the Constitution, and for the processes of government seem borne out by the willingness of trade unions and local governments to refuse to cooperate with government policy or in other ways to challenge its authority (Punnett, 1988, p. 24).

The ability of groups to use direct power to obtain new benefits or defend their privileges reflects the loss of initiative by both the government and the union leadership. Challenges came from the backlash against incomes policies. From a strategy aiming to facilitate increased growth, incomes policies by the mid-1960s were the main instrument of deflation in the battle to stabilize the pound sterling and reduce inflation. Free collective bargaining led to the strike wave of 1968-1974, revealing its incompatibility with the maintenance of full employment and financing the welfare state (Jenkins, 1989, p. 12). Between 1964 and 1970 unemployment rose from a quarter to over half a million and after 1967 inflation took off, ending the decade at 8 per cent. In part America's involvement in the Vietnam war led to an exporting of inflation and excess of global money supply, but increasingly inflation was seen to derive from trade union wage settlements. The Wilson government established the National Prices and Incomes Board (NPIB), exemplifying a faith in the expert and tripartite policy-making, to investigate pay conflicts and encourage pay restraint. The numbers of strikes, especially unofficial strikes, increased sharply after 1968, showing rank and file impatience with pay restraint. In 1972 the Heath government conceded a 27 per cent wage rise to the miners, defeating their anti-inflationary efforts. The October 1973 Yom Kippur war and the quadrupling of oil prices pushed up inflation and encouraged unions, the miners included, to see what they could extract when conditions made their labour more important than ever. Rank and file pressure pushed miners' leaders into another confrontation with the government in late 1973 and early 1974.

Government pressures on the TUC and trade unions to support its economic policies encouraged these groups to contest government strategies and to propose their own policy options (Crouch, 1979, p. 64). The trade unions significantly influenced the parliamentary leadership when Labour returned to office in 1974. When inflation and government finances got out of control between 1974 and 1976, the Labour Government relied on TUC initiatives on incomes policies to restrain wage rises. With Jack Jones, the powerful leader of the Transport and General Workers Union (TGWU), leading the way, the TUC proposed a package of measures consisting of a commitment to reduce inflation, price controls, a flat-rate pay rise, and no pay increase for those on high incomes. Agreed to by the CBI, this proposal became government policy with only minor amendments in 1975 (Crouch, 1979, p. 97). The Chancellor's 1976 Budget speech proposal trading wage restraint for tax cuts symbolized just how politicized and corporatist economic policy-making had become. The process of negotiation and the substance of policy (linking taxes to wages) required public debate (Crouch, 1979, p. 99). With the leftward drift in policy deriving from the alliance between the left and the unions, Prime Minister Wilson grew ever more isolated from the party conference, its executive, and found even the parliamentary party unmanageable (Morgan, 1992, pp. 415 and 502–3).

This loss of state initiative can also be seen in efforts to reform industrial relations. The first important attempt was the 1969 Labour government's White Paper, *In Place of Strife*, which intended to legislate conciliation pauses, strike ballots, an investigatory commission for inter-union disputes, and a compulsory register for trade unions. This effort to legislate restraints on unions, despite the support that the 1968 Donovan commission gave to voluntarism and free collective bargaining, aimed to make incomes policies less important and reassure creditors abroad (Crouch, 1979, pp. 68–70). Strong objection from the TUC joined by a revolt in the parliamentary Labour party forced Employment Secretary Barbara Castle, the chief architect, and Prime Minister Harold Wilson to abandon their legislation.

The Heath government in 1970 attempted a second time to use the direct force of the state to weaken trade unions. For two years Prime Minister Heath pursued a radical strategy of abandoning the postwar settlement in favour of a free market approach. The Industrial Relations Act, passed without union consultation, intensified antagonism between unions, the membership, and the government. Unofficial strikes in the public sector increased, being politicized in some cases by ministers' declarations of states of emergency and public condemnations. Public sector strikes included action by the local government manual workers, electricity workers, postmen, health service manual staffs, coal miners and railwaymen, while private sector action included the dockers, building workers, and Ford motorcar workers (Crouch, 1979, p. 74). The miners developed mass picketing, the building workers flying pickets, with some picketing turning violent. Yet, the government backed down in all cases except in the dispute with the postmen. Making these many industrial disputes even more intense was the conflict over the Industrial Relations Bill (Crouch, 1979, p. 75). The Act provided further incentive for industrial and political action, with industrial relations becoming ever more politicized. In the end, the unions' strategy of passive resistance paid off, furthering their confidence in making demands. This was so particularly since the Industrial Relations Act was abandoned as the Heath government, facing mounting unemployment and inflation, made a dash for growth and legislated an incomes policy (Crouch, 1979, p. 82).

The ability of the left-leaning unions dominating the TUC to take initiative in a wide range of public policy matters became most obvious with the fourth Wilson government's trade union legislation. The 'social contract', an effort by the Labour Party to revive a national consensus through a bargain between the Labour Party National Executive and the TUC's General Council in 1972 committed a future Labour Government to repealing the Conservative's Industrial Relations Act and statutory incomes policy, to extending price controls, to introducing new legislation to enhance union and worker rights, and to a number of other measures in exchange for union consideration of the state of the economy when advancing wage claims (Crouch, 1979, p. 89). The Employment Protection Act of 1975 and the Trade Union and Labour Relations (Amendment) Act of 1976 fulfilled the Labour Government side of the bargain, extending for individuals protection against unfair dismissal, redundancy payments, paid time for union work, and maternity leave for women and for unions, immunities from common law actions, legal procedures for obtaining recognition, new rights to information pertinent to bargaining, and a new arbitration facility, the Advisory, Conciliation and

Arbitration Service (ACAS) (Crouch, 1979, p. 92). Constituting a significant shift in the balance of power toward unions, these measures advanced the use of the law and state institutions, revealing a new confidence on the part of organized labour about its ability to use the state.

The remaining vestiges of authority of the social democratic governing formula finally crumbled with the trade union revolt against Labour Prime Minister Callaghan's incomes policy during the 1978–79 Winter of Discontent, a series of unofficial and localized strikes that revealed starkly the breakdown of the old formula. Trade union rank and file, having aggregated power during the 1970s under Labour's social contract policy, exposed the lack of consent for economic policy and the government's vulnerability in the face of group pressures. The events of the Winter of Discontent revealed an upsurge of self-interest and pettiness, not working-class cohesion and common aspirations. According to Peter Jenkins, 'The country seemed to be in the hands of self-appointed Gauleiters, pickets and strike committees, who officiously decreed who and what should pass' (1989, p. 27). The accompanying media spectacle and daily experiences of Britons seemed to corroborate neoliberal arguments that the social democratic formula could not maintain order or control industrial conflict. As Jenkins concludes, 'If there was something aspiring to be called a "consensus", in the sense of a general disposition to uphold the Post-war Settlement by co-operation across the class divide between government, employers and trade unions, it was the events of the winter of 1979, not Margaret Thatcher, which put an end to it' (1989, p. 28). In short, by the 1970s collectivist pluralism was becoming a mix of excessive group representation and state concessions and was clearly failing to foster public authority or to provide effective economic management.

Decision-Making Processes

The main elements and processes of policy-making associated with the postwar collectivist consensus were collapsing or discredited as state-society relations of direct power became conflictual and political. By the late 1970s only two elements of the postwar consensus remained, although even these now functioned in a different manner. The trade union leadership was more than ever intimately integrated into state policy-making and economic institutions, though their role was now highly politicized. Similarly, there was a continuity of liberalism in the form of a priority on free collective bargaining, 'shown in the reluctance of all concerned to move away from a model of the two sides of industry confronting each other in bargaining and accommodating their conflicting interests without external regulation' (Crouch, 1979, pp. 106–7). And parliamentary government seemed to have been further weakened by party dealignment. A decline in support for the two main parties at the general elections and in public opinion polls show an increased volatility among voters, and identification with a political party dissipated (Kavanagh, 1990, pp. 143–5). This is associated with a decline in the class bases of the major parties (Sarlvik and Crewe, 1983).

For the most part the key elements of the postwar consensus – state intervention to guarantee full employment, to expand the welfare state, and to integrate functional groups whose expertise in running the economy was needed – were gone, former partners in consensus now operating to new rules and for different ends. The agreement to keep industrial relations out of politics gave way to intense politicization. The government's neutrality, permitting a measure of mediation and conciliation, ended, the state now itself a major player as a benefactor and supplicant. The commitment to full employment went after 1975. The ability of a centralized leadership to dominate the trade union movement with a national policy largely disappeared (Crouch, 1979, p. 106). And the commitment to growth and the welfare state as a universal service came under attack, as looming economic disaster forced retrenchment.

The loss of control of the economy led to an International Monetary Fund (IMF) rescue package in December 1976, stabilizing sterling through elements of austerity and Keynesianism. Incomes policy and tax cuts mixed with spending cuts, reduction of public sector borrowing requirements, and cash limits for government spending and targets for money supply. By 1979 unemployment rose to 1.2 million. A new realism took hold after Prime Minister Wilson removed Tony Benn as Minister for the Department of Industry following the June 1975 EC referendum. Wilson and Chancellor Healey returned to an incomes policy to contain the inflationary pressures of excessive money wage raises. After taking over as Prime Minister in 1976, James Callaghan continued this package, boldly announcing the end of Keynesian economic management to the autumn Labour Party conference.

The effort to control the economy through public ownership continued in limited fashion. The Heath government had sold off Thomas Cook's travel agency and the Carlisle state brewery, but took over Rolls-Royce and prevented the closedown of the Upper Clyde shipyard. The Labour government's return in 1974 promised large-scale nationalizations. While in opposition a Labour Party working group called for the nationalization of 25 of Britain's largest companies and a renationalization without compensation of the firms the Conservatives had sold off. The 1974 Party manifesto called for the nationalization of specific industries like the ports, shipbuilding, and aircraft, the institution of planning agreements between government and industrial firms with a view to promoting investment and employment, and the creation of a National Enterprise Board (NEB) to buy shares in companies to promote investment, exports, and other national interests (Stewart, 1978, pp. 215–17). New calls for nationalization and planning agreements were made by a party policy statement in 1976. Yet, while nationalizing parts of the specific industries identified in 1974, only one planning agreement had been made by 1979 and the NEB simply took over the shares of companies that previous governments had taken up in order to prevent their collapse (Kavanagh, 1990, p. 138).

After 1976, the Labour government applied cash limits to welfare services. Between 1953 and 1973, social welfare, encompassing social security, education, the health service, and other personal social services, benefited from an increase of 12 per cent, while programmes covering housing and the environment, transport, employment, agriculture and food increased by only 6 per cent. Public expenditure on the military, law and order, debt, finance, and external affairs decreased dramatically, by 18 per cent over the same period (Kavanagh, 1990, pp. 45 and 141). Pressures for moving from a universal provision to a selective one had been increasing even earlier as prosperity grew for the majority, while a core of real poverty remained (Marwick, 1968, pp. 430 and 433). For the left, poverty continued, since it was defined in relative terms, and led to criticism of the Labour governments in the 1960s and 1970s. After 1975, the right demanded that costs be cut, services be privatized, benefits be made selectively so as to generate a moral incentive for work. In the 1970s, doubts about the moral and material utility of the welfare state grew. Julian Le Grand (1982) argued that the welfare state actually benefited the better off, failing in its aim of redistributing life chances. The attack on 'big government' mounted in Britain's slow growth economy, with limited resources heightening the clash between social policy and collective bargaining and government policy failure producing some modesty about the prospects of solving complex problems by the expenditure of resources (Kavanagh, 1990, pp. 132–41).

The conflict between the effects of full employment on living standards and bargaining power of workers and the consequences of unrestrained collective bargaining strained the corporatist bias on which policy-making stood. As Peter Jenkins summarizes this process of attitude change:

> In order to defend full employment, promote economic expansion and avoid policies of crude wage restraint, trade unions were drawn into

5

44   *Power and Privatization*

sharing responsibility for the management of the economy. To their members this appeared as a collusion with the government and employers for the purposes of reducing real wages. The authority of national leaderships was undermined, the power of shop stewards enhanced, and the fires of militancy fuelled. By the same process the government came to be held responsible for what people were paid, not only for the general level of wages but for the disparities between the pay of a nurse and a miner, a general and a policeman. Government soon found itself carrying a can of worms marked 'social justice'.   (Jenkins, 1989, p. 10)

The emergence of these new connections and the transformation between members, unions, and the government led to still other new demands and strategies, constituting a wholesale reorganization of the postwar patterns of coordination and control.

Since state intervention and planning entailed extending the 'corporatist bias' that had been evolving since WWI, a 'process of government by bribery' ensued. It involved a 'whole syndrome of threats and inducements, in which the threats became less and less credible, and the inducements more and more lavish, until Keynesian social democracy ended in industrial anarchy' (Skidelsky, 1988, p. 13). As David Marquand argues, Britain's social democrats lacked a theory of the political economy which would give them effective control of group pressures or legitimate the distributional consequences of incomes and industrial policies (Marquand, 1988, pp. 58–61). Alternatively, Peter Jenkins pictured the contradictory and unstable relationship between ends and means facing the Labour movement. He asked how it was to reconcile its goals of full employment, welfare, and price stability with its commitment to free collective bargaining (Kavanagh, 1990, pp. 129–30). With the growth of bargaining power and the heightened importance of the shop floor in decision-making, policy-making depended on gaining the consent of the trade unions. As a result, the state lost power to producer groups, whom it depended on for the success of its policies, but whom it could not persuade or coerce.

CONCLUSION

The postwar consensus involved a collectivist pluralism, in which policy-making drew on expanded group representation and benefit distribution. Emerging from the need to sustain state autonomy after WWII, the extension of direct policy-making power to groups succeeded in expanding representation and improving material conditions of life. The pattern of power became dysfunctional by the 1970s, evolving into a system that limited the ability of governments to deal with the challenges of greater international economic competition and heightened material demands at home. As producer groups gained policy making influence, the government lost initiative and authority to effect policy. Power relations became more politicized, more conflictual, and more stalemated, as the consensus and cooperation of the early postwar year turned into dissension and self-aggrandizement.

The problem facing collectivist pluralism by the early 1960s was not a question of limited resources, too many demands, legitimation, vested interests, or a romantic rebellion against authority. The question was its inappropriateness as a means of providing solutions and control in an environment demanding greater efficiency in the use of limited resources (Wolfe, 1989, pp. 168–72). Collectivist pluralism had proved effective at satisfying expanding group wants and giving groups' influence after WWII. But it failed to work in an increasingly competitive and hostile domestic and international environment. This ineffectiveness produced the unwanted consequences of rising inflation and unemployment and government fecklessness. The postwar policy-making process, responding to the need for social integration, proved unable to cope with the need for greater efficiency, competitiveness and productivity.

3 The New Right and State Power*

The fundamental difficulty facing British politicians in the late 1960s and 1970s was a failure of state power, not simply economic and geopolitical decline. Both political parties had been discredited by the end of the 1970s. As the crisis deepened, so ideological debate intensified. For the Conservatives, the 'undermining of the traditional authority of the state that was thought to be occurring in the 1970s' led to the development of the new right or Thatcherism (Barry, 1990, p. 21). This, along with efforts by the Labour Party to renew socialism marked what Raymond Plant refers to as 'a tacit admission of the failure of the British state to govern efficiently, justly and authoritatively' (1988, p. 9). Carried out in the discourse of economic language, this debate posed the question of how political control was to be reestablished.

This chapter examines the development of the neoliberal elements of the New Right as a prescription for restoring state power and control. In examining what the key ideas were, where they came from, what changes they went through, and how they triumphed, it is clear that the Thatcherites had no fixed plan or even ideology. Their chief concern was with ways of restoring state autonomy in Britain's parliamentary democracy and searching for ideas that pictured an alternative and workable pattern of power. Raymond Plant states in reference to recent ideological debates, 'Right across the political spectrum political parties are looking for ways to replace government as the major agent of allocation of values, goods, services, benefits, burdens and cost' (1988, p. 9). To examine how the Conservative Party turned to neoliberal ideas, this chapter studies the rise of monetarism, analyzes its picture of power, describes the turn toward privatization, and examines the model of power in arguments justifying privatization.

---

*Parts of this chapter draw on my previous research in 'Privatization and the Reshaping of Pluralist Democracy: The British Case', presented at the 1985 American Political Science Association Annual Meeting, and my chapter, Wolfe, 1989a.

THE RISE OF MONETARISM

Thatcher's monetarism emerged in the early 1970s from a conversion of leading opponents of twice defeated former Conservative prime minister Edward Heath to a broadly monetarist viewpoint. There was a general questioning of the postwar achievements from the 1960s onwards that contributed to the search for alternative governing philosophies; but, it was the conversion of Sir Keith Joseph and Margaret Thatcher to monetarist neoliberal ideas that made them important. Rather than the imposition of a ruling class, than a response to popular pressures for fundamental restructuring of the political economy, or than the institution of state interests, the rise of monetarism, privatization, and deregulation rests on the decisions of individual leaders. They faced the need to come to terms with the immediate and long-term needs: a Conservative Party confronting subordination to a Labour Party agenda and a series of electoral defeats, a nation suffering from the problems of inflation and industrial decline, and a failure of state intervention, planning, and bureaucratization. The result of these problems was to ideologize Conservative and party politics and to bring to the foreground a debate about how to recast Britain's way of governing.

In 1974 Sir Keith Joseph became the most important convert to and proponent of monetarism and neoliberal ideas. He had been (Secretary of State for Social Services, DHSS) in the Heath government of 1970–74 and had gained large increases in funds for his department. After the Conservatives' February 1974 election defeat he abandoned collectivism altogether. Sir Keith Joseph took up the task of renewing Conservative political philosophy and policy. With the conviction of a born-again fundamentalist, he provided 'the nearest statement of a "New Right" credo' by bringing together monetarism and the neoliberal themes expressed by Friederick von Hayek and the public choice economists (Kavanagh, 1990, pp. 115 and 117).

Helped by friends like Alan Walters, Alfred Sherman and Peter Bauer, Sir Keith converted to monetarist neoliberalism. He attacked excessive state spending in the form of deficit financing and borrowing as the primary source of inflation and the loss of a 'private enterprise dynamic'. He advocated instead a decentralized, profit-seeking, competitive economic system (Keegan, 1984, p. 46). He preached that the state could create the environment for market capitalism by expanding the individual freedom to make choices as much as possible (Kavanagh, 1990, p. 116). Besides attacking deficit financing and demand management as the source of decline at a time when global inflation and a loss of markets to developing states were forcing structural adjustment, Sir Keith challenged the idea that unemployment was in itself evil, criticized incomes policies, and spoke of the 'great havoc' caused by excessive money supply. His speech at Preston Town Hall on 4 September, 1974, became an 'historic event, the final, considered Josephite onslaught' on the postwar framework, written with the aid of Alfred Sherman, Samuel Brittan, and Peter Jay (Young, 1990, p. 88).

To advance his new ideology, Sir Keith organized the Centre for Policy Studies (CPS). He became its founder and chairman with Margaret Thatcher as President and Alfred Sherman as Director. The CPS's avowed purpose was to 'reshape the climate of opinion'. Thatcher, with her Grantham grocer's daughter background that centred on hard work, family responsibility, ambition, duty, and patriotism, was a willing convert to Sir Keith's crusade. The CPS joined the Institute for Economic Affairs (IEA), a market-oriented propaganda organ formed in 1957, in the gathering effort to proselytize. The IEA, also emphasizing limited government and virtues of the market, was particularly important in publicizing the ideas of Hayek and American public choice theorists (Kavanagh, 1990, p. 81–3). Other groups formed later to propagate Josephite ideas included the Adam Smith Institute, founded in 1977, and the Social Affairs Unit, founded in 1980, to bring new right ideas into discussions of social policy. Business groups, such as the Aims of Industry, dating from 1942, and the Institute of Directors, originating in 1906, also joined in promoting the liberal economic views of the emerging Thatcherites.

The formation of the CPS, genuine though its educational purpose was, signalled a challenge to Heath's leadership. William Keegan contends, 'before the prospect of the leadership arose, [monetarist] ideas were conspicuous only by their absence' (Keegan, 1984, p. 47). Heath's election losses in February and October 1974 dominated the 1975 Conservative Party leadership contest, not new right ideology. However, Sir Keith raised doubts about his own leadership ability by undermining the Party at a crucial moment in an election campaign with his Preston speech and by advocating contraception for the poor in a later speech. Thatcher fortuitously stepped into the breech. With the leading moderate or 'middle way' contenders, such as William Whitelaw and Edward du Cann, refusing to stand against Heath in the first ballot. Thatcher became the alternative. She was backed by both a majority of Conservative Members of Parliament dissatisfied with Heath's ineffective leadership and a committed minority of right-wingers and monetarists.

While a few academic economists like Milton Friedman had long crusaded for controlling inflation by controlling the money supply,

monetarism rose to prominence with the help of leading financial commentators in the British press and a handful of British economists. Peter
Jay at *The Times* and Samuel Brittan of the *Financial Times*, former
Keynesians who had been impressed by Friedmanite explanations of the
correlation between the growth rate in money supply and inflation under
the Heath Government, began shifting to monetarism in 1968 and 1969
(Smith, 1987, p. 36). The *Times* editor William Rees-Mogg also joined
the monetarist movement. Economist Harry Johnson, who held posts at
the University of Chicago and the London School of Economics (LSE), set
up the Money Study Group in 1969, a forum for disseminating monetarist
ideas. Others academics, like David Laidler and Michael Parkin at
Manchester University, Alan Walters at the LSE (and later Thatcher's
economic advisor at No.10), Brian Griffiths at City University, and Patrick
Minford at Liverpool were among the first to espouse monetarist explanations. By mid-1974 monetarism was gaining popularity and influencing
the political debate out of proportion to its status in the economic
profession as a whole or in the Bank of England and Whitehall, where
there were only a few converts.

The mass media also assisted by mounting a campaign to disseminate
new right monetarist ideas. Editorial support came from *The Economist*,
The Times, *The Spectator*, and *The Daily Telegraph*. Sympathetic voices
like Paul Johnson, Roger Scruton, John Hoskyns, Digby Anderson, Walter
Goldsmith, and John Vincent wrote columns in the press. Some commentators, including Woodrow Wyatt, Hugh Thomas the historian, John Vaizey
the economist, and Paul Johnson the former editor of the *New Statesman*,
moved rightwards ideologically. Former Labour Cabinet ministers, such as
Lord George-Brown, Lord Marsh, Lord Chalfont and Reg Prentice, joined
them. With the core supporters advocating monetarism in the *Daily
Telegraph* and the *Spectator*, lecturing at IEA lunches or working at the
CPS, personal and institutional connections among proponents multiplied,
facilitating policy making influence (Kavanagh, 1990, p. 96).

The Labour government's monetarism during the mid-1970s was a
pragmatic and emergency response to the failure of demand management.
But monetarism fitted uneasily with the Keynesian elements (like incomes
policies) that were fundamental to Labour's economic policy until its
defeat in 1979. Monetarism was adopted not because it had a foundation
in Labour ideology but because monetarist ideas mattered to external
creditors and seemed useful in regaining control of public finances (see,
Brittan, 1987, p. 249).

With the loss of faith in demand management and the Labour
Government's ad hoc adaptation of sound money policy alongside its

planning and incomes policies, the Thatcherites consolidated their hold on
the Conservative Party and strengthened their commitment to monetarism.
Sir Keith gained converts among some members of Tory Party research
institutions and committees and among ideologically predisposed party
followers (Keegan, 1984, p. 30). They purged some Heath supporters at
the Central Office and replaced them with Thatcherite loyalists. In the
Shadow Cabinet, Thatcher moved her most loyal supporters into the key
economic policy jobs and retained heavyweight 'wets', such as William
Whitelaw, Lord Carrington and Francis Pym, in non-economic posts
(ibid., p. 71). The Heath loyalist Jim Prior, who shadowed industrial relations as Employment spokesman, moved slowly but steadily toward
accepting the necessity of giving Thatcherism a try (Young, 1990, pp. 117
and 167). With the conversion of Sir Geoffrey Howe, Nigel Lawson,
David Howell, John Biffen and John Nott, the ranks grew. But it was the
alignment of Thatcher as leader, Sir Geoffrey Howe as Shadow
Chancellor and Sir Keith as sage that set the course.

MONETARISM: MARKET AS DIRECT STATE POWER

The Thatcher plan from the start was to replace a faltering postwar governing formula based on pluralist collectivism with a neoliberal alternative. Yet, to appreciate the sources and meaning of monetarism and
privatization it is necessary to locate it in its larger context of overall political strategy, which aspired to provide an alternative governing formula.
Events challenged the Keynesian orthodoxy and left it wanting. With the
emergence of stagflation, simultaneous rising prices and rising unemployment, Keynesian recipes for unemployment threatened even higher
inflation (Smith, 1987, p. 45). With the old formula yielding only greater
disorder, the search was on for a new paradigm to provide a means for
restoring order. How did monetarism, or Thatcherism in its initial phase,
propose to alter power in Britain?

Monetarism, first, prescribes markets as a foundational framework by
relying on economic forces in the form of gains and losses to impose discipline. A stable, non-inflationary free-market capitalist regime, it proposes, requires 'a binding and inescapable monetary discipline such as had
been imposed by the Gold Standard or fix exchange rates' (Hoover and
Plant, 1989, p. 26). The quantity theory of money holds 'that, in the long
run, the main determinant of monetary demand or the total level of spending, and thus the main influence upon the Gross Domestic Product (GDP),
is the quantity of money circulating in the economy' (Hoover and Plant,

1989, p. 24). Consequently, contrary to the Keynesian view, monetarism contends that expansionary policies, designed to curb unemployment, only generate more inflation and increase unemployment.

Monetarism purported to provide a framework which would enable the government to force groups to accept limits on their claims. The state acts as the 'trustee of the whole community in any economic system, holding the balance between different interests' (Conservative Party, 1976, in O'Gorman, 1986, p. 226). The government, by controlling the money supply, establishes a nonpolitical framework that imposes economic discipline through its effects on trade-offs and by creating credibility in the rules of play (Willetts, 1992, pp. 126–7). The government's control of the money supply imposes physical limits on economic transactions. In fixing the money supply, the government makes the relationship between public spending and service levels depend on available resources. More specifically, if inflation is to be minimized, expansion of money supply must be in line with output growth, assuming that a free economy maximizes output. According to David Willetts, inflation 'is caused by governments running too loose a financial policy, thus allowing the total amount of money circulating in the economy to increase by more than real output can grow' (1992, p. 125). This implies that the state bears the responsibility for inflation, since it influences the total spending through public sector deficits, interest rates, intervention in foreign exchange markets and the like.

By reducing the money supply the government could compel people to reduce their spending. This implied, first, that it could bring inflation under control, while making trade unions and monopolistic firms bear responsibility for unemployment. Increased costs could cause inflation only if government matched it by increased spending; alternatively, if spending were held down in the face of rising costs and prices', the result would be unemployment (Dunn and Smith, 1990, p. 28) A second implication was that cutting government borrowing was the most efficient way to control money supply. Since government bonds are sold to finance public spending and function as assets 'backing' commercial bank loans, the less government borrowed the less commercial banks would be able to make loans. In short, an iron-clad money discipline, requisite for a sound economy, required an act of political will that would simultaneously revive state autonomy.

Simply put, monetarism theorized an anchor for a non-inflationary and stable economy. In consequence, it shifts the grounds for public spending, away from the Keynesian focus on how levels of spending affect output and employment to questions about how to finance current and future public expenditure (Hoover and Plant, 1989, p. 26; Dunn and Smith, 1990, p. 29). Limiting public spending involves either cutting programmes or raising taxes. Monetarism permits either choice. The supplementary arguments contending that public spending and taxation erode the efficient functioning of markets and lead to privileges for vested interests, dependency, and tyranny make spending cuts the preferred way to reduce state spending (Hoover and Plant, 1989, p. 26).

Second, the monetarist idea offered the Tories a vision that would enable them to reset the political agenda. The New Right believed that monetarism would reverse a decline in the electoral fortunes of Conservative Party, which held office for only four years between 1964 and 1979 in comparison with thirty-seven years between 1918 and 1964 (Jacques, 1983, p. 52). Moreover, the 1970–74 Heath government had failed to restore growth without inflation, rejuvenating the old collectivist formula after two years of a free market strategy (Gamble, 1983, p. 116). Even worse, Prime Minister Heath seriously miscalculated in calling a general election over the Miners' strike. In response to their own and the nations' conundrums, Conservatives from the mid-1960s moved rightwards, yet monetarism does not seem to have captured their attention (except for Enoch Powell) until 1974.

Monetarism, then, offered the Party and a prospective Conservative government a means for taking the initiative in setting the political agenda in a time of rising inflation and declining competitiveness. Control of inflation became the key to reversing Britain's long-term decline during the 1970s despite a record low unemployment by 1980s and 1990s standards (Pym, 1984, p. 138). According to monetarists, the pursuit of full-employment caused inflation and undermined competitiveness. They rejected outright the conjectures of Keynesian demand management that governments could control the level of unemployment by selecting monetary and fiscal policy. Rather they argued that the labour market determined the minimum level of unemployment, with any attempt to push unemployment artificially below its 'labour market' level producing inflation. By implication that trade unions caused unemployment by demanding concessions that priced people out of jobs (Keegan, 1984, p. 42). In linking selfish and overbearing group influence to rising inflation and rising unemployment, monetarists identified political weakness as the source of economic decline, seen in a halving of Britain's share of world trade between 1955 and 1980 (Howe, 1983, p. 6).

With their attacks on public spending and focus on the threat to freedom of the corporate state, Sir Keith and Thatcher shifted the political ethos and policy agenda towards a fundamental break with postwar collectivism.

At one level, monetarism attacks the evil of inflation deriving from public expenditure and excessive wage increases, which increases the price of commodities without increasing their value. In reducing productivity and competitiveness, inflation destroys jobs and erodes entrepreneurial incentives.

At a more fundamental level, monetarism challenged the power relations between groups and the state which had evolved since WWII. Monetarism proposed to mount a direct attack on interest group representation. Unions in particular threatened liberty. Sharing public power with private interest groups through social contract agreements established a corporatist state and made parliamentary democracy illusory. The monetarists believed that previous concessions to power grabbing interest groups that were responsible for economic decline, openly repudiating the Tory paternalist and collective 'middle way' tradition of Disraeli and Macmillan. By making concessions to unions, Conservative were put on the defensive, always working from a weak position. William Keegan characterizes this viewpoint, 'by searching for the middle ground, the Tories were allowing the rules to be dictated by their opponents' (Keegan, 1984, p. 84). In consequence, the managed economy and welfare state were, according to monetarist philosophy, the source of common ailments – the too large public sector, the faltering of entrepreneurialism, the wasted subsidies for nationalized industry, and the failing of private firms.

In reality, then, monetarism provided the emerging Thatcherites with a way to recast political debate and to gain political advantage. Monetarists asserted their claim to lead based on their political vision. This is evident in their call to alter the power relations that had evolved since 1945. It meant a radical break with the postwar consensus and with the 'middle way' tradition of Ted Heath and Francis Pym, which argues for consent, compromise and balance. The political aim implicit in monetarists' goals of restoring the market and the authority of property owners, social institutions, and Parliament to their 'rightful' places was to gain political initiative. In saying that collectivism ironically reduces the ability of governments to secure citizens' public interest, monetarists claimed that their programme offered a more effective programme of governing (Atkinson, 1984, p. 8).

Third, monetarist processes would purportedly limit the power of interest groups by establishing the criteria defining exchanges or trade-offs, compelling efficiency of means and optimization of returns in decision-making. For monetarists, an environment unleashing and encouraging economic forces would discipline individual and group choices. Market

processes would act as effective forces but had to be fashioned and protected by the government. Individual choice was central to market discipline but the substance of the choices were controlled by political will.
Monetarists held that refashioning the environment shapes individual and
collective action or choice, in turn determining how groups relate to each
other and the government.

To achieve the economic circumstances compelling readjustment of
group and individual behaviour requires a strong state, one willing and
able to intervene in civil society in order to impose the conditions and
rules for expanding capitalist processes. To constrain self-serving interest
groups, to create a prosperity generating market order, and to liberate individuals from bureaucratic oppression, monetarism pictures a government
using direct force (Gamble, 1985, pp. 22–4). Thatcher said, in reference to
improving the economy, 'My job is to let the country begin to exist within
sensible and realistic economic disciplines' (cited in Young, 1990, p. 207).
In short, a strong state directing the reconstruction of a liberating environment is necessary to change individuals' motivations and habits. While
monetarism emerged as an economic policy in response to the failure of
the social democratic formula to control inflation, its political significance
lay in its model of politics, in which a strong state restructures the environment of politics in order to make costs rather than benefits the imperative
of group behaviour.

FROM MONETARISM TO PRIVATIZATION

The Thatcher administration took office in 1979 committed to the monetarist approach to economic policy to bring down inflation. The first
'enthusiastic' phase extended from May 1979 until late 1980, relying on
M3 (cash plus current and deposit accounts) as the target indicator affecting interest rate decisions (Riddell, 1989, p. 18). The government, believing that controlling the money supply would restrain the growth of public
spending, sought to reduce the Public Sector Borrowing Requirement
(PSBR) and to cut public spending. These goals gave rise to the Medium
Term Financial Strategy (MTFS), announced on March 20, 1980, which
set strict monetary guidelines for the rate of money growth and reductions
in public spending and borrowing. This innovation promised a 4 per cent
reduction in planned expenditure between 1979/80 and 1983/84, continued
cash limits, and the first real cuts (as opposed to reductions in planning
increases) to start in 1981/82 (Hoover and Plant, 1989, p. 157). In addition
to expressing the monetarist proposition that there is a direct link between

money supply and inflation, the MTFS intended to bind the government to an immovable course (Hoover and Plant, 1989, p. 156). Local government spending became tightly regulated, nationalized industries were denied funds for investment, charges were raised for public services, and prices raised in government-run commercial operations.

Yet monetarist policies failed to control the supply of money and the overall level of public spending, showing that the market was no more effective as an instrument of direct force than any other means. The money supply indicator, sterling M3, increased 70 per cent in contrast to 46 per cent projected over the period. Other indicators were then suggested, but the government started to move away from money targets by 1982. In the autumn of 1980 vociferous complaints by industrialists about high sterling and excessive interest rates, led the government, despite its failure to keep within monetary targets, to reduce interest rates (Smith, 1987, p. 98).

The attempt to control money supply produced an increase in interest rates and attracted foreign funds. Sterling rose, reinforced by growing North Sea oil exports and foreign investors' favourable view of government policy. The higher sterling rate made imports cheaper and exports dearer. The reduced competitiveness of British manufacturing produced draconian job losses, falling almost a quarter during the first Thatcher administration. Union power collapsed in the face of severe recession, though firms remaining in business were much more productive (Dunn and Smith, 1990, p. 30). Between the second quarter of 1979 and the first quarter of 1981, industrial production fell by 12.8 per cent and manufacturing output by 17.5 per cent. Unemployment rose from 1.2 million in May 1979 to 2 million by the end of 1980 and to over 3 million by the autumn of 1982 (Smith, 1987, p. 90).

However, a strong pound and a deep recession moved the government to adopt in early 1981 a more flexible or second strategy, which combined a flexible monetary strategy with fiscal restraint. Tighter fiscal control was introduced in the March 1981 Budget in spite of rising unemployment. It was intended to facilitate lower interest rates and to stop the rise in the pound (Riddell, 1989, p. 19). In this second phase, while monetary targets were modified to compensate for past overshooting, the key policy tools became the exchange rate and the PSBR. The March 1982 Budget started the trend toward easing monetary supply. It meant the end of simple monetarism and the phased 'unwinding of the policy, beginning with a pragmatic monetarism that was to give way to total pragmatism' (Smith, 1987, p. 106). The 'death' of monetarism occurred in January 1985 with the shift to pragmatism and the rejection of Friedmanite ideas (Smith, 1987, pp. 122–3).

This second phase, lasting until 1985, drew on another version of monetarist thought, one that favoured developing privatization. This took into account the impact of the flow of money between exchange markets on inflation. If money flows out through the foreign exchange market, currency exchange rate will fall, causing rises in import prices and forcing up overall prices and wages. According to Dunn and Smith, 'This approach implied that the key to controlling inflation lay in maintaining the exchange rate, and this depended on pursuing policies that encouraged an appropriate flow of funds across the foreign exchanges' (1990, p. 32). The key factor in regulating exchange rates, prior to joining the European Exchange Rate Mechanism (ERM), was interest rates. By helping to reduce government borrowing, the revenues gained from privatization helped the government keep interest rates lower than they normally would be.

Between 1979 and 1986, despite a 'decrementalist' approach to reducing expenditure, growth in public spending matched overall economic growth. Cuts in education, housing, transport, trade and industry, and the EEC were offset by increases in defence, agriculture, unemployment benefits, health services, social programmes, and law and order (Hoover and Plant, 1989, pp. 162–3; Dunn and Smith, 1990, pp. 30–1). Public sector employment remained stable, but cash limits necessitated cutting back on the quality of services and investment.

In a third phase, the government, acknowledging its inability to control M3 effectively through continuing to announce targets, turned to exchange rates as the basis for financial discipline (Riddell, 1989, pp. 21–2). Riddell states, 'policy was still guided by monetary indicators such as the price of assets, the exchange rate and interests rates ... [T]he Government believed that ... macro-economic policy should be primarily concerned with fighting inflation' (1989, p. 25). Never reverting to Keynesian demand management, the government put a priority on managing inflation, despite abandoning strict monetarism in favor of 'discretionary' monetarism.

These pressures combined to create an imperative for furthering privatization. First, it offered a means to reduce public spending and borrowing (Dunn and Smith, 1990, p. 32). While Samuel Brittan (1984, p. 113) rightly questions whether the privatization programme was motivated simply by a desire to reduce the PSBR by raising funds, Thatcherism held above all that cutting spending would make room for tax cuts, allow interest rates to fall, help control inflation and put an end to the 'socialist ratchet effect' (Holmes, 1985, pp. 40 and 105). As it became clear during the first few years that the recession was making it harder to cut public expenditure, privatization was given a greater impetus (Riddell, 1983,

p. 138). In autumn 1981, the government decision to raise public spending by £5 billion higher than originally planned elevated the concept of privatization in the neoliberal programme. According to Riddell, the 'inescapable upward pressures on expenditure exerted by the recession (increasing the deficits of nationalized industries and expenditure on unemployment)...[not] a successful campaign by the "wets"' necessitated the extra spending (1983, p. 46).

Second, privatization promised to replace the direct political control of the public sector with the methods typical of business practices – consumer choice, producer competition, and productive efficiency. Contracting out and denationalization would make managers and workers cut costs and improve delivery in services (Dunn and Smith, 1990, p. 31). When Nigel Lawson put forward the sponsoring Ministers' case in September 1982, he argued that nationalized industries were not accountable to anyone and satisfied no one (Riddell, 1983, p. 174). Young concludes, 'As time went on, ministers became more solidly convinced than they had been in 1978 that the wholesale removal of state control, rather than tinkering with the financial regime imposed on state industries, was as politically popular as it was economically necessary' (1990, p. 360). As a consequence, from 1981 on the government turned to privatization to improve financial and constitutional relations between Whitehall and the nationalized industries. And Peter Lilley (1989) confirms this pragmatic character of privatization: 'We were originally attracted to the idea of privatisation not because of any abstract theory or party ideology, but because of a simple pragmatic observation. By and large, free enterprise worked and nationalisation did not ... nationalisation failed its workforce, its customers, and its investors (the taxpayers), and failed to reconcile commercial and wider national interests'.

Third, privatization was the means for increasing supply-side measures, using market transactions to generate efficiency and increased productivity. In the mid-1980s an effect of the shift to using a strong exchange rate to discipline the economy was to make more apparent the need for supply side measures at a time when unemployment remained high and the economy improved. To lower labour unit costs and to price workers into jobs, workers and firms would have to respond more sensitively to market conditions. Chancellor Lawson stated in his 1989 Budget speech: 'Strong sustainable growth is achieved...by allowing markets to work again and restoring the enterprise culture' (cited in Dunn and Smith, 1990, p. 33). Reducing state intervention and creating a free market in labour meant using the freedom of unencumbered choice to create opportunities and jobs.

Fourth, privatization satisfied the needs of the leading Conservative Party policy-makers as recession replaced inflation as an overriding policy problem. One reason Thatcher and her loyal followers, such as Sir Geoffrey Howe and Sir Keith Joseph, emphasized privatization after 1981 was the failure of monetarism to appeal to party activists and supporters. Privatization would reward Conservatives' supporters with increasing profit opportunities and turn attention from the recession (Brittan, 1984, pp. 111–12). Thatcherites faced grave problems in considering the 1982 Budget. The Government was unpopular among their traditional supporters and the public at large, as unemployment reached high levels. Moreover, the world recession was getting worse and British industry was taking a beating. Ministers on the Economic Strategy Committee, feeling that they could not reject their neoliberal ideology and that the falling inflation rate had been their one major achievement, thought that privatization and more anti-union legislation would shift attention to future accomplishments (Keegan 1984, pp. 73–4). Economist Michael Bleaney elaborates: 'The disillusionment with monetarism did, however, lead to a search for new initiatives in other directions. The two which standout are the sale of state assets and industrial relations legislation' (1983, p. 145).

The Conservative administration, in sum, gradually adopted privatization as the central element of its alternative to collectivist pluralism. The privatization programme grew in comprehensiveness at a time when monetarist economics proved ineffective and unpopular, becoming the symbol of the Conservative's radical approach to governing. Privatization obviously fit Thatcher's vision of society, a belief in sound money, family virtues, and private enterprise linked to strongly anti-union and anti-public sector prejudices (Riddell, 1985, p. 231). Yet, the inability of monetarism to halt upward pressures on public spending and to rejuvenate growth and create jobs turned the Thatcherites toward privatization.

While retaining the monetarist commitment to sound money, along with other New Right ideals like individual self interest, a strong state, and diminished union power, privatization replaced monetarism's narrow focus on control of the money supply with a broader supply-side concern. Private ownership and competition promised to make markets for goods and services more efficient, improve the efficiency in the labour market, provide a cheaper means for providing public services, help reduce government spending and borrowing, and so help reduce interest rates. Privatization aided the monetarist objectives of reducing public spending by dismantling the stagnant bureaucratic system that had evolved during the postwar period, and increasing employment opportunities. Once monetarism as a technical notion faded, the macroeconomic anchor with which to discipline public finance became the exchange and interest rates. Yet, New Right commitments to reducing public spending, smashing trade unions, and rolling back state intervention remained and privatization became the chief strategy for implementing these neoliberal objectives, developing a long-standing strand of neoliberal thought into a tool for reviving state autonomy.

If monetarism focused attention on controlling public spending and the money supply, among the core new right notions was a firm and original if latent commitment to privatization as a means for correcting the political distortions of the postwar consensus. Willetts, discussing monetarism, writes 'that the only way to improve the underlying rate of growth of the economy is by measures which liberate the supply side' (1992, p. 127). According to Hugo Young, 'Mrs Thatcher had always said, when asked to crystallise the essence of the British disease, that the nationalised industries were the seat of it: where monopoly unions conspired with monopoly suppliers, to produce an inadequate service to the consumer at massive cost to the taxpayer' (1990, p. 353). In 1977 John Hoskyns and Norman Strauss, encouraged by Sir Keith and Thatcher, drafted a programme, 'Stepping Stones', that called for fundamental reform of trade unions as basic to breaking with the collectivist consensus and linked deregulating the economy, reducing inflation, controlling public spending, attacking unions and particularly public sector union power into a coherent package (Young, 1990, pp. 115 and 117). The 1978 Ridley Report proposed a strategy for denationalization and weakening public sector unions, such as the miners, but the 1979 Party's election manifesto made only a few specific commitments (Keegan, 1984, p. 127). In July 1980, Thatcher expressed her conviction that 'the two great problems of the British economy are the monopoly nationalised industries and the monopoly trade unions' (cited in Young, 1990, p. 207). Later in summarizing the attitudes of her first Cabinet in May 1983, she said: 'We all wanted strong defence, more resources for law and order, lower taxation, more private enterprise, less government control' (Riddell, 1985, p. 42).

At the time of the 1979 election and even just before the 1983 election, then, there was no hint of the political potential of privatization, or of its future role in the Conservative Government's programme. Yet, privatization promised to provide the supply-side component in New Right thinking. In his 1984 Mais Lecture, Nigel Lawson reverses the Keynesian relationship between macroeconomic and microeconomic policies:

> But the proper role of each is precisely the opposite of that assigned to it by the conventional postwar wisdom. It is the conquest of inflation, and

not the pursuit of growth and employment, which is or should be the
objective of macro-economic policy. And it is the creation of conditions
conducive to growth and employment, and not the suppression of price
rises, which is or should be the objective of micro-economic policy.
(cited in Willetts, 1992, p. 128)

Privatization was the key micro-level mechanism for freeing-up the
growth generating private sector at the expense of the inefficient public
sector.

PRIVATIZATION AS FREEDOM FROM DIRECT CONTROL

Privatization promises to free economic decisions from the direct control
of political, bureaucratic and administrative forces. Privatizing public
activities institutes private market transactions or business practices as the
mechanism for organizing activities and so making use of resources.
Proponents argue that privatization enlarges freedom and democracy by
giving individuals the means and the alternatives to make voluntary
exchanges that are always self-rewarding. New Right rhetoric justifies
privatization as the disengagement or withdrawal of public enterprises
from the state and their replacement by the freedom of voluntary mutually
advantageous exchanges of the marketplace.

David Heald and David Steel's analysis of Conservative leaders' state-
ments in favour of privatization reveal the link between privatization and
market freedom or choice. First, freedom is increased because privatization prevents public enterprises with statutory monopoly powers and
monopoly market strength from competing unfairly and thereby limiting
consumers' freedom of choice (Heald and Steel, 1982, p. 337). Second,
efficiency is enhanced because the private sector firms have to confront
the discipline of capital and product markets. Public sector firms are insu-
lated from these forces and use or make use of political pressures instead
that lead to inefficient allocation of resources (ibid., pp. 339–40). Third,
privatization ends the ability of unions to hold the nation 'by the jugular
vein', since workers in the private sector know that excessive pay agreements will lead to bankruptcy. Further, liberalization or deregulation prevents firms from passing pay rises on to consumers (ibid., p. 341). Finally,
privatization contributes to restraining public sector borrowing and
slowing monetary growth (ibid., p. 342). The sale of assets directly contributes to the Exchequer, since the creation of hybrid companies permits
the Government to exclude their external finance from the PSBR, while

the imposition of charges for public services rendered through contracting-out reduce public expenditure and so remove pressure on the PSBR.

The aim of privatization, then, is to replace political and bureaucratic modes of decision-making with economic modes involving free choices based on calculations of rational self-interest. New Right thinkers contend that market processes harness the individual pursuit of self-interest in a constructive way, yielding greater efficiency and productivity. Beesley and Littlechild, leading academic proponents of privatization, argue: 'the underlying idea is to improve industry performance by increasing the role of market forces' (1983, p. 1). While some economists deem other factors like greater competition to be especially necessary more fundamental for the New Right are the effects of a change in ownership. These occur, they argue, because privatization changes the motivations of managers and employees to the benefit of consumers. Privately-owned firms are motivated by profit-seeking and are responsive to consumer choices (ibid., p. 4).

In the model of power implicit in privatization strategies, property rights provide the foundations for individual choice, freedom, and initiative. Private property, the exclusive rights of control resources and assets, makes a person accountable for his or her action, linking action explicitly and directly to costs and benefits or risks and rewards. Private property provides the 'institutional mechanism' producing efficiency and liberty. In the words of Cento Veljanovski, 'Privatization...involves the transfer and redefinition of a complex bundle of property rights which creates a whole new penalty-reward system which will alter the incentives in the firm and its ultimate performance' (1987, pp. 77–8). Similarly, Nigel Lawson records:

> The widespread ownership of private property is crucial to the survival of freedom and democracy. It gives the citizen a vital sense of identification with the society of which he is a part. It gives him a stake in the future – and indeed, equally important, in the present. It creates a society with an inbuilt resistance to revolutionary change. (Lawson, 1992, p. 206)

From this perspective, socialism fails because the 'collectivisation of production diffuses responsibility and clouds the objectives of organisations' (Veljanovski, 1987, p. 81).

Privatization also changes the relations of agency and clearly defines the criterion of choice. According to Veljanovski's exposition, by creating interactions or exchanges based on the disciplines associated with property ownership, privatization is more productive than bureaucratic forms of power relations. In addition to giving control to individuals and making them responsible for its preservation, property rights facilitate individual choice and initiative. Property rights confer the means to take risks that can increase their wealth. Shareholders' ability to trade ownership rights, for example, enables them to monitor and then control management's behaviour through their own commercial choices. Veljanovski writes:

> The tradability of shares in the private corporation constrains management from acting against their shareholders' wealth-maximisation goal. The mechanism that does this is the takeover, especially the hostile takeover bid.   (1987, p. 87)

Moreover, property rights establish the criterion of decision-making, namely, optimizing profits. Veljanovski continues:

> If management pursue policies that do not maximise profits or if they run the company badly, shareholders will begin to disinvest, with the result that the share price will begin to fall. This provides a signal to the market which sets in train a self-correcting sequence of events.   (ibid.)

In short, markets constitute an explicit, if indirect, form of control or power. Freedom and choice manifest in voluntary, mutually beneficial trade-offs control behaviour. Individual preference stimulated by property rights grounds choice, self-interest motivates initiative, and optimization determines preference fulfilment. As Veljanovski points out, the claim that private monopolies are more efficient than nationalized producers '...relies on these pressures in the capital market [profit maximization] being stronger than the explicit control mechanisms which were applied to the nationalised industries' (1987, p. 89). Privatization changes the way firms or organizations are controlled, as objectives shift from welfare to profit and its maximization, information becomes better, and senior and technological managers are driven by self-interest to take initiatives in markets (Bös, 1991, ch. 3; see, Vickers and Yarrow, 1988).

Privatization supporters claim that increased competition maximizes consumer benefits by creating consumer sovereignty. The consumer with several alternative providers or products to choose from is free to make the exchange which is most advantageous. According to John Moore, MP, the Financial Secretary at the Treasury in the early 1980s and Government Minister responsible for coordinating the privatization programme, 'The primary objective of the Government's privatization programme is to reduce the power of the monopolist and to encourage competition' (1983). Peter Lilley argued that while the desire to 'look after oneself and one's family is a characteristic of human nature...at least under competitive private ownership the self-interest of employees and managers is harnessed to the satisfaction of customers and the efficient use of resources' (1989). In short, private sector firms facing competition are compelled to be responsive to consumers (Moore, 1983, pp. 9–13).

The benefits of private commercial transactions stimulate economic growth. By replacing the administrative control of conduct with the real market transactions (Moore, 1983), managers become free to manage and to follow opportunities when they emerge (Bruce-Gardyne, 1984, p. 84). In addition, employees and managers, as in the case of the National Freight Corporation among others, benefit by taking up ownership in the firm they work for, a situation that increases their performance. Financial remuneration is then linked to economic success, pay bargaining is compelled to respond to the balance book, and job satisfaction and morale can be raised. Moreover, whereas nationalization preserved outmoded jobs, privatization compels adaption to technological and market developments that creates real jobs and provides entrepreneurial efforts with the opportunity to succeed.

The Government also attempted to broaden share ownership, to foster a people's capital market, and to change relations between employees and employers in order to obtain wider support for market decision-making. Ministers hoped that privatization would end traditional class conflict between workers and management in newly privatized firms and to create a synergetic harmony based on more people to play by the rules and norms of property ownership. Only 7 per cent of adults in the United Kingdom own shares compared to 25 per cent in the US, and the proportion of UK company shares owned directly by individuals fell from 37 per cent in 1975 to 28 per cent in 1981. Having created 'a new army of capitalists' with the British Telecom sale in 1984, John Moore believes that new attitudes are being formed. He writes: 'When employees commit their capital as well as their labour to the company for which they work, it becomes apparent that they and the management have a common interest in the success of the company' (Moore, 1984, para. 4). According to Thatcher, the government's aim is to harmonize class relations through spreading wealth and ownership via public sale of assets and employee share schemes. She states: 'Don't talk to me about 'them' and 'us' in a company ... You're all "we" in a company. You survive as the company survives, prosper as the company prospers – everyone together. The future lies in cooperation and not confrontation' (cited in Hall, 1983, p. 31).

Politically, privatization's proponents justified its benefits in terms of freedom, competition, and efficiency. In praising privatization one observer claimed that it is 'a means of changing how policy is conceived and executed – a means of changing expectations about the nature of government and the nature of politics' (Letwin, 1992, p. 107). Neoliberal advocates picture it as freedom from oppressive direct power. Replacing direct state power with market modes of decision-making, proponents viewed privatization as freedom from direct state intervention and the institution of more individual choice and autonomy. Privatization became the means for implementing the monetarists' goal of introducing restraints on collectivist politics. By disaggregating or dissipating the power of privileged pressure groups and making them more responsive to market conditions and processes, market relations were to stimulate and expand economic activity and growth. The effect would be to reduce direct political responsibilities and public accountability as well as improve the government's public finances.

CONCLUSION

Privatization became central to the Thatcherite or neoliberal programme because monetarism failed as a policy for controlling money supply and, more importantly, because the need to achieve the break with pluralist collectivism intensified. Monetarism proposed using market relations to force groups to live within limits. Governments could impose restraint on inflationary claims by controlling the money supply and making claimants endure the negative effects of excessive demands. Privatization, according to its advocates, uses market trade-offs to check excesses, improve efficiency, and compel innovation. Privatization fosters individual freedom and choice, consumer sovereignty, and greater efficiency. Where monetarism projected the core state as the ultimate guardian of order, privatization hailed individual rationality in market trade-offs as the stimulus of discipline and prosperity, breaking away from reliance on oppressive direct state power.

As theories, monetarism and privatization thus developed and evolved as responses by leading politicians and intellectuals to political crisis and uncertainty. These politicians turned or, perhaps more accurately in the case of Thatcher and Sir Keith, converted to the monetarist frame of politics because they saw no hope and effectiveness in the old rules of the game. Kavanagh encapsulates the linkage between ideas and events: 'Events in the "real" world, particularly the growing concern over inflation, the obvious shortcomings of incomes policies and successive governments' management of the economy, and the intellectual crisis of Keynesian economics, encouraged policy-makers to look for new ideas' (1990, pp. 112–13). Thus, the reshaping of state-society relations comes from individual politicians adopting political ideas as solutions to both personal and structural problems.

4 Power and the Public Sector Sell-off

Freedom, choice, competition are neoliberal ideals. They promise more democracy, more productivity and more prosperity. Choice would unleash individual energies and initiatives, making for more efficient and effective use of resources and skills. More freedom and individual autonomy would mean engaging and redirecting individual behaviour into processes that were more efficient. Yet, freedom and choice would mean the peculiar freedoms and choices of the market. The new freedoms and choices were exercised in market activities, processes that had their own particular rules and norms. These would be dependent on the motivation or incentives of the players and the flux of engagement in response to serial activity. In practice, the choice and competition created by privatization uses the market as an indirect type of control, as a distinctive type of activity which itself functions to control behaviour.

Monetarism failed because it used the money supply as a direct force, constraining choices and coercing austerity. Privatization worked because it used the market as an indirect means of control, developing participation in market activities which in themselves define and regulate options, risks, and opportunities. As a type of indirect power, market transactions are instrumental rather than substantive, objective rather than intuitive, and exclusive rather than inclusive. This implies that they are limited to participants with calculative attitudes, know-how and technical skills, and financial resources. As a form of decision-making, market-guided activities vary. This chapter examines privatization as a process of selling state assets, while the next chapter deals with its subsequent implementation. Subsequent chapters explore other forms of market-shaped decision-making, deregulation and pricing.

In privatizing, Thatcherites learned how to turn neoliberalism to their advantage and to enhance state control by expanding the market economy as a medium of indirect social control while maintaining their hold over the electorate. Using market accountability as a means for redrawing the rules regulating the practices of interest formation and representation, New Right ideas led to a significant change in state autonomy and British democracy. In writing about sales of state assets Peter Riddell concludes: 'The privatization programme deserves considerable attention, both because it has been a novel initiative and because it has fundamentally changed the boundaries of the public sector in Britain. Yet perhaps its real significance lies in its being the prime example of the broader economic trends of the 1980s, the assertion of managerial power, the weakening of trade union influence, and the spread of share ownership' (1989, p. 112). Moreover, New Right ideas worked to significantly enhance the authority of the state. While the competence and credibility of every government ebbs and flows, the contrast between the weakness of the Wilson and Callaghan governments and the autonomy of the Thatcher governments in relations to group pressures is remarkable. Thatcher governments set the public agenda and implemented significant changes in the balance of power. These changes bear out Kenneth Wiltshire's explanation of the link between privatization and the question of power relationships in British democracy: 'privatization is only one component of new right economic and political strategy, whose basic objective is to bring about a fundamental and not easily reversed change in the power balance in society' (1987, p. ix). In contrast to Keynesian social democracy, neoliberalism has provided a relatively successful solution to the puzzle of how to restore the capacity of central state authority to control the interest pressures arising from the political economy. As Jim Bulpitt (1986) argues, the chief goal of the Thatcher governments was to win elections and achieve governing competence. This meant regenerating a measure of relative autonomy insulating central state leaders from the interference of group pressures and enabling them to control and resolve conflict.

This chapter examines the programme of selling-off state assets. It assesses the way Thatcherite politicians used the neoliberal ideas to enhance their control of interest representation and policy-making (Wolfe, 1989a). It shows, by partly focusing on the story of British Telecom (BT), how new right ideas provided the state with the means to privatize state industries. The process reveals a narrowing and intensification of control, rather than an enlargement of democracy and freedom. Key governmental ministers, managers of state industries, and city advisors became the architects and instigators of the reform, while the participation and influence of workers, consumers, and voters was reduced.

GROUNDING PUBLIC SECTOR SALES PROGRAMME

The inspiration and justification for privatization in general drew on the New Right thinking discussed in the last chapter. Its rhetoric of individual freedom, anti-statism and efficiency projected business practices as a more effective way of operating public affairs than the postwar collectivist package. For the asset sales programme, discussion of the virtues of property rights and private ownership were paramount.

The justification of privatization starts with the critique of nationaliza-tion and bureaucratic rule. Nigel Lawson, as Energy Secretary, stated in a talk in September 1982: 'What public ownership does is to eliminate the threat of takeover and ultimately of bankruptcy, and the need, which all private undertakings have from time to time, to raise money from the market' (1992, p. 202). Furthermore, he said that the private sector was the only means to real change, since the introduction of property rights would 'provide managers with an incentive to respond the right way' (Lawson, 1992, p. 203–4). Privatization, in the view of M.E. Beesley, ends political interference and motivates management to seek profits: 'Privatization implies the political decision to give up the direct responsibility *and* accept drastically diminished direct influence on the industry' (1992, p. 51).

In November 1983, John Moore, Economic and then Financial Secretary to the Treasury, provided the first official and intellectually coherent government justification for privatization (Grimstone, 1990, p. 5). After the 1983 General Election victory, Prime Minister Thatcher 'took a continuing interest in ensuring that the programme remained on track' (Grimstone, 1990, p. 5). Moore's appointment at the Treasury gave form to her intention. His effort to give privatization a philosophical coherence aimed to give the programme 'conviction in economic and political terms and to be seen as other than a purely financially-orientated exercise' (ibid.). Purportedly privatization would boost public finance, end the politicization of nationalized industries by bringing about the end of government involvement in industry, make the firms accountable to private sector rules and disciplines, and strengthen the climate for business through wider share ownership, stronger capital markets, employee share ownership.

Underlying particular stated objectives was a belief in the virtue of property ownership as a mechanism of control. Veljanovski lists govern-ment objectives in selling state assets in the order in which they were emphasized: reducing state interference in industry, facilitating the raising of funds on the capital markets, raising government revenue, promoting wider share ownership, creating an enterprise culture, encouraging workers' ownership of shares, increasing competition and efficiency, and introducing state oversight by economic regulation (1987, p. 8; Wiltshire, 1987, p. 29). After listing nine reasons for privatization, Letwin (1988) argues that 'distrust of the state as a manager of commercial enterprise' is a general assumption behind various specific reasons. He continues: 'The proponent of privatisation begins with the supposition that, all other things being equal, it is likely that the state will not be a good manager of any given commercial entity; in each particular case, he looks for the specific advantages which a specific privatisation could bring, and these become his reasons for that particular privatisation...' (Letwin, 1988, pp. 28–9). These arguments of government supporters counter the assertion that privatization lacked a clear rationale (Kay and Thompson, 1986).

New Right ideas about using market accountability idealized property rights as the key to efficiency, competition, and democracy. The role of ownership in controlling enterprise behaviour were the working tools of leading Thatcherite politicians holding core state offices. From the start, they wanted greater privatization. Nigel Lawson recounts:

> The exiguous references in the 1979 conservative manifesto reflected partly the fact that little detailed work had been done on the subject in Opposition; partly that the enthusiasts for privatization were Keith Joseph, Geoffrey Howe, John Nott, David Howell and me, rather than Margaret herself; and perhaps chiefly Margaret's understandable fear of frightening the floating voter. But privatization was a central plank of our policy right from the start.   (1992, p. 199)

Geoffrey Howe stated his commitment to privatization in his first Budget Speech, referring to a substantial scope for asset sales and the goal of widening share ownership (ibid.).

Justifying the Sale of BT

To illustrate the central role of property ownership in establishing a market regimen, I turn to the sale of BT. The new right rhetoric condemned state control of public enterprises. It proposed that improving the economy's supply side could be achieved by 'setting enterprises free' (Dunn and Smith, 1990, p. 34; Heald, 1985). Supported by Sir Keith, Howe, and Lawson, Thatcher expressed repeatedly her ideological belief that private ownership was a solution to collectivist immobilism (Wolfe, 1991, pp. 247–8). The case of BT shows how the decision to sell assets drew on the belief that property rights were basic to establishing a market behaviour.

The first attempt by a Thatcher government to use market controls to modernize British telecommunications introduced a degree of liberalization alongside increased ministerial control, drawing on management support while taking advantage of division between Post Office unions. In September 1979 the Minister of Industry (Sir Keith) announced a review of BT's monopoly. On July 21, 1980, in the House of Commons, he stated the government's intention to liberalize the telecommunications industry. In November 1980, he introduced the Telecommunications Bill (Newman, 1986, p. 3). The resulting British Telecommunications Act of July 1981, guided through Parliament by a newly appointed Minister of Information Technology (Kenneth Baker), separated postal and telecommunications services, created BT, and made some competition possible in equipment markets, network operation, and services (Vickers and Yarrow, 1988, p. 204). The Labour Party opposed the Bill, forecasting a deterioration in postal services. However, the Post Office unions split: the Union of Communications Workers (UCW) opposed it and the Post Office Engineering Union (POEU) favoured it (Moon, Richardson and Smart, 1986, p. 343). The government also conceded to BT the right to supply the first telephone in the home. The Act enlarged the power of the Minister to license companies other than BT to run transmission systems (Mercury was licensed in February 1982 and launched in April 1983), to provide equipment, to use BT's network for value-added networks services (VANS), and even to mandate BT's behaviour if needed.

By separating telecommunications from the Post Office, the Government sought 'to free those concerned with the fast changing and commercially potent telecommunications industry from the 'service' function of running the Post Office, in the hope of increasing profitability' (Moon, Richardson, and Smart, 1986, p. 343). The Government was anxious about the outdated technical capacities of the telecommunications network, the loss of export earnings, demands for more public financing at a time when it was trying to lower the Public Sector Borrowing Requirement (PSBR), and the power of the POEU (now the National Communications Union [NCU]). In 1977 the Carter report had questioned the sincerity of the Post Office's desire to digitalize, pointing out that data transmission was slow. The City, requiring fast data transmissions for its future moves to stay at the forefront of international finance, complained about poor service, while IBM demanded the right to compete in the provision of public exchanges, given its success in selling PABX (Hills, 1986, p. 90).

The Government used its authority to make BT internally more market driven and to protect its profitability. Appointed BT chairman in 1980, Sir George Jefferson introduced a business-oriented organizational structure, dividing the company into four distinct profit centres, recruiting new sales staff, opening new sales offices, making tariffs more reflective of real costs, and introducing commercial accounting and management systems (Moon, Richardson, and Smart, 1986, p. 343; Pitt, 1990, pp. 63-5). The idea underlying the reorganization was to link tasks to results in order to make the company more competitive against Mercury and attractive to the privatization market. After privatization further reforms opened the international area to commercial activities and introduced total quality management in order to increase the productivity of staff (Hallett, 1990). This process of adapting the corporate structure and culture to the commercial world still continues, however, more than ten years after the first liberalization. In April 1991, a corporate reorganization designed to serve customers more efficiently went into effect (Financial Times, March 27, 1991, p. 12). The Government furthered BT's privileged position when it announced in October 1982 its 'duopoly policy', giving BT and Mercury exclusive rights to provide basic telephone services until 1990, yet protecting it from cable operators (Veljanovski, 1987, p. 193).

These were the first efforts by a Thatcher government to apply New Right ideas in telecommunications. They legislated limited competition and imposed internal restructuring under increased but ineffective state supervision, giving BT greater initiative and facilitating the assertion of its organizational interests. The result enhanced the dominance and independence of BT and led to increased conflict with the Ministry of Information Technology, which itself had been given increased discretionary powers. Ministers were frustrated when BT resisted efforts to introduce competition. Critics charged that BT still had the capacity to block potential competitors (Hills, 1986, p. 97; Pitt, 1990, pp. 59–60). BT stalled when given responsibility for approving equipment that would be compatible with its system, resisted extending interconnection rights to Mercury, and tried to prevent licensing the use of its network for VANS it was not supplying. Moreover, BT demanded new Government funding to finance its modernization, bringing it into conflict with the Government's aim of reducing the PSBR. Finally, BT offered special deals to City firms and introduced new business services. Overall, while the first efforts yielded limited liberalization of the telecommunications sector and encouraged BT to undertake some internal restructuring, it confirmed the ineffectiveness of state supervision.

Privatization became the next step in the attempt to solve the problems of making BT and the telecommunications industry more accountable and dynamic. Ideas about ownership of property rights inspired and justified BT's privatization as a viable option. These hold that private ownership would redirect the proclivities and energies of key participants into the reform process and motivate the firm's modernization and competitiveness.

The decision to sell BT drew on ideological and pragmatic business-oriented beliefs about the role of property ownership in motivating innovation and efficiency. According to Hills (1986, pp. 121 and 124), 'the major impetus to privatisation came from the ideological framework of the Thatcher government, from a belief in monetarist policy which demanded a decreasing share of public expenditure with GDP'. In addition, the Government believed that the private sector could better control the unions. Bulford warns, 'it was also clear that they [the Government] are intent on using privatisation as a means of "increasing efficiency" in BT via a greater concentration of profitable services and by job reductions, etc.' (Bulford, 1983, p. 132; *Financial Times* October 7, 1991, p. 1). Privatization, according to three observers, '...was becoming a more central element in the Government's economic policy, associated with the desire to inject an enhanced competitive and entrepreneurial spirit into British industry whilst also raising much needed funds for the public purse – the latter point becoming of increasing importance as time passed' (Moon, Richardson, and Smart, 1986, pp. 344–5). It would free the BT managers of ministerial supervision of its tariffs, its wage settlements, its investment programmes, and appointments to its Board (Baker, 1993, p. 78). Finally, the 1984 Telecommunications Act articulated the Government's ideological position. It stipulated that the telecommunications system should be operated with the aim of promoting effective competition, efficiency and economy, research and development, the international competitiveness of UK firms supplying telecommunications services and apparatus, and the interests of consumers, purchasers, and other users (Vickers and Yarrow, 1988, p. 208). Privatizing BT, thus, would institute ownership rights and profits as the grounds for the corporation's decisions, while providing revenue for the government.

ADVANCING THE ASSET SELL-OFF PROGRAMME

Failure to control the nationalized industries as well as their failure to serve consumers, a crisis of standards in education, inability to control local authorities spending or programmes, and the funding dilemmas for the National Health Service led Thatcherites to introduce forms of market accountability to regain a measure of state supervision and control. The success of ad hoc measures of introducing market accountability in limited areas led Thatcherites to generalize the introduction of market-led decision-making. Through assimilating different areas of the political economy to the neoliberal model, they evolved a coherent programme.

Peter Riddell argues that Thatcherism took shape as a 'response to events rather than the execution of a clearly prepared and argued-out blueprint' (1989, p. 11). More cynically, Heidrun Abromeit writes that privatization reveals the self-developing logic of incrementalism, showing 'the dynamics a short-term programme, put up for pragmatic and fiscal considerations, may develop in the course of its implementation' (1988, p. 83).

Yet, Riddell forcefully elaborates how the Thatcher government's struggle to gain control over policy-making in the nationalized sector led to the sell-off programme:

> In domestic policy, Mrs Thatcher's political victories in 1981–2 enabled her to regain the initiative in a number of areas where previous approaches had not worked. In particular, the failure to get to grips with the large deficits of the nationalized industries led to the development of the privatization programme. As often during the Thatcher decade, what turned out to be a far-reaching initiative developed in an unexpected fashion in response to a particular problem, rather than as a result of some pre-ordained plan. It is certainly true that Mrs Thatcher and her close allies had an ingrained hostility to nationalized industries which they regarded as less efficient than the private sector. But even the most radical private thinking of the Conservatives in opposition ... had not envisaged the sale of the major monopoly utilities, as happened in the second half of the 1980s. The programme which transformed the boundaries between the public and private sectors was in response to a policy crisis. (1989, p. 10)

As neoliberal New Right ideas operated successfully, it became clear to core Thatcherites that the way forward was to use economic thinking and processes as a guide to redesigning policy-making processes, not as an imposed constraint but as a way of problem-solving. Moreover, as market-driven policy-making proved successful as a tool, it inspired the future sequence of events in the same policy area or it led to their application in another problematic area. With successes in privatizing BT and British Gas (BG), the Government moved after the 1987 election to privatize the great water and electricity monopolies, believing that, as Lawson puts it, '[t]he tide of ideas was now flowing strongly in favour of the market economy' (1992, p. 230).

Soon after becoming Energy Secretary in a Cabinet reshuffle in September 1981 that gave further impetus to developing privatization as a programme, Nigel Lawson declared principles setting out the approach to privatization he followed in his time in office. The first rule is: 'The

Conservative Party has never believed that the business of government is the government of business'; the second is 'No industry should remain under State ownership unless there is a positive and overwhelming case for it so doing. Inertia is not enough. As a nation we simply cannot afford it' (Lawson, 1992, p. 211). By 1983, Industry Secretary Patrick Jenkin and the other economic ministers in the Cabinet 'concluded that there is no sense at all in having productive industries subject to direct political influences under the authority of the Treasury' (Taylor, 1983, p. 57).

Other considerations encouraged a step-by-step approach to radical change, in which 'a private monopoly is better than a public one' became a leading precept. As pressure for technological innovation is greater, private monopoly lacks the political influence of state monopoly, and private monopoly can be eroded over time (Pirie, 1988a, p. 183; Minford, 1988, p. 94). Accordingly, enhancing competition is only one motivation and less important than extending property ownership. Moreover, privatization gained force because its advocates justified initiatives in terms of the truths of economic science and the objective realities of market forces and because early instances provided policy makers with experiences of successes that made privatization appear both natural and inevitable, which in turn led to its elaboration as a policy idea.

Government strategies sought to change the circumstances of action as well as the subjective criterion of assessment. Officials brought into play interest groups, like small investors and employees, as allies in the privatization process (Letwin, 1988, p. 89). In building a coalition of supporters for privatization, the Government drew upon postwar trends toward greater prosperity and ownership. Slogans about popular capitalism and the enterprise culture fed on an individualist enthusiasm for choice and reward that conflicts with postwar collectivist policies. Riddell writes:

> The reality of a property-owning democracy may have much more to do with the long-term post-war build-up of owner occupation, and inheritance, than the post-1979 initiatives of giving council tenants the right to buy their homes or attractively priced share offers. But the Tories have identified with, and taken considerably further, these successful and widely accepted developments. The result will not be a shift in economic powers – since managements may ensure that there is more independence for owners rather than less as a result of wider and less concentrated shareholdings. The true significance may be to give greater control to individuals over their own lives...Popular capitalism has become a central part of the individualist challenge to collective

provision – while the extension of ownership has given people something to defend.   (1989, p. 126)

While home ownership increased from 56 to 64 per cent between 1979
and 1988 and share-ownership from 3 million to 9 million over the same
period (from 7 to 20 per cent of the adult population), the real significance
lies in a new attitude about market methods of social control rather than in
distributing wealth to more shareowners, many of whom are in the market
for a short time or hold small stakes.

According the Letwin, the success of Thatcher's housing policy was
crucial to the creation of the privatization programme: 'This remarkable
experiment in privatisation carried the Thatcher regime across the great
divide between mere attempts to reduce the public sector and a much
bolder, positive policy of promoting the private sector' (1988, p. 90). The
disposal of council housing showed Thatcherites that the sale of assets
would be easier than deregulation. Graham and Prosser contend, 'It could
be implemented with relatively little political cost to *central* government
and it had important electoral advantages, in particular through breaking
up the traditional constituency' (1991, p. 24). Madsen Pirie (1988c, p. 16)
confirms that success in privatization made a truth out of a tentative
hypothesis. He explains: 'We privatized first and used the success of
privatization to win the argument. We didn't have to win it in theory in
advance. We didn't get public opinion to support it until after it was done.
So, in that sense, it was an act of leadership'. Privatization grew as
decision-makers learned that it could be successfully implemented and
worked to their advantage.

In its initial stages, the Thatcher government's programme concentrated
on profitable firms at the periphery of the public sector. After selling
shares in BP, ICL, and Suez Finance Company in 1979–80, it sold
Ferranti, Fairey, British Sugar, and a majority of its holdings in British
Aerospace in 1980–81. The government then sold Britoil, Amersham
International, and the National Freight Corporation in 1981–82, and
Associated British Ports, BR Hotels, International Aeradio, and parts of
Cable and Wireless in 1983 and 1985. At the same time, the Thatcher gov-
ernment found that promoting housing ownership was a popular way to
advance its radical agenda.

From 1981 on a second phase of privatization emerged, as leaders
broadened an already viable programme to include the major public utilities (Heald, 1989, p. 37). According to David Steel, the programme
gained new momentum 'because it provided a unifying theme for a
Conservative Party deeply divided on macroeconomic policy and, later,

from the post-Falklands realization that the government would win a second term' (1984, p. 102). More specifically, it was in response to the economic crisis of 1981 in which recession combined with upward pressure on public expenditure due to the nationalized industries' deficits and the cost of unemployment insurance that Thatcher, encouraged by Keith Joseph, decided to deepen and broaden the privatization programme. She reshuffled ministers in September 1981 and set each of them the task of privatizing as much of their business as possible (Riddell, 1985, pp. 48–9). In July 1981, Sir Geoffrey and Sir Keith spoke in favour of more privatization, and in September 1981, Energy Secretary Lawson confirmed that privatization was the government's priority (Riddell, 1985, p. 172; Young, 1989, p. 360; Baker, 1993, p. 80). A year later Sir Geoffrey promised a significant extension of privatization, concluding 'that state ownership and control should be displaced or supplemented, wherever sensibly possible, by the discipline and pressure of the market place and by some degree of private ownership' (Howe, 1982, p. 20; Riddell, 1985, p. 170). The resulting sales of major public corporations started with BT, which in 1984 was the first and largest flotation of a public sector firm and became the model for BG (1986), British Airways (1986), Enterprise Oil (1984), Royal Ordnance Factories (1986), Sealink (1984), National Bus Company (1986), and parts of British Shipbuilders (1985) (Heald, 1989, p. 38–9).

The government, even more confident of its capacity to reform state institutions after winning an unprecedented third term in 1987, initiated a third phase. This extended privatization to most types of activities remaining in the public sector. The search for candidates grew. These privatization initiatives depended on the priorities and opportunities of the particular ministers and departments involved. Privatization proposals emerged from the particular sponsoring department. In the water industry, Roy Watts as a Chairman of the Thames Water Authority encouraged ideologically predisposed Cabinet members. He restructured the industry on the model of an American utility company, rather than a British public service organization and in early 1985 called for independence from the government. With powerful allies in the industry and confident after the BT privatization, government moved forward with the initiative (Richardson, Maloney, and Rudig, 1992, pp. 160–1).

This phase led to new initiatives to unload the government's remaining shares in already privatized firms (BP in 1987 and BT in 1991) and prepare the disposal of firms still in the public sector (Heald, 1989, p. 42). The privatization of major public utilities like water (1989) and electricity (1990) advanced the reform programme dramatically. The third phase also included British Airports Authorities (1987), Royal Ordnance (1987),

Table 4.1   Main public asset sales

Year Company	(% shares)	[method of disposal]	
1979/80			£ million
BP	(5%)	[stock market flotation]	276
ICL	(25%)	[private sale]	37
Suez Finance Co			57
1980/81			
Ferranti	(50%)	[private sale]	55
Fairey Engineering	(100%)	[private sale]	22
British Aerospace	(51%)	[stock market flotation]	195
British Steel Corporation		[private sale]	44
Automation & Technical Services, etc.			91
Pretcold	(100%)		9
Motorway Service Stations		[private sale]	28
1981/82			
British Sugar	(24%)	[private sale]	44
Cable & Wireless	(50%)	[stock market flotation]	182
Amersham International	(100%)	[stock market flotation]	64
National Freight Corporation	(100%)	[private sale]	5
1982/83			
Britoil	(51%)	[tender offer]	225
Associated British Ports	(49%)	[stock market flotation]	46
British Transport Hotels	(100%)	[private sale]	40
International Aeradio		[private sale]	60
1983/84			
United Medical Enterprises		[private sale]	17
Twinlock		[private sale]	4
National Enterprise Board (misc. holdings)		[private sale]	125
BP	(7%)	[tender offer]	565
Cable & Wireless	(25%)	[tender offer]	260
1984/85			
J.H. Sankey			12
Scott Lithgow		[private sale]	12
Lye Tinplate			16
Enterprise Oil	(100%)	[tender offer]	392
Wytch Farm Oil	(50%)	[private sale]	215
Associated British Port	(48.5%)	[tender offer]	51
Inmos		[private sale]	95
Jaguar Cars		[stock market flotation]	295
Sealink		[private sale]	66
BT	(51%)	[stock market flotation]	3700

Table 4.1   *Continued*

Year Company	(% shares)	[method of disposal]	
1985/86			
Britoil	(48.8%)	[stock market flotation]	450
Royal Ordnance Factory, Leeds		[private sale]	11
Hall Russell shipyard		[private sale]	–
Cable and Wireless	(22.7%)	[stock market flotation]	558
Trustees Savings Bank		[proceeds to bank itself]	1000
Warship building yards (Vickers, Yarrow, Swan Hunter, Vosper)			140
British Aerospace	(48.8%)	[stock market flotation]	400
1986/87			
National Bus Company		[private sale]	250
BA Helicopters		[private sale]	13.5
Unipart		[private sale]	52
Leyland Bus		[private sale]	4
Royal Ordnance			190
Leyland Trucks	(40%	holding new venture with DAF)	–
DAB		[private sale]	7
Istel		[private sale]	26
British Gas (offerings in 1986, 1987, 1988, 1989)		[stock]	7720
British Airways		[stock market flotation]	900
British Technology Group			–
1987/88			
Rolls-Royce			1080
British Airports Authority		[stock flotation and tender offer]	1275
BP	(31.7%)		–
Dockyard management			–
Ship repair yards			20
1988/89			
Travellers Fare		[private sale]	20.6
Govan shipyard		[private sale]	–
Professional and Executive Recruitment (first civil service unit sold off)			–
British Steel		[stock market flotation]	2500
Girobank		[private sale]	300

Table 4.1 *Continued*

Year Company	*(% shares)*	*[method of disposal]*	
1989/90			
12 electricity distribution companies		[stock flotation]	5200
Electricity Generating Companies		[stock market flotation]	5400
Short Bros.			30
Property Services Agency			10
Water Companies		[stock market flotation]	5300
1990/91			
Speke and Luton airports			–
Port of Bristol			36
90 state-owned ports authorized for sale			–
New toll roads and second Severn Bridge			–
BT	(27%)	[stock market flotation]	1800
1992/93			
National Express			90
Naval dockyards			–
BR Freight and Parcels Divisions			–
BR's 2,500 stations			1000
BR's passenger services franchised			–
Post Office: Parcelforce; Counters			–
BT	(22%)	[stock market flotation]	3200
National Power	(40%)	[stock flotation]	1200
Powergen	(40%)	[stock market flotation]	800
Scottish Electricity			835
Marketable debts, e.g., BT			1000
100 canal and riverside properties			1.5
Northern Ireland Electricity			1000
Northern Ireland Water			–
Docklands Light Railway			–
Remaining 38 bus companies' property			11
Property Services Agency			–
24 local airports			600
British Technology Group			–
1993/94			
British Coal		[private sale]	–
Electricity Debt			850
Forestry Commission			2200
Approximate Total:			50 billion

Sources: Lee, 1994, Appendix; Graham and Prosser, 1991, pp. 96, 106–7; Johnson, 1991, Table 33.

British Airways (1987), British Steel (1987), BL (1987), Rover Group (1988) and British Coal (1994). British Rail is being privatized in 1996, and the Post Office is a possible target. Over half the total privatization proceeds came from the energy sector, including the sales of BP (1979, 1983, and 1987), Britoil (1982 and 1985), Enterprise Oil, BG, and the Central Electricity Generating Board (CEGB) (Johnson, 1991, pp. 158 and 300). Overall, the scope of the sell-off programme was wide, with almost all state-owned industries becoming private sector businesses.

The Initiative to Sell-off BT

While ministers' initiative for privatizing BT stemmed from ideological principle, the privatization decision also provided a concrete solution to practical problems of financing BT's modernization. The Telecommunications Act 1981 introduced a measure of deregulation into the telecommunications industry and into the supply of services and separated the telecommunications functions from the Post Office. Various actors in the telecommunications industry had been participating in an ongoing debate about how to achieve fair competition and regulation in the face of liberalization and the creation of the fledgling private sector Mercury (Moon, Richardson, and Smart, 1986, pp. 344–5). These discussions involved informal contacts between the Department of Trade and Industry and individual firms, bypassing the established consultative apparatus in order to achieve fair competition between private operators and the government-owned BT. The Beesley Report in 1981 advocated complete freedom of use of the national network to provide services to third parties, similar to the US. But BT opposed the breaking of its monopoly and expressed interest in raising capital on its own, outside the PSBR restraints. Liberalization, favoured by all except the unions, produced no consensus about how to regulate BT or whether its monopoly should be broken.

When BT's management contended that technical improvements should be made prior to facing competition, implying a greater burden on the Exchequer, and called for higher domestic charges, Ministers started to think about the practical value of savings for the PSBR in privatization (Moon, Richardson, and Smart, 1986, p. 345). Since it was separated from the Post Office in 1981, the Government and BT management had attempted to find ways around the PSBR constraints in order to finance BT's £1.2 billion modernization programme (Veljanovski, 1987, p. 192; Hills, 1986, pp. 122–3). The inability to BT to raise investment capital and the failure of the 'Buzby bonds' initiative meant that BT would only borrow the amounts of money it need if it were in the private sector (Baker, 1993, p. 79–80). Frustration over financing investment funds within the PSBR encouraged the prospect of the sale.

After achieving the passage of the 1981 Telecommunications Bill, Kenneth Baker along with David Young, ministers at the Department of Trade and Industry under Sir Keith, initiated the sale of BT. In July 1981, they proposed legislation for the sell-off by early 1983, a regulatory agency, increased competition from Mercury and other providers, the actual sale in 1983 and 1984, and more competition by 1990 (Baker, 1993, p. 78) After the September 1981 Cabinet reshuffle, they enlisted new Secretary of State, Patrick Jenkin, and by late 1981 the sale of BT was government policy (Baker, 1993, p. 80). The Cabinet supported the sale because it would enable BT to raise its own funds and enhance government revenues. In July 1982, Jenkin announced the intention of sell off 51 per cent of BT shares when he introduced the new Telecommunications Bill. Due to a hiatus caused by the 1983 election, the legislative process was not completed until April, 1984 (Moon, Richardson, and Smart, 1986, pp. 344–5).

IMPLEMENTING PRIVATIZATION

The sale of state assets involved political control by indirect means. It operated through a patchwork of interconnected but divergent participants, drawn into a commercial process by motives of immediate benefit and future advantage. Critical to its success was the ability of the government to translate privatization into a matter of business dealings, shaped by market calculations and trade-offs. According to Wiltshire, his 'study has revealed that the sale process is heavily driven by the expectations of the market' (1987, p. xi). The sale process limited policy-making involvement and accountability to business players, the sellers (Government, managers and advisors) and buyers (City institutions and individual purchasers of stocks). The process reflected the Government's aim to transfer control to the private sector and to create support for that transfer (Buckland and Davis, 1984, p. 50).

Using business practices to regulate interest formation and group pressure made the interests of those owning property rights primary, transforming asset sales processes into commercial transactions and deflecting conflict over questions of substantive values. Lewis and Harden write, 'This particular pattern tends to subordinate the decision-making process to the decisions themselves as if they were, in some sense, already the outcome of consensual politics, which they manifestly are not' (1983, p. 228). In short, the marketizing of the political process largely shaped the method of the sale, the form of the privatized firm, and the role the government will play after the sale.

The policy was highly controlled from the centre, not by imposing but by constructing and maintaining the process of the sale. According to Gerry Grimstone, Treasury assistant secretary responsible for privatization from 1982 to 1986, 'A strong political will, and tight central control and co-ordination, are essential'. The Treasury dominated the process, 'because of the nationalised industries' public expenditure impact and their effect on macro-economic policies', with sponsoring departments, such as the Department of Energy or Transport, taking responsibility for day-to-day implementation (Grimstone, 1990, p. 7). Wiltshire recounts the centralized process:

> the privatisation process begins with a collective discussion by minis-
> ters outlining the general framework, and an agreement on the candi-
> dates for privatisation and the aims to be pursued in each sale. The
> Treasury assumes responsibility for the timing of the sale including an
> assessment of the readiness of the enterprise for sale and the capacity of
> the market to absorb the flotation. After these matters are settled it is left
> to the sponsoring department to implement the sale. The Treasury keeps
> a guiding hand firmly in place, however, since many of the sales have
> run into practical difficulties as well as political antagonism from
> interest groups, which might tend to swamp the department with
> difficulties. It is the Treasury that keeps the momentum going and, with
> the department and the enterprise, prepares any necessary legislation
> and helps to decide the method of the sale (fixed-price or tender, for
> instance).   (1987, pp. 53–4)

Moreover, steering committees comprising the department, the enterprise, and the Treasury and their advisors oversaw each phase of the
process, with subcommittees dealing with special issues, such as marketing or the prospectus. Regulation decisions involved Treasury officials,
sponsoring department ministers, other affected departments, and the
enterprise itself (Wiltshire, 1987, p. 54). 'Thus the normal procedure is to
employ merchant banks to act as financial advisers and to give advice on
the price to be set; the Secretary of State in some cases also appointed an
independent adviser to act as a means of cross-checking' (Graham and
Prosser, 1991, pp. 91–2). The advantage of centralized control through
'a small caucus of officials at the centre who would be involved in each

and every privatisation', was a specialization of knowledge and institu-
tionalization of initiative, backed by cohesion and discipline (Grimstone,
1990, pp. 7–8).

Market imperatives limited bargaining to business issues and sector
practitioners. Government ministers dealt with enterprise managers, each
of whom relied extensively on City advisors, to the exclusion of consumers, unions, and citizens. Decision-making focused on business
matters, having an 'essentially private nature'. Bishop and Kay (cited in
Graham and Prosser, 1991, p. 92) write:

> This mechanism of advice and representation is at once extensive and
> patchy...mainly conducted behind closed doors. Interests of consumers,
> for example, are represented only to the extent that such interests are
> among the Government's concerns. Senior management interests, by
> contrast, are represented very strongly indeed. Employees of the
> concern to be privatized play no part in the process...Very little of the
> expensively purchased advice and analysis is available to Parliament in
> its legislative scrutiny of the proposals.

Yet, MPs have been extensively lobbied by the enterprises being privatized, and the public courted through expensive and sophisticated sales
campaigns. Public scrutiny can occur only after the privatization process is
completed, and is limited to the House of Commons Public Accounts
Committee and the National Audit Office, which examine whether enterprises were sold too cheaply and other aspects of the sales (Graham and
Prosser, 1991, pp. 93–4; Wiltshire, 1987, pp. 94–7). In the post-privatization phase, Parliamentary scrutiny is denied, despite 'the fact that the government is still actively participating in the affairs of the new enterprises
through nominated directors, the regulatory system, the aftermath of the
share sales, licensing processes, and a direct and substantial shareholding
in the case of the hybrid enterprises' (Wiltshire, 1987, pp. 94–5).

The imperatives of the market (preparing for sale and interesting
buyers) meant that the sale of assets went through various distinct phases
of selecting, 'dressing-up', and selling business concerns. Over a two or
three year period, government ministers selected suitable enterprises,
decided on what organizational changes were necessary for it to function
effectively in the private sector, passed the required enabling legislation,
and then determined how and when to sell.

The ease and speed of a sale corresponded to the potential cooperation
of major participants, favouring companies trading in competitive markets
which could be disposed of through trade sales and assimilated to existing

competition law (Beesley, 1992; Grimstone, 1990, 8; Letwin, 1988). Yet such sales did little to break up the collectivist arrangements that had developed in the public sector. To make a difference, policy had to extend to the core public utilities, such as BT, BG, Water and Electricity. Even in these more politically important and sensitive enterprises the Government moved with speed to ensure the transfer to the private sector, choosing appropriate methods of sale, forms of the privatized industry, and its regulation.

Legislation provided a framework for the detailed negotiations among key participants. Statutes gave broad powers to the Secretary of State to license operations and details of the company's financial structure (Graham and Prosser, 1991, p. 79). As Graham and Prosser elaborate:

> Noticeable absentees from the legislation are any regulation of the sale procedure, in which...the discretion of the Secretary of State is almost total, and provisions on the design of the successor company. Even the most important of such provisions are left to the company's articles of association, including those setting out the relations with government after privatization through such devices as the golden share. In the case of regulated companies, the operating environment will also be determined not by the legislation itself but by the license or authorization issued by the Secretary of State, and, especially in the case of the electricity industry, contracts between different enterprises within the industry and with its suppliers will also establish its structure.   (1991, p. 79)

In several cases, questions, however, emerged over the legality of enterprises as subjects of privatization. In the case of TSB, they involved rightful ownership; in the case of water, they involved the authority to sell and meter water. According to Graham and Prosser, parliamentary sovereignty limits potential constitutional challenges, while other aspects of sales fit under private law, limiting issues concerning the public interest (1991, p. 81).

The final form of the privatized enterprise reflected the effects of the asset sale policy process. Its grounding in property rights drew in the support of crucial actors, such as managers, while excluding factors unacceptable to the market and minimizing the role of unions, consumers, and the public at large. The form which each privatization took resulted from the ability of the government to engage the participation or acquiescence of key actors. Usually industry managements supported privatization because they would benefit by being released from the harsh financial control of the government, and in the cases where industry chairmen did resist, the government used its power of appointment to replace them with enthusiastic supporters of its programme (Steel and Heald, 1985, p. 77). Veljanovski writes, 'the managements of the nationalised industries have emerged from the privatisation process as a separate and influential pressure group...who will support the government but only on terms that reflect their own economic and political self-interest' (1987, p. 119). According to Abromeit, 'the process of privatisation is mainly a bargaining process going on behind closed doors, in which the state industries' managers (or chairmen) are of paramount importance: their support is needed, hence actual privatisations are shaped according to their ideas' (1988, pp. 76–7).

Because management exercised considerable influence, the government often neglected the goal of increased competition in favour of the other benefits of transferring assets to the private sector (Kay and Thompson, 1986, p. 29). In the cases of BT, BG and BA, they acquiesced in the sell-off of the industry as a monopoly rather than breaking it up into competitive parts. BT's chairman George Jefferson effectively opposed the company being broken up. BG chairman, Sir Denis Rooke, resisted the government's attempt to privatize parts of the industry and stalled over the sale of its showrooms and its Wytch Farm oilfield in Dorset, representing the most noteworthy instance of management (backed by its unions) winning concessions from the government. Rooke, supported by Peter Walker, who became Energy Secretary after Nigel Lawson, insisted on maintaining a monopolistic and integrated gas industry. He successfully opposed Lawson's (now Chancellor) and presumably Prime Minister Thatcher's desire to break the company up along regional lines and then separate the gas and appliance businesses before selling them (Lawson, 1992, pp. 214–16). In addition, British Airways's Lord King resisted efforts to reduce the firm's dominant position by increasing competition in the British airline industry (cf. Reed, 1985).

In the case of water privatization, the government initially gave in to the managers' wish to maintain integrated control, as specified by the Water Act of 1973. This made the prospective private water companies responsible for managing rivers and controlling pollution, fisheries, environmental conservation, recreation and navigation. Yet, the White Paper announcing water privatization drew strong opposition from a small group of Tory backbenchers, Labour MPs, the Confederation of British Industry (CBI), trade unions, conservation groups, the fishing community, and local governments (*Guardian*, July 4, 1986). An EC Commission challenge to the status of the privatized water authorities to regulate environmental and other issues led to Environment Secretary Nicholas Ridley postponing the legislation until after the 1987 election.

The CBI's reasons for opposing the proposed legislation confirm the view that the sell-off process was 'market driven'. The CBI and the Country Landowners Association opposed the idea of privatized water authorities' controlling environmental regulation, arguing 'that it was "wrong in principle that one privatised company should exercise statutory control over the affairs of another private company"' (Richardson, Maloney and Rudig, 1992, p. 164). A host of problems – criticism of metering water use, large debts, a legal challenge over the Water Authorities ownership (the local councils or the government), as well as the questions about a profit maximizing private water company's ability to protect the environment – combined to introduce political controversy into the commercial processes (*Guardian*, July 5, 1986). By July 1986, it was becoming clear that this politicization would make water privatization unpopular and undermine a successful sale.

But once Ridley and Lawson agreed that 'the obvious route was to privatize the water and sewerage business and hive off the regulatory and environmental responsibilities into a separate State-owned National Rivers Authority', they moved forward, recreating the 'market' for the firm and dispensing with opponents supporting non-market values (Lawson, 1992, p. 232). The run-up to privatization in July 1988 witnessed a reestablishment of close and exclusive cooperation between the government ministers at the DOE and industry leaders in the Water Authorities Association (WAA), the latter proving very effective in bargaining advantages for their industry. Despite the development of a larger group opposing the initial privatization proposals, the WAA now reestablished effective working relations with the government, because other 'groups in the network lacked the technical expertise and were less likely to play a role in the implementation process' (Richardson, Maloney and Rudig, 1992, p. 171). The resumption of the policy process meant a return to a private transaction between the key players, the government and the industry leaders, interested in moving the corporation into the private sector. In short, despite opposition among unions, conservationists and anglers, the proposal to flout the norms of market practices that separate politics and economics provided the only serious challenge to the privatization of water, which finally occurred in December 1989.

The privatization of electricity offers another example of how market processes shaped policy outcomes. In privatizing electricity, the government needed the cooperation of industry leaders who insisted on including nuclear power in the package and potential buyers who found nuclear power generation a non-starter. The conflict became serious only after the legislative package had passed in July 1989. The key provisions of the legislation reflected the government's sense that privatization of electricity had to be different from that of BT (where poor service led to loud complaints) and BG (where private monopoly seemed to favour shareholders), that is, it had to appear to favour consumer interests by introducing a measure of competition (Riddell, 1989, p. 102). Rejecting the CEGB's desire for unity after privatization, the February 1988 White Paper proposed the breakup of the CEGB, ending its monopoly on generation by shifting 30 per cent of its capacity (coal, oil and gas fired stations) to a competing company, PowerGen, and 70 per cent to a company named National Power, including the nuclear stations. The decision to privatize nuclear power necessitated this proportioning as well as a requirement that distributors purchase a minimal quota from nuclear generators (Vickers and Yarrow, 1991, p. 489). The national grid would be jointly owned by the 12 new regional distribution companies, which had been the 12 area boards. These new distributors could generate their own electricity, as long as this did not lead to monopoly of production and supply (Riddell, 1989, p. 103; Roberts, Elliott and Houghton, 1991, pp. 57–8). The little competition introduced into the generation side of the Electricity Supply Industry (ESI) reflected the Secretary of Energy Cecil Parkinson's need to be 'semi-radical' in the face of determined lobbying for keeping generation integrated and unified, including the influence of the powerful nuclear energy lobby (Roberts, Elliot and Houghton, 1991, ch. 6).

Yet, opposition to the government's acquiescence to industry leaders' wish to include nuclear power generation in the privatization of electricity generation came from the 'market'. This pressure stalemated the government's initial proposals, forced a significant modification, and then dissipated, facilitating a return to concentrated decision-making. In July 1989, Parkinson withdrew the aging Magnox nuclear stations from the sale and in November the new Energy Secretary John Wakeham pulled the rest of the nuclear programme out of the sale of the electricity supply industry, thereby signalling the government's overriding concern to complete the sale without further complications. According to Roberts, Elliot and Houghton, this meant that the 'Security of supply, research and development, the future of the coal and of the power plant industries were ignored because of ideology...combined with the pragmatics of privatisation' (1991, p. 97).

What forced the withdrawal of the nuclear component of the industry was its unattractiveness to investors and the weakness of the old nuclear power lobby. According to Roberts, Elliott and Houghton, 'Just as the economics of nuclear power are incompatible with the private sector, so the fracturing, by privatisation, of the corporatist ESI caucus destroyed the

political support on which the continuance of the nuclear power programme depended' (1991, p. 100). Overall, the government's concern
with ownership and structure dictated the process of marketing the ESI to
potential buyers. This process rejected the inclusion of nuclear power
because of its poor commercial future and neglected key post-privatized
issues, such as regulation and the coordination between distributors and
generators (Vickers and Yarrow, 1991, pp. 492 and 494).

The emphasis on property rights gave the managements great influence
over the form of most sales and also shaped the method of sale, designed
to win the support of a variety of groups for stock ownership. The
Thatcherites intended to widen share ownership 'in the belief that this will
improve the economic efficiency of companies and alter people's voting
habits', widen employee shareownership, enlarge the capital market itself,
and get a good return of the sale of shares (Wiltshire, 1987, p. 48). A high
percentage of employees purchased shares, usually at a discount or with
interest-free loans (Veljanovski, 1987, p. 104). Private or trade sales to
other firms, management buy-outs (parts of the former NBC), worker buy-
outs (National Freight) are among the methods used to sell public assets.
However, the most common has been the fixed price offering and then the
tender, where the price is determined by the response. The fixed price
method enables the government to appeal to small investors and to create
interest in the issue, which results in active trading once the sale is completed (Veljanovski, 1987, p. 132). The government favoured this method
because it led to underpricing and enabled small shareholders to cash in on
their premiums. From the government's point of view, this was good.
According to Nigel Lawson (1992, p. 210), 'The enormous publicity given
to the profits enjoyed by subscribers to the issue conveyed the clear
message to the general public that investing in privatization issues was a
good thing'. The fixed price became the norm, though criticism of 'asset
stripping' came from many quarters (Abromeit, 1988, p. 77; Wiltshire,
1987, pp. 64–6). Yet, proponents like Grimstone (1990, pp. 9–10) argue
that by at least doubling shareholding privatization contributes to widening and deepening the capital market. In short, the government gained
public support for expanding private ownership in firms, even though it
did not raise the highest financial returns possible.

Further, market accountability meant that government would exercise
indirect continuing control over the privatized companies. While companies entering the competitive sector fall under competition law, the sell-off
of the large utility companies led to the creation of new regulatory agencies. The government, starting with BT, commissioned an expert economist to recommend the most effective way to control the privatized

enterprise. In the case of BT and water, Stephen Littlechild, a University of Birmingham economics professor, recommended a price control mechanism backed by licensing agreements enforced by an independent regulatory agency (Veljanovski, 1987, p. 126). Accepting these recommendations the government included in its privatization legislation clauses establishing the regulatory authorities. Furthermore, the government applied other means to prevent a privatized enterprises' takeover by an undesirable or unwanted agent. Most notable is the 'golden share' retained by the government, preventing a takeover or change in a firms' articles of association without the government's agreement. In addition, government uses competition law, environmental regulations, and contracts with firms to exercise continuing control (Graham and Prosser, 1991, ch. 5).

Opposition to privatization per se (in contrast to its form) has proven ineffective, revealing just how successfully neoliberalism has been able to define policy-making in terms of ownership rights and to limit policy processes to issues and participants conforming to the ideological imperatives of market accountability. The process of engaging individual participation in corporate ownership advantaged some, while denying access and benefits to others. Unions have consistently opposed privatization, though some unions and workers have gained from privatization while others have lost (Thomas, 1984, p. 74). Union action, sustained by BG management, postponed the sale of gas showrooms, but this was the only exception. Strikes have been limited, with the largest BT union, the POEU, carrying out the most significant industrial action, while only token stoppages occurred in the gas industry, the Royal Ordnance Factories, and Sealink (ibid., p. 64). Unions also carried out publicity campaigns, but despite arousing public sympathies these have had little impact. Even their use of political influence through the Labour Party proved ineffective, as the party was itself moving away from defending nationalization, lacked a broader ideological alternative to Thatcher's neoliberalism, and was overwhelmingly outnumbered in Parliament.

From the government's perspective, it has been extremely successful in passing its legislation, reflecting its large majorities and the enthusiasm of its backbenchers for the initiatives (Steel and Heald, 1985, pp. 78–9). The impact of public opinion seems negligible, as it opposed the BT, BG, water and electricity sell-offs (Crewe, 1988, pp. 41–2; Saunders, 1995). Only nationalistic sentiment evokes enough opposition to block the sell-off of British firms to foreign multinationals, illustrated by the dropping of plans in 1987 to sell Austin-Rover to Ford (Heald, 1989, p. 43).

In short, privatizing state industries meant private market processes and expertise were able to control behaviour, thereby diverting attention away from direct political contests into the endless and self-governing pursuit of private commercial dealings. According to Cento Veljanovski, the 'crucial difference [between nationalized and private firms] that lies at the heart of the privatization debate is that in the privatized company there are tradable private property rights' (1987, p. 92). This ability to control a firm's behaviour by buying and selling ownership rights in it, in particular through the potential for the hostile takeover bid, became the main method of deciding policy, diminishing the interference of non-market pressures. Thus, though the form of the firm, the number of competitors, the suppliers, and unions may all be different after the sell-off, profiting from the new ownership rights became the primary criterion guiding decision-making. While BG was transferred to the private sector as a monopoly and the sale of BT was preceded by limited deregulation and competition, each focussed on developing its profitability. Justified by the idea that property rights provide a superior mode for controlling firms, the sell-off of state assets was a reform or transitional process. The key to its success was the ability of a private commercial transaction process to redirect thinking and activities into operations that in themselves designated how energies were to be translated into particular results.

The Sale of BT

To return to the case study of BT, the main stages of the sale process were the split from the Post Office by the British Telecommunications Act in 1981 and BT's licensing as a limited company in April 1984, following passage of the Telecommunications Bill. The government initially introduced this legislation in July 1982 and then reintroduced it in July 1983 after the June election (Graham and Prosser, 1991, p. 78; Veljanovski, 1987, p. 191). The business of the corporation was transferred to the company in August 1984, shares issued to the Secretary of State and debts removed. The public sale or stock market flotation occurred on 16 November 1984 when 'the Secretary of State's advisers offered 50.2 per cent of the ordinary shares for sale on his behalf' (Graham and Prosser, 1991, p. 79).

The Government's strategy of reform involved making the transaction as much as possible into a private sector market exchange that drew on the self-interest of potential owners and executives. This meant narrowing negotiations about key issues to those who agreed on the inevitability of privatization and who were capable of being drawn into the privatizing process. Overshadowing the long and controversial legislative process was the behind-the-scenes preparation to create a marketable product and to generate a large market for the product. This involved changes within BT itself, such as the creation in July 1983 of a marketing committee involving BT and the government for the purpose of developing and maintaining the conditions for successfully selling BT. Because it was the first sale of a major public utility, the main and sub-working groups set precedents time after time. To create interest among institutions and the public at large, many lawyers, bankers, brokers, marketing and public relations and advertising specialists, and the government, BT and their advisors worked closely together. To achieve the sale, the meetings 'merged the cultures and requirements of occasionally almost incompatible interests into a force which was to achieve one of the greatest marketing conditioning achievements on record' (in Clutterbuck, 1991, p. 103).

The result of the marketing efforts was a coordinated but comprehensive campaign, covering the media, MPs, major customers, key opinion formers, the BT employees and the public. The committee monitored every action, utilizing continuous market research. Incentives were used to raise support by making shareownership widely possible and effectively marginalizing opponents with fundamental differences in values. Moreover, complicated and wide-ranging negotiations with the government and its advisors 'helped shape the legislation, the content of the new long-term operating licences so crucial to our commercial and competitive future, and, of course, the sort of price at which the newly-created nominal 25p shares might be sold' (ibid., p. 102).

Different conceptions of the means for ensuring actors' future wellbeing, that is, the ways groups defined their business interests, influenced the form of the privatized BT and the political conflict over privatization. First, different criteria for decision-making led to a change in relationships among key players. During the time up to privatization, the 'partnership' between the unions, the Post Office, and the Department of Industry in making policies collapsed. The unions took an 'outsider' strategy in a campaign against privatization and the formation of a new coalition favouring privatization (Moon, Richardson, and Smart, 1986, p. 345). The main benefactors and participants in the new coalition were the BT management, the City, new shareholders, and the Government.

Further, the adjustment of divergent standards for interpreting self-interests influenced the form of the privatized BT. It's management wanted to prevent a break-up of the corporation (as happened with AT&T), limit competition, and minimize regulation. BT argued that these aims dovetailed with the Government's hopes to maximize its return on the sale of shares (while remaining the largest shareholder) and to ensure the success of the privatization for ideological reasons (Vickers and

Yarrow, 1988, p. 210; Hills, 1986, p. 126; Pitt, 1990, p. 60). The Government's desire for a successful sale and its need to subject the privatized BT to a regulatory regime led it to accommodate BT's management. Thus, BT preserved its horizontal and vertical integration and limited its competition, which gave it a pricing formula that ensured profits often double that of its international competitors (Vickers and Yarrow, 1988, pp. 235–6; Kay, 1984, pp. 77–8; *Financial Times*, January 15, 1991, p. 16).

The Government also rewarded the City firms giving professional advice or purchasing the largest proportion of shares issued, while providing benefits to the 2.3 million initial shareholders in an effort to garner popular support (Hills, 1986, p. 130). Public relations efforts contended that the sale would benefit telephone users, for whom special incentives were given for the purchase of BT shares, including rebates. The sale, costing £323 million, was oversubscribed; many shareholders made large profits (Hills, 1986, p. 130; Newman, 1986, ch. 10). Differing perceptions of self-interest led to the negotiating over future advantages that would accrue from privatization, striking accommodations among those supporters who would gain benefits, while excluding losers. Hawking writes,

> Many decisions were reached by a process of interaction – not negotiation exactly, but accommodation – amongst the interested parties, and often represented the outcome of political (in the loosest sense) processes – relations between brokers and institutions, favours owed to clients, relations between banks, the views of Ministers, etc. In addition, of course, more or less all of the parties involved had a financial stake in the outcome.   (cited in Graham and Prosser, 1991, p. 90)

The Government's policies of price regulation and incremental increases in competition also depended on BT's and other interested groups' acceptance and active participation in the new regime. BT executives strongly supported the government policies and worked effectively with its officials who reciprocated by favouring BT's interests (Vickers and Yarrow, 1988, p. 210; Newman, 1986, pp. 12–3). The 1984 Act adopted the principle of price regulation and the RPI-X price formula, following the 1983 Littlechild Report's suggestion that price rises on monopoly services be restricted by less than the retail price index (RPI) measure of inflation. It also gave Mercury more room to compete while assuring BT's dominance, ended BT's monopoly of maintenance on new equipment and prevented the simple resale of BT capacity. Competing networks interconnecting through BT, like Mercury and the cellular telephone operators, would have to pay BT an access fee. However, the government rejected Littlechild's proposal that cable TV should compete with BT (Hills, 1986, pp. 127–8). After privatization, the main business of negotiating the RPI-X pricing formula ensued, settling on RPI-3 per cent.

Finally, differences in interpreting the purposes of telecommunications also affected interaction and conflict among those involved in making-policy. Those initially favouring public control lost. Taking the lead among opponents, the POEU worked with an umbrella organization, called the British Telecom Unions Committee (BTUC), to organize publicity campaigns, parliamentary lobbying, and industrial action (Kay, 1984, p. 78). The objectives of the BTUC were 'to amend the Bill, protect services, and thereby save jobs, and to keep BT as one unit' (BTUC, 1984, p. 23). Its strategy was to arouse business to voice their fears, fight the Bill in the Commons at the committee stage, and then fight for changes in the Lords. Able to gain the cooperation of the National Farmers Union, the BTUC gained passage of an amendment in the Lords preventing price discrimination against rural users (BTUC, 1984, p. 27). Along with guarantees for BT workers' right to strike and against breaking up BT, the BTUC claimed other victories in the Lords: 'There were victories on uneconomic services, services for the blind and disabled, Directory Enquiries, the defence of UK manufacturers, rural prices, bringing BT's licence before Parliament, advisory councils for consumers and telephone tapping' (BTUC, 1984, p. 28).

The Society of Telecom Executives (STE) representing some 25 000 BT managers opposed privatization (STE, 1983). Union opposition to privatization was strong but was undercut by job losses and internal restructuring prior to privatization. Job cuts weakened workers' bargaining position, and generous incentives for BT employees to buy shares diminished their hostility (POEU, 1984). The telecommunications equipment manufacturers – GEC, Plessey, and STC – opposed the privatization bill, fearing correctly that BT would no longer favour domestic suppliers and lead to an uneasy post-privatization relationship (Moon, Richardson, and Smart, 1986, p. 353; Hills, 1986, p. 127).

The legislative process revealed substantial controversy about the ends of telecommunications services, but the transformation of noneconomic values into differences in benefit mollified opposition. On July 19, 1982, in the White Paper, *The Future of Telecommunications in Britain* (Department of Industry, 1982), the Government announced its intention to sell 51 per cent of its shares in BT and to create a new regulatory body (OFTEL). The subsequent Bill, reintroduced after the Conservative victory in the June 1983 General Election, provoked the longest debates in the Commons (taking up 321 hours) since WWII, substantial contro- versy in the Lords, and even industrial action by the POEU. Consumer groups were among the most vocal opponents of privatization. The National Farmers Union, Scottish local authorities, and Welsh users protested against the loss of rural services. The Post Office Users Council protested that OFTEL could not take over its function and still be respons- ible for guaranteeing a profitable BT (Hills, 1986, p. 127). These demands to protect the public service function of telephones yielded some conces- sions during the legislative process. The 1984 Act, consequently, provided greater protection for consumers and user-groups, such as the disabled, the elderly, small businesses and people in rural areas, and improved privacy protection against wiretapping.

CONCLUSION

This chapter, including the case study of BT, shows that the Thatcher gov- ernments' sale of state assets supports the model of indirect state control through market activities. The ideas of the New Right projected the substi- tution of market modes of decision-making for the more open and unstable processes of collectivist pluralism. New Right ideas make individual self- interest the ground for choice and charge individuals with the responsibil- ity of advancing their well-being. Choice in market processes is about optimizing gains and reducing costs, reducing decisions to instrumental matters of calculated process. The standard of choice is rationality, linking input to benefit, and the objectification or commodification of costs and rewards provide precise measurement. Faith in New Right ideas simulta- neously generated a self-righteousness that steeled the core Thatcherites' resolve to move forward with the privatization programme and to exclude those who disagreed about its correctness.

The state's power increased by drawing those who would gain, or those who thought they would gain, into market activities, but marginalized those whose participation was not critical or whose worldviews oppose the private sector. Being central to the privatizing the process of policy- making advantaged the state, senior executives, City advisors, and City institutions. Those outside the commercial transaction counted for little. Privatizing decision-making disadvantaged those who held opposing views, lacked specialized business experience and knowledge or wealth. John Ernst comments, 'On the major [consumer] issues – such as those concerning the priority to be accorded to the interests of ordinary con- sumers in the regulatory system, the balance between equity, service quality and company profitability considerations, and the ability of domestic consumers to achieve a strong independent voice – the community sector campaigns had a limited impact' (1994, p. 34). Market policy-making eliminates opposition by denying non-market criteria a hearing.

The Thatcherite economic objectives and methods initiated an alternative to state interventionist bureaucratic methods of control. Dramatically reshaping the boundary between society and itself by selling off its assets did not result from the influence of capitalists, pressure groups based on inequalities of wealth and power, or state institutional capacity. It did not involve directly imposing losses on outsiders, such as workers, unions, citizens, though these were indirect consequences.

Rather, effective and enlarged state power emerged from engaging participation in market transactions, letting participation in the process itself control behaviour, maintaining surveillance from a distance, and then redirecting the processes of market-led policy-making as required. Rather than imposing changes on the participants, privatization made use of the control deriving from participation in market transactions. In recasting choices as market outcomes, the government participated as a market player along with financial and business experts and ensured the completion of the commercial transactions. It assumed a role of seller in a process involving a host of commercial advisors, advertisers, and buyers, but a seller determined to make a sale. In short, the government relied on an indirect type of power: a commercial process that was initiated, participated in, and overseen by the government itself.

5 Regulation and Control

How does the government exercise control over private sector monopolies and subcentral governments when direct political decisions, hands-on bureaucratic administration, and imposition of financial limits prove feckless? The neoliberal solution is to emphasize that competition would enable consumers to hold the producers accountable and reduce the need for government intervention. Yet, there are many situations in which competitive processes do not exist or cannot be easily created. In these circumstances, governments rely on some type of regulatory policy, specifying a principal-agent relationship designed to effect the principal's ends despite differences in interests and information.

While neoliberal regulatory theory assumes that material incentives are the most effective means for getting agents to perform stipulated tasks, this chapter argues that the most important controls arise indirectly and internally from participation in social activities. Rather than the direct or external force of incentive or legal penalties, compliance depends on strategic behaviour, emerging from involvement within a situation, directed by a controlling purpose, and relying on the use of explicit ideas about risks and rewards in view of what others are doing. The regulator, as principal, succeeds in gaining compliance with government-stipulated standards, not by demanding or negotiating incentives, but through the way ideas or meanings defining acceptable activities determine the way constituents refer their way of behaving to the action of others and work to make it fit in. The controlling effect of market-utilizing forms of regulation emerges from engagement within commercial or economic processes, situations requiring the adjustment of action in response to what others have done or are about to do. Understandings or dispositions about the way markets work and the boundaries of the approval or disapproval, favour or disfavour, voiced by other players drive and shape market-driven participation. The use of direct force takes on a secondary role, with government intervention being occasional and limited to preventing conflict from causing a breakdown.

This chapter analyzes indirect state control at work in two major forms of delegation typical of neoliberal regulation. First, it considers the regulation of private sector public utilities. This focuses on the processes of using an independent agency to promote increasing competition and industrial modernization. In regulating what initially were private monopolies or near-monopolies, regulators are both agents of the government and participants in a market-driven process of self-administration. Second, it examines the use of competitive tendering throughout sub-central government, the process of competition for monopoly, as a means to improve economic efficiency. In this case, the government is at a distance from the agency administering spending and provision programmes. The government maintains surveillance in order to ensure that agency behaviour conforms to its stipulations. On occasion, it intervenes directly.

REGULATING PRIVATE MONOPOLIES

Enforcing Market Incentives

The successful sell-off of the major public utilities pushed regulatory policy into the limelight. In turning major public monopolies into private monopolies or near-monopolies from 1984 to 1990, Thatcherites ensured successful sales but created regulatory policy dilemmas (Maloney and Richardson, 1992, p. 15). Veljanovski writes:

> The overriding purpose of privatisation was to propel the new entities into the private sector with new and greater freedoms to pursue commercial objectives and improve efficiency. Yet, unfettered, they have every incentive to charge customers high prices, reduce the quality of services and prevent competition. Regulation is required but invites other difficulties.   (1991, p. 5)

Among these difficulties are regulatory uncertainty, pressures for increased controls, and 'due process'. Remedying such 'market failures' is, then, the primary rationale for regulation. Economists focus on the effects of market power, externalities, and asymmetric information as the sources of internal and allocative inefficiencies. Regulation aims to constrain monopoly behaviour, limit destructive competition, and promote desirable competition (Kay and Vickers, 1988, pp. 301–8). Yet, market failure has to be balanced with the possibility of regulatory failures (Helm and Yarrow, 1988, pp. ii–vii).

Post-privatization regulatory agencies replaced nationalization as a failed form of direct regulation. Nationalization relied on institutional and political criteria, expecting boards to pursue the public interest. A 1976 National Economic and Development Office study reported that the control system in nationalized industries revealed a 'lack of trust and

Table 5.1   Regulatory agencies

	Year	Industry
Economic Regulators		
Civil Aviation Authority	1971	Airports
Office of Telecommunications	1984	Telecommunications
Office of Gas Supply	1986	Gas
Office of Water Services	1989	Water
Office of Electricity Regulation	1990	Electricity
Quality Regulators		
National Rivers Authority	1989	Water
HM Inspectorate of Pollution	1987	All
Independent Television Commission	1991	Terrestrial, Cable & Satellite TV
Radio Authority	1991	Radio
Broadcasting Standards Council	1990	Broadcasting
Competition Regulators		
Office of Fair Trading	1951	All
Monopolies and Mergers Commission	1948	All

Source: Veljanovski, 1991, p. 11.

mutual understanding between government and management, confusion about roles, and the absence of an effective system for measuring performance and managerial competence' (Veljanovski, 1991, p. 7). In addition to being monopoly providers, then, the nationalized industries became regulated by ministers for political ends.

An unregulated privatized monopoly would be able to charge higher prices and produce lower outputs (e.g., unreliable and outdated products) than a firm facing tough regulation and competition. In the words of C.D. Foster, 'Thus the economic case for the regulation of natural monopoly derives fundamentally from the propositions that there are monopoly industries where such an advance in competition cannot be relied on and that, in so far as price discrimination is technically impossible or legally impermissible, that means, in the absence of regulation, under all circumstances higher prices and under almost all lower outputs than under competition if the firm sets its prices and output so as to maximize its profits' (1992, p. 198). In short, regulation policy acts as a proxy for competition.

In instituting an alternative type of indirect and internal control, regulation uses market incentives as the standard of accountability. Supervising market transactions enables the regulator or principal to maintain incentives for efficiency where he or she lacks information available to the agent and to induce the agent (the regulated firm) to act in the public interest (Vickers and Yarrow, 1988, pp. 92–9; Kay and Vickers, 1990, pp. 230–3). According to economist Ray Rees (1986, p. 19), 'Regulation by government Department, through direct control of capital allocations, investment plans, borrowing requirements and pricing policy, is to be replaced with regulation by a quasi-governmental public agency, backed up by competition policy'. Regulation formulates the delegation of government functions to designated agents in terms of principal/agent problems, usually relying on a public agency.

The new regulatory structures, which were the result of the selling off of public sector monopolies, reflected departmental preference for marketizing policy-making without public debate. Economist Stephen Littlechild, now Director General (DG) of the Office of Electricity Regulation (OFFER), provided academic advice, drawing on his economist training and projecting his New Right politics. As Walker (1990, p. 150) puts it, 'But the advice supplied... has come from a single discipline, economics, and had a dogmatic, prescriptive, rather than analytic flavour'. The Office of Telecommunications or OFTEL, the first new regulatory agency, was modelled on the Office of Fair Trading and then became the model for subsequent regulatory agencies.

Post-privatization regulation, then, replaces direct state involvement with public agencies responsible for improving the productive and allocative efficiency of a particular industry. While overtly reducing the directness and inevitability of ministerial intervention, the ends guiding the new regulation permit state officials to maintain and even tighten control, because government principals, the regulators, attempt to entice their agents, the providers, to 'set prices equal to short-run marginal costs ... and expand output until price equals long-run marginal cost' (Foster, 1992, p. 198). In contrast with aiming to serve the public interest through nationalization, the economic goal of enhancing internal and allocative efficiency determines more intermediate and explicit ideas, conflicts, and debates, dispensing with the need for direct government intervention and responsibility. Industry participants engage in a game governed by economic modus operandi, yet are indirectly supervised and guided by the regulator who acts more as a leading player than a sovereign power.

Direct government involvement remains as a potential and occasional option.

Objectives in Regulating Telecommunications

The post-privatization telecommunications regulatory regime comprises such a quasi-market-driven game. Players include the Director General of Telecommunications (DGT), BT and Mercury Communications (MCL) as well as the cellular phone, mobile (PNCs), satellite, cable, private mobile radio (PMR) and radiopaging companies and other new entrants, such as the private networks operated by British Rail (BR), and the fuel and power companies, the transmission systems operated by the BBC and the former Independent Broadcasting Authority, and various consumer and advisory bodies. Telecommunications industry decision-making centres on implementing the obligations of the DGT to ensure that companies fulfil their licence conditions and to promote competition while maintaining the economic viability and vitality of the industry's enterprises.

In telecommunications, as in the gas, water, and electricity sectors, the Government shaped policy-making by providing the basis for enlisting and organizing the support of constituent firms and for deciding the criterion for approving decisions. The Telecommunications Act 1984 stipulates the DGT's ends. They are essentially economic, specifying improvement of productive and allocative efficiency in the industry. According to DGT Bryan Carsberg (1991, p. 99), 'It seems to me that most important regulatory activity falls into two main categories: the promotion of competition and the development of incentive regulation'. OFTEL attempts to foster new competition, monitoring BT's behaviour for possible predatory pricing yet not being overly restrictive. In product areas in which BT continues to have monopoly power, OFTEL relies on the price cap formula to encourage internal efficiency (Hartley and Culham, 1988, p. 3). OFTEL also oversees provision of socially necessary services, in the interest of providing universal basic services. As the leading participant in a regimen of economic interplay, the DGT controls by offering incentives and providing opportunities.

The purpose of corporate policy became increasingly to secure a profitable future. Iain Vallance, BT Chairman, articulates the viewpoint of firms under the new regulatory regime. First he doubted that a nationalized monopoly like BT 'could have adapted itself to such an environment, given that the government was determined to push through market competition even faster than it was being achieved in the United States through the break-up of the Bell conglomerate' (in Clutterbuck, 1991, p. 100; Riddell, 1989, p. 96). Rejecting any return to state ownership, 'when we were so very much a political football, at the mercy of stop-start pricing, investment and planning policies which characterised our state sector era', Vallance portrays BT as responding to changing domestic and international markets. He writes: 'During the 1990s, as we look forward, among other things, to the implementation of the Single European Market and to inevitable liberalisation and change in other telecommunications markets, we expect to see any number of new opportunities for generating extra earnings growth – provided that we choose and understand our market well and succeed in putting customers first' (in Clutterbuck, 1991, pp. 109 and 110).

For BT employees, the changes in the corporation's status and environment coincided with the introduction of commercial practices, eroding the past foundations of industrial relations (Haywood, 1987). The centralized pattern of physical planning based on a commitment to provide the resources necessary to develop the phone network became a decentralized system of profit centres with evaluations of managers' performance based on the costs and income of every activity. Labour costs were carefully scrutinized, as cash limits put downward pressure on manpower levels. This was in contrast to the previous system of estimating the needed manpower and then requesting the necessary finances to hire the requisite workforce. At the same time, the traditional open and consensual public sector style of industrial relations gave way to resistance to trade union organization and to reluctance in negotiating concessions, bargaining becoming divisional rather than corporate.

The Regulators: Directing Social Control

Law and the market define a situation in which regulators act as leaders or guides of sectoral activity rather than as external bosses. Each privatization Act established the framework in which the privatized entity operates, stipulating the licence and its conditions and the supervising public agent. These were the DGs of the five economic regulatory agencies (OFTEL, OFGAS, OFWAT, CAA, and OFFER).

The privatization Acts give the government some direct powers for involvement in regulation. Golden shares and competition law enable the government to interfere directly in shaping shareownership and corporate control (Graham and Prosser, 1991, p. 172). Secretaries of State grant licences, but are required to consult the DG, who also has the duty to keep the Secretary of State informed. But once the licence is granted, the

Secretary of State cannot change it. However, the DG can amend the licence through agreement with the licencee or by referring it to the Monopoly and Mergers Commission (MMC) (Graham and Prosser, 1991, p. 191). The MMC and the Secretary of State can decide to appeal. The DGs, heading non-ministerial government departments, enforce licences and their conditions and can also modify the conditions. In addition, they approve contractors, the apparatus required, and the record-keeping. Finally, they investigate complaints about services and apparatus, and enforce competition laws.

Given the reserve character of formal power, most policy-making involves bargaining among the key constituent firms. While DGs review licence conditions and the price cap formulas, giving notice of changes, reasons, and permitted time for representation by concerned parties, changes can be made only with the consent of the individual companies. Even in cases in which the regulator fails to come to agreement with the industry and the Secretary of State or MMC gets involved, as seen in BG's reference to the MMC, the policy recommended by the Secretary of State still depends on its acceptability to the industry (Beesley, 1992, p. 360; Veljanovski, 1991, pp. 13–14). While the DG can enforce licence terms by issuing provisional or final orders, permitting any party affected by failure to comply to sue for damages, the procedure has never been used (Graham and Prosser, 1991, pp. 213–15).

The Acts place duties of protecting consumers and promoting competition on the person of the DG, not the agency. The regulatory agencies then are 'personal regimes' in which officeholders have wide discretion and the use of public relations facilities (Walker, 1990, p. 152; Ernst, 1994, pp. 62–3). Sir Gordon Borrie, director general of the Office of Fair Trading (OFT), and Sir Bryan Carsberg, the DGT, provide public accountability by creating a public persona. James McKinnon, former DG of OFGAS, and Stephen Littlechild, DG of OFFER, pursued less public styles. If style contributes of the 'elastic powers' of the regulator, the regulators benefit also from being 'fully part of the state machine; their administrative culture is Whitehall's' (Walker, 1990, p. 154). Assessments on the industry finance the regulators' expenditures, though Parliament and the Treasury approve their budgets. Staffed by civil servants and supervised by the relevant Department, agencies assisting the DGs fit into the socio-cultural traits of the senior civil service, making them different from, while still part of, the sectoral business activity. With wide discretion and quasi-judicial functions, regulators are 'rule-makers' who operate by renegotiating the framework of economic activity in order to achieve their economic (and social) objectives (Walker, 1990, p. 157).

The regulators of the recently privatized utility companies have been important agents for advancing competition and ensuring fairer pricing in their industries. The effort to expand competition in these industries now seems greater since the 1987 political backlash from the sale of the British Gas monopoly and the deterioration of BT services. Yet, the problem started with privatization. Veljanovski writes,

> The present regulators have clearly not been 'captured' by their industries but they do operate within a regulatory system which was the outcome of an earlier capture. This happened in the very formulation of the agencies and the structure of the industry itself. This is seen by the failure to restructure all but the electricity industry and by the setting of prices for the operation of the price cap at their initial nationalised levels. (1991, p. 22)

This has led regulators to reshape the initial 'regulatory bargain' favouring the monopoly utilities by extending control more widely and deeply and providing profit incentives for new entrants. To change the initial bargain, 'regulators are encroaching on more areas – prices, quality of service, access, rate of return – and scrutinising and probing more of each utility's activities' (Veljanovski, 1991, p. 22).

The growth of regulatory control has gone hand in hand with efforts to encourage greater competition. The broad economic ends assigned to the DGs enable them to implement government ideology about increasing competition. The DGs use the bargaining process to change internal and external conditions in which player and potential entrants operate and exercise their discretion to make deals that satisfy all parties, yet widen competition. Beesley and Littlechild (1991, pp. 50–1) write that the regulator must attempt to identify entry conditions 'from the point of view of the potential entrant' and predict how changes in regulation will affect their behaviour. Drawing on the Austrian school's focus on utilizing profit opportunities to maintain and advance market processes, Beesley and Littlechild (1991, p. 51) contend that 'there is more scope for promoting competition than has hitherto been recognised'. Peacock (1991) believes that regulators can counter monopoly power by competition but this requires that they not only stimulate competition but encourage new entrants.

The regulated producers, however, are not passive but actively manoeuvre in order to improve their advantage. In the words of Alan Peacock (1991, p. 83), 'The regulated concern is not a Pavlovian dog reacting to stimuli supplied by the regulator'. Certainly George Stigler's theory of regulatory capture – that producers invariably influence regulations for their own benefit – assumes producer initiative. This complicates the regulatory process and implies that the relation between regulator and regulated producer is a bargaining relationship. Veljanovski (1991, p. 25) points out that this generates opportunities for 'gaming the system': 'because regulation is operated in a discretionary way, each party has an incentive to operate strategically to obtain an advantage or avoid losses'. Despite gaming by producers and regulator latitude, informal bargaining predominates, with few matters leading to deadlock and referral to the MMC.

While some strategic initiatives and anticipatory responses by industry aim to 'outwit the regulator', others are genuine efforts to respond to new opportunities in a changed environment. The privatized utilities expansion into overseas markets, illustrated by BT's 1993 purchase of 20 per cent of MCI's shares, is one important response to regulators' squeezing domestic sources of profits. These initiatives prompted regulators to call for including these foreign operations under their remit. Regulators hoped to prevent the firms from financing such expansion at the customers' expense (*Financial Times,* October 11, 1993, p. 15).

In short, regulators are the government's agents, but in their role as principals supervising an industry, they have wide discretion and must act in their own right. They act as leaders of their particular industry's business, not imposing decisions from outside but encouraging and developing constituent members' participation and involvement in those activities. The personal and nonlegalistic framework of the regulators provide them with the capacity to take initiatives that encourage increased competition and maintain appropriate business initiatives by the regulated. Yet, the regulator cannot rule by imposition. DGs must succeed through credibility with their constituents, through principled argument and demonstration as part of a bargaining exchange. C.D. Foster (1992, p. 204) emphasizes that the regulator should engage in debate with all concerned about what he thinks are the best options for increasing efficiency: 'But in the end he will be wise if he insists only on what he can demonstrate and what is widely accepted to be reasonable'.

Using Incentives to Lead in Telecommunications
The Director General of Telecommunications (DGT) has the statutory duty of promoting competition under Section 3 of the 1984 Act, an objective that the first incumbent Sir Bryan Carsberg personally took to be his main objective. He supervises the OFTEL, a non-ministerial government

department, modelled on the Office of Fair Trading, with a staff of 143 in 1991 (OFTEL, 1992). Backed by the MMC and the Secretary of State for the Department of Trade and Industry (DTI), the DGT enforces licences and expands competition. Sir Bryan Carsberg, the DGT until 1992, stated his pro-market objective in his first annual Report: 'I attach a high priority to my duty to promote effective competition and I have quickly come to believe that this is one of the most important and urgent of the duties laid upon me by the Act' (cited in Vickers and Yarrow, 1988, p. 217). Favouring a proactive strategy, Carsberg used incentives, edicts, and threats of changes in licensing conditions by referrals to the MMC to gradually increase competition. This process of 'regulated liberalization', purportedly aiming for eventual self-regulation through market forces, relies significantly on the acceptance and involvement of BT and other participants themselves.

The proactive regulation of the first DGT kept the goalposts shifting in order to encourage increased competition. It led, in turn, to initiatives by BT, the dominant player, designed to secure its future and by Mercury, Hull and other new players aiming to take advantage of the new opportunities. Carsberg's initiatives show how the independent regulatory agent is both the government's agent and the principal overseeing and directing the industry's constituents' individual and collective behaviour. Encouraging competition meant fostering conditions which make entry profitable, a strategy that depended on the interplay and cooperation of the regulator and major firms in the industry. As Beesley and Littlechild (1991, p. 49) put it, 'The regulator therefore has to be selective – that is, to take a view about where entry might be most likely, if encouraged, and hence most effective in producing net benefits to consumers and producers, as they will be refined by the impact of entry'. Carsberg formulated the idea of entry assistance to characterize the way he encourages new entrants. In order to increase efficiency and greater variety in services, Carsberg gave concessions to new entrants, offering these favourable locations, specializations, or interconnection discounts. His scheme for access deficit contributions waived the contributions of new entrants to BT's non-usage-sensitive costs until they reached 10 per cent of the market share (Carsberg, 1993, p. 92–3).

Even the framework set by the duopoly policy for basic telephone services and the pricing formula aimed systematically to increase competition. It encouraged Mercury by protecting its initial but high cost efforts. Control of prices by price caps is a form of incentive regulation, 'setting a ceiling on prices for a number of years, thereby giving the regulatee the opportunity to make a higher profit by exceeding the efficiency target implied in the price cap' (Carsberg, 1991, p. 100). After a major review of the price cap in 1988, controls were widened and the main cap tightened to 4.5 per cent. In 1991 the DGT worked out a further bargain with BT in which international calls were to be included in the price cap, while the main cap was increased further to 6.25 per cent (Foster, 1992, p. 217). Incentive regulation also can be seen in the Customer Guarantee Scheme and the publication of information about the quality of service. Despite the formal commitment to incentive or price regulation, the concern about excessive profits led regulators to address issues about the appropriate rate of return for the particular type of business.

As DGT, Carsberg, though gaining a reputation for being pro-competitive and tough on BT, achieved advances in introducing new market-oriented incentives absent from the original bargain, as encapsulated in the 1984 legislation. He gave advice and suggestions, rather than imposing his views, as the means for redirecting and guiding constituents' initiatives. His first major action recommended that the Minister block a proposed VANS network between IBM and BT. He said that it would forestall competition because IBM's System Network Architecture would prevent the use of equipment made by other manufacturers. The Minister subsequently announced that all VANS use the Open System Interconnection standards, which makes possible the interconnection of all makes of equipment (Hills, 1986, p. 131). Next, the Government took OFTEL's advice in preventing BT from entering the mobile radio communications services. Further, when BT announced its intention to take over Mitel, the ailing Canadian PABX producer, it posed a threat to British equipment manufacturers by furthering the vertical integration of its operations, which had already produced its own line of telephones and microcomputers. OFTEL recommended approval with safeguards, though suggesting that the MMC review the sale. The MMC recommended against the merger, but the Minister (Leon Brittan) preferred OFTEL's suggestion, approving the sale with restrictions (Hills, 1986, p. 132; Vickers and Yarrow, 1988, pp. 220–3).

Overall, the regulator acts as leader of the industrial groups' activities. By means of advice and incentives, the constituents' initiatives, taking the plans and actions of others into account, control developments. In terms of economic theory about principal-agent relations under asymmetric information, the optimal incentive arrangement for all players is mutual interdependence: for the reward of each to be contingent upon the performance of all (Vickers and Yarrow, 1988, p. 116). The way the DGT fosters competition and renegotiates the price cap formula appear to be just such a structure of expectations. In short, regulators' initiatives only work through the initiatives of the regulatees.

Decision-Making: Profit-Oriented Bargaining

The regulatory process involves informal, secretive negotiation among the regulator and the regulated firms, with the state retaining substantial potential capacity for redirecting what is a commercial process. Veljanovski (1991, p. 13) emphasizes the informal in contrast to the legal characteristics of the UK's bargained regulation: 'Rather the law operates as the sanction of last resort against which compliance is sought through negotiation, bargaining and threats. *Regulation in practice is better understood as operating in the shadow of the law* [his emphasis]; as a complex interaction between politicians, civil servants, industry, consumers, interest groups and regulatory bodies'. Informality and commercial haggling predominate. This insulates the government from direct control, though it does retain reserve powers. The Secretary of State, for example, has the ability to stop a proposed licence modification or to refer such proposals to the MMC (Graham and Prosser, 1991, p. 219).

The UK-style of regulation gives a DG considerable room to negotiate a deal requiring economic efficiency improvements. In contrast to the United States, where regulation is characterized as rigid, rule-bound, adversarial and open, the UK-style is informal, discretionary, cooperative and closed. Veljanovski characterizes it as 'quick, cheap, and flexible' (Veljanovski, 1991, p. 15; Stelzer, 1991). Informal methods and negotiations prove cheaper and yield gains to the regulator and the industry (Veljanovski, 1991, p. 16). At the same time, the formal process for modifying licence terms and conditions or of resetting price control formulae through reference to the MMC is 'clumsy, time-consuming and unpredictable' (Veljanovski, 1991, p. 15).

In addition to the informal structure of regulation, the negotiation power of regulators derives from the legal character permitting DGs discretion and secrecy. This negotiating capacity emerges from the licensing procedures and the price-cap mechanism. The RPI-X or price level system, in contrast to the US-style rate-of-return or profit-level regulation, permits the regulator to propose a modification at any time during the term of the licence. However, the regulated firm cannot initiate a change, is 'forward-looking' by being based on forecast of possible productivity improvements, provides more degrees of freedom in negotiations, and enables regulators to make decisions without giving reasons or being subject to substantive challenges in court. Beesley and Littlechild write:

> The consequence of these four differences – exogenous risk period, forward-looking approach, degrees of freedom, and less requirements to

explain – is that there is greater scope for bargaining in RPI-X than in rate-of-return regulation. The level of X can reflect negotiation with the company, not only about the scope for future productivity agreements, but also about other matters affecting the company's future, including the details of the price constraint formula, the rate at which competition is allowed to develop, the provision of information, and so on. In short, X may be thought of as one of several variables in a political and commercial bargaining process.   (1991, p. 41)

Together these features of UK-style regulation give the regulator greater scope to negotiate with an upper hand than any United States counterpart.

The extent of the regulator's discretion seems to be critical to maintaining his or her independence and effectiveness in negotiating efficiency improvements. Avoiding legal processes and appeals, limiting ministerial intervention to occasional occurrences, providing for inexpensive and flexible resolution of disputes, and giving the regulator considerable power to determine and follow through on offences as well as to gain information provides wide discretion. These features may provide a way to forestall regulatory capture (Foster, 1992, chs 8 and 11). Foster concludes, 'The new British regulatory system ... has realized, again without obvious explicit recognition, that an absence of precise laws or rules, and the use instead of discretion, is necessary for effective regulation: it has given the regulators the greatest possible discretion in the interpretation of the licences and, for the most part, the independence to use it' (1992, p. 419).

Yet, the DGs' discretion in the decision-making process revolves around making a private commercial bargain. This process marginalizes all but the key players and makes shareholders' interests primary. Not only do the privatization Acts target profitability as the regulator's top priority, but the regulatory process itself – the tendency for firms to downplay the possibility for efficiency, the inability of regulators to precisely workout possible efficiency gains, and the fear of service disruption from overzealous regulation – favours shareholders against consumers (Ernst, 1994, pp. 60–1; *Financial Times*, September 14, 1994, p. 15; Helm, 1994).

Moreover, these bargains are not democratic. Graham and Prosser report that in setting the initial terms and conditions of the licence in the electricity industry 'negotiations over the contracts between the generating industry and the distribution companies, which will determine the effectiveness of competition in the industry, have been treated as private commercial transactions and, for example, large energy users were excluded from the discussions' (1991, p. 211). Further, consultation processes in telecommunication provide the illusion of wide representation. The DGT's commitment to open representation takes the form of advisory committees, consultative documents calling for responses, policy-specific forums, and the Telecommunications Forum which debates general issues among a many interested parties. However, the variety of issues being negotiated exclusively between BT and the DGT, the lack of necessity for BT to respond to third parties, the DGT's failure to give reasons for his decisions limit the decision-making process. Referring to OFTEL's 1988 review of BT's price-cap, Graham and Prosser point out that 'Although the DGT discussed issues underlying his decision, when it came to the question of the new rule he simply described the decisional procedures undertaken and then stated that it should be RPI-4.5' (1991, p. 216). The two authors conclude, 'the standard form of decision-making in this area is likely to be based on bargaining and negotiation between the agency and the regulated company, with little chance for third parties to make their views known' (Graham and Prosser, 1991, p. 219).

The DGs treated demands to open up the process in the late 1980s, in particular to give consumers a voice, as additional commercial factors compelling producers to improve their allocative efficiency. When BT's quality of service deteriorated in 1987 because of a BT engineers' strike and trouble with new technology, DG Carsberg gained agreement from BT to publish targets and actual performance results and to introduce a system of contractual liability, under which BT would pay £5 per day minimum 'liquidated damages' after two days if a fault was not repaired. These measures followed Carsberg's belief that 'BT needed additional incentives to improve its performance on this front' (Carsberg, 1988, p. 15). Such a stance is certainly consistent with his testimony to the House of Commons Energy Committee concerning the relationship between social and economic responsibilities:

Economic factors are ... the appropriate balance between prices and costs taking account of the wish to enhance the value of the network for all the users, and that gives us some pointers. 'Social' factors might be, for example, the need to protect people on low incomes, and they are quite different. It seems to me that the regime I administer deals very effectively with economic factors. I do not think it deals with social factors... My view is that politicians have to decide what they think should happen as far as social aspects are concerned, and the regulator has to deal with the economic side of things.   (cited in Wiltshire 1987, p. 83–4)

Treating social or political concerns as economic issues underscores the argument that the regulators are part of a mostly exclusive private commercial exchange process.

Liberalizing Telecommunications

Further, OFTEL's decision on the interconnection of the BT and Mercury networks shows how Carsberg's strategy of increasing competition within the duopoly framework by encouraging and redirecting the participants' profit-seeking behaviour mixed indirect controls of commercial deal-making with the occasional direct intervention. Mercury negotiated its first licence in February 1982 to provide services to large businesses in London, Birmingham and Manchester. It was unwilling to provide unprofitable services to poorer areas without subsidy (Hills, 1986, p. 133). In order to succeed, however, Mercury needed access of BT's local networks. As stipulated under BT's licence, it had to negotiate a connection agreement with any licensed operator and the DGT had the power to decide the deal if the parties failed to agree. Mercury asked BT to arrange a connection agreement, but the two companies could not agree. Mercury then turned to the DGT to adjudicate, though this was delayed when BT went to court, contesting an interim agreement made the previous year and arguing that the DGT did not in fact have the power to decide. The Court's decision that this 'Heads of Agreement' document was no longer binding enabled the DGT to adjudicate the dispute (Vickers and Yarrow, 1988, p. 218). In October 1985 in what was hailed as a pro-competitive result favouring Mercury, Carsberg 'ruled that the two networks must have full interconnection for both domestic and international calls', specifying a timetable for its accomplishment, and a price structure that encouraged Mercury's expansion (Vickers and Yarrow, 1988, p. 219; Veljanovski, 1987, p. 185). Interconnection disputes continued, however, leading OFTEL to censure BT for failing to interconnect Mercury customers reliably and ruling that Mercury's service should be extended nationwide (Graham and Prosser, 1991, p. 198). These decisions were most important in demonstrating the way the DGT acted through negotiation and the occasional directive to shape the pathway to competition.

Regulation through commercial negotiations decided the outcomes of the duopoly review of 1991 and the BT price reviews of 1988 and 1992, offering further evidence of the marketization of public policy power relations. In these decision-making processes, OFTEL initiated opportunities for increased competition alongside tighter regulation, yet it was careful not to offend BT's support for the regulatory regime. Competing firms readily took advantage of the changing context, while BT responded to the threat of diminished market share by moving toward providing global services. In sum, OFTEL's decisions reflected the neoliberal ideal of enhancing competition, yet compensated for the way economic incentives distort public services and injure the industry's long-term interests. BT's policies suggested acknowledgement that maximizing self-interest would mean further internal restructuring and market innovation.

In January 1988 a price review started. The DGT published a consultative document on price regulation discussing options for replacing the price cap formula in BT's licence due to expire in July 1989. Nearly a hundred submissions by interested parties followed and 'two or three weeks of very tough negotiation' between OFTEL and BT over not only the setting of X in the RPI-X formula but also the scope of the basket of prices, quality of service targets and other matters (Graham and Prosser, 1991, pp. 196 and 216). The new agreement called for increasing the price cap to RPI-4.5 per cent. BT undertook to limit increases in exchange line rentals, connection charges for new lines, and charges for installation to RPI + 2. It also accepted that new charges on previously free services, would be included in the basket of regulated prices and that international calls may need regulating. The DGT publicly stated the issues involved in his decisions and published a summary of the responses to his consultation paper. Yet, his negotiations with BT were in secret, and BT was not obliged to respond to third parties. In announcing his decision, finally, the DGT described the procedures followed and stated his conclusion, giving no reasons (Graham and Prosser, 1991, p. 216).

The debate on the duopoly policy examined how patterns of economic accountability could be changed to influence gains to consumers and producers. It posed the possibility of increasing competition by ending of the duopoly policy and permitting new entrants to apply for licences. The review had started in 1989 with the publication of a document setting out the criteria of the review and significance of recent events. Beesley and Laidlaw's *The Future of Telecommunications* first published in April 1989 significantly influenced the Department of Trade and Industry's 1990 consultation paper, *Competition and Choice: Telecommunications Policy for the 1990s*. Beesley and Laidlaw (in Beesley, 1992, p. 345) called for the end of the duopoly policy, since it 'tended to produce less competition than is now possible and desirable, and unless modified will continue to do so'. They recommended price controls that protect customers at risk from price changes and a liberalization of 'own-account' operations (private circuits), increasing Mercury's incentive to develop its network, licensing local and regional operations, and ending restrictions on resale of leased transmission capacity.

After a policy review and consultation process involving 219 submissions, the Secretary of State for Trade and Industry (Peter Lilley) in a White Paper on March 5, 1991 continued the trend to increase competition and tighten regulation through a process of mutual and informal negotiation, adjustment and testing (Maloney and Richardson, 1992; Veljanovski, 1991, p. 22). While contending that privatization, competition, and regulation had already provided wider customer choice, lower prices, and better responsiveness to consumers, the review exposed the overwhelming dominance of BT and advocated its correction by requiring more competition (*Survey of Current Affairs*, 1990, pp. 432–4 and 1991, pp. 108–9). *Financial Times* correspondent Charles Leadbeater revealed the strategy of expanding trade-offs that informed Government policy in reference to the 1991 White Paper:

> At the end of the day none of the contestants will be unhappy. OFTEL's role will expand. The government will get more competition without devaluing its shareholding in BT. The company recognised that competition was coming, will be nowhere near as handicapped as it once feared to meet it. (*Financial Times*, March 6, 1991, p. 8)

The government's objective in bargaining for competition succeeded by engaging firms in a private transaction that involved redirecting the profit-maximizing goals of enterprises rather than imposing losses.

The outcome meant that large international companies would benefit, since BT and Mercury would have to become more competitive in their services. In local networks, the White Paper encouraged cable television companies, many owned by American telecommunications companies (the Baby Bells), to compete with BT by carrying telephone services as well as entertainment. Cable companies, however, would be protected for up to ten years from BT and Mercury in the entertainment market. The White Paper also encouraged other local competition from mobile telecommunications networks, such as cellular, telepoint, and personal communication networks. One projected new beneficiary of this deregulation was British Rail, which has 2,500 kilometers of fibre optic cable running beside its tracks (*Economist*, March 2, 1991, pp. 55–6; *Financial Times*, March 6, 1991, pp. 1, 8 and 16).

OFTEL, moreover, extended price capping to cover international calls, getting BT to agree to cut prices by 10 per cent, and tightening the price cap from RPI-4.5 to RPI-6.25. Yet, BT won concessions from the

Government, including special tariffs or discounts for large users and a 're-balance' of local tariffs, producing lower costs for calls and higher costs for providing residential exchange lines. The White Paper also favoured BT in calling for companies interconnecting through BT to pay a share of the cost of meeting social objectives. However, the DGT decided in July to waive these access charges for those with small market shares (OFTEL, 1992, pp. 12–13; *Financial Times* July 4, 1991, p. 8).

A deal between BT and OFTEL in July 1991 on how competition should be introduced cleared the way for the Government to sell off another portion of its stake in BT and to implement its new telecommunications competition policy (*Financial Times*, July 4, 1991, p. 8). In December 1991, the Government sold 1,350 million shares reducing its ownership from 47.7 per cent to 25.8 per cent. Ministers claimed to have obtained the true market value of the public assets, while allowing small investors some profit (*Financial Times*, December 4, 1991, p. 27; December 9, 1991, p. 14; December 10, 1991, p. 21). In addition to the sell off, OFTEL took steps towards further competition without alienating BT, whose cooperation in the liberalization process was needed. In August, the Government issued two new telecommunications class licences, permitting businesses to establish their own telecommunications networks and any kind of satellite link not connected to the public system (*Survey of Current Affairs*, 1991, pp. 347–8).

By January 1992, OFTEL prepared to license new international telecommunications companies, which would purchase cable and satellite capacity from BT and Mercury and then resell it to customers. However, it was not clear that it would license firms, such as US Sprint, that applied for a licence to build its own network (*Financial Times*, January 27, 1992, p. 12 and January 28, 1992, p. 14). Meanwhile, BT has been involved in negotiating global communications networks for business users, involving possible collaboration with America's MCI and Japan's Nippon Telephone and Telegraph (*Financial Times*, January 27, 1992, p. 6 and May 22, 1992, p. 24).

In late January 1992, OFTEL initiated its most thorough price review of BT since the privatization of 1984, having increased the X-factor and included international calls in the regulated basket of prices the preceding year. Already extending regulatory control to cover services that generate 70 per cent of BT's revenues in contrast to an initial 50 per cent in 1984, the DGT's review proved more interventionist and harsher than expected, extending regulation even further into controlling monopoly profits, helping residential customers, and encouraging BT's competitors. OFTEL raised the price cap to RPI-7.5, lowered connection charges from £152.75

to £99, cut back the proposed hike in rental charges from 8 to 2 per cent above inflation, and ordered investment in infrastructure by demanding that BT lay optical fibre and provide digital services to 99 per cent of its customers by 1997 (*Financial Times*, June 10, 1992, pp. 6, 12, 14).

With BT still holding 95 per cent of the UK market, making enormous profits, and resisting newcomers' attempts to cut into its market share, the DGT's task of using competition and economies of scale to benefit the consumer and to encourage BT to respond increasingly to market pressures became more complex (*Financial Times*, 1991, p. VI; Pitt, 1990, p. 74; Foreman-Peck and Manning, 1988, pp. 54–67). Price-based regulatory incentives encouraged BT to cut service quality, investment, research and development, and staff, without making products affordable to average residential customers, unless the DGT used other incentives to redirect behaviour, as in the case of service quality after 1987 (Hills, 1992). Still, despite the delay in plans by among others, US Sprint, National Network of the UK, and British Rail to compete with BT and Mercury, new competitors numbered 17 by 1991. Many of these new competitors used radio and satellite technologies for individual telecommunications services (*Financial Times*, April 23, 1992, p. 19).

The DGT's strategy of bargained liberalization advanced the Government's goal of making the telecommunications industry more accountable to commercial standards and practices, facilitating the adoption of new technologies, cost reduction, a greater range of consumer options, and the movement into global markets (*Economist,* October 5, 1991, Survey p. 14; *Financial Times,* March 6, 1991, p. 8). The regulator's ideal of enlarging the circle of private sector winners while making telecommunications services more widely available depended on changing the way agents were held accountable. This meant supplementing the indirect controls of business practices with expanded and tightened regulation of monopoly activities (*Economist*, October 5, 1991, Survey p. 14).

Summary

In short, the post-privatization regulatory regimes operate largely by means of indirect controls, whereby economic ends and processes become the medium grounding motivation and action, determining the character of participants and their economic initiatives, and then engaging the industrial sector players in economic deal-making. Direct control remains at arm's length, as a threat of direct imposition of the decisions of a higher-level non-ministerial examination or the choices of the Secretary of State.

THE POLITICS OF COMPETITIVE TENDERING

A second important form of neoliberal delegation involves the separation of the authorization from the production of services. This is another form of principal-agent regulation, involving the awarding of a product or service market to the competitor offering the lowest price. In economic terms, competition for monopoly eliminates problems with undesirable monopoly of information and with administrative price setting (Vickers and Yarrow, 1988, pp. 110–115). Its success, however, depends on particular conditions. These include having numerous potential but real competitors in order to ensure competition, low sunk costs in order to facilitate asset handover if there is a change in contractor, and minimal technological and market uncertainty in order to make the contract between franchisor and franchisee simple and easy to administer (Kay and Vickers, 1988, pp. 327–8).

Increasingly subcentral governments have become 'enabling' authorities, that is, principals with responsibility for authorizing and monitoring the activities of direct providers. Along with rearranging many of subcentral government's functions, limiting its resources and reformulating the bases of its financing, the central government introduced and then mandated the use of competitive tendering or franchising for provision of services or servicing markets as the strategy for controlling local and other subcentral authority relations with service providers. Relying on in-house or private sector contractors, this strategy focuses on competing for monopoly (and the product markets and jobs that come with it) rather than competing within markets. Its attraction for neoliberal Conservatives lies in its capacity to use choice and competition, its greater efficiency in the provision of public services, its ability to reward private companies and undercut unions (Cousins, 1990, p. 98).

In public sector agencies accused of yielding too generously to the interests of unions and administrators, competitive tendering produces internal efficiencies. Separating authorization from provision makes the public authority agency into an enabler, supervisor, and adjudicator of contracts and the private or in-house contractor the agent producing or delivering services. Competition among contractors bidding for a tender compels them to cut costs and improve productivity in order to offer their services for lower prices (Hartley, 1990, p. 185). Local authority or NHS managers become an 'administrative rump', which chooses among the competition for the product market (Thomas, 1988, p. 157).

Separating the roles of authorization and actual public service provision through competitive tendering redefines the internal power relations in

subcentral agencies. Managers of the authorizing agency rely on the standards of private commercial transactions to decide outcomes. Managers
bargain for lower costs and anticipate increased efficiency from providers,
which encourages workers and their unions to produce more for less
money. This type of marketizing politics dispenses with previous pluralistic practices of consultation and negotiation (Rhodes, 1992, p. 53). Sylvia
Horton observes, 'It is evident that the partnership which once dominated
central-local relationships has become much more a principal-agent
relationship' (1990, p. 183).

Using competitive tendering as the decision-making method for
choosing service providers formally increased direct central government
intervention. However, in practice, it reduced practical involvement to surveillance and policing and enlarged the informal sphere of policy-making
in which managers, contractors, and workers operate through the indirect
control arising from the processes of business transactions. By stipulating
franchising as the mode of delegating duties to subcentral government, the
central government turned to economic rationality to regulate principle-
agent relations between the subcentral units and the service providers.
Requiring the use of competitive tendering mandated the efficient use of
increasingly constrained resources. Making subcentral agencies responsible for authorizing and scrutinizing the actual provision of services
through competitive tendering replaced the overt politics of inclusive bargaining with a marketized method of indirect control. In effect, choice and
competition in the form of franchising made marketized decision-making
into an effective vehicle for improving efficiency in subcentral service
provision.

New Right Grounds

While contracting-out can be viewed as 'an aspect of public procurement
policy' (Hartley, 1990), what distinguishes the current boom is the use of
tendering to achieve neoliberal aims. The use of private sector providers is
not new. In the 1950s when it was difficult to recruit and maintain the
labour needed to provide key services, public sector agencies turned to the
private sector. In this early period contractors provided services at a rate
more expensive than in-house providers. Contractors managed an
agency's employees or rehired them on a management fee basis. Thereby,
they avoided conflicts over job and wage reductions and the monitoring of
service quality (Ascher, 1987, pp. 179–80). Concern to control costs
mattered little. The second Wilson government contracted out cleaning
services for central government departments in order to cut costs after the

1967 devaluation, a policy that gave private contractors an opportunity they have not abandoned. During the 1970s, private contracting opportunities were few and gained little attention (Ascher, 1987, pp. 23–5).

When winning the election in 1979, the Conservatives had done little to make contracting-out an important aspect of their neoliberal programme. During the winter of discontent, hospital ancillary workers and local government employees went on strike, producing chaos and gaining wide publicity. As a result, contracting-out became a prominent and an attractive alternative to direct public sector provision. The 1979 Conservative government was more than ever determined to curtail trade union power. Public opinion was now more accepting of Tory initiatives, including the acceptance of private sector providers who had stepped in during the turmoil (Ascher, 1987, p. 26). Moreover, the Conservatives were ideologically committed to reducing public spending and public sector employment, to rolling back the state, to building up the free market, and reigning in inflation.

Competitive tendering became a strategy for readjusting power relations between local authorities and trades unions. Applying competition to the public sector through franchising exposed waste and inefficiency, while opening the door to private sector operators who replaced some public sector direct labour organizations (DLOs) (Ascher, 1987, pp. 48–9). The threat as much as the reality of private sector firms brought lower wages, more flexible working hours, less overhead, and more part-time workers (Foster, 1993, p. 58). Thus, private sector providers undercut unions, usually refusing to hire members of the previously unionized in-house labour force and thereby reducing the likelihood of industrial action. Moreover, competitive bidding for contracts prohibited public sector employers from colluding with union-dominated DLOs and eliminated the possibility of shielding labour from market competition.

The Thatcherite government gained confidence from new right think-tanks, the contractors, and Tory backbenchers, and the professional associations (Cousins, 1990, p. 99). Michael Forsyth became a leading advocate. A Conservative Westminister City Councillor and later MP, in 1980 he wrote *Reservicing Britain*, which called for competitive tendering for local government services and in 1982 *Reservicing Health*. He later formed a public relations firm to advance contractors' interests. Supported by Christopher Chope, who came from Wandsworth, Forsyth proved instrumental in getting the government to accept competitive tendering (Ascher, 1987, p. 39). Soon groups on the left and the right of the Tory Party demanded competitive tendering (Ascher, 1987, p. 50). However, the fragmented trade union movement, the chief opposition to competitive tendering and contracting out, lacked a vision that would provide it with a counter-initiative. Workers lacked enthusiasm for or interest in opposing reforms, relying on inaction for lack of any alternative (Ascher, 1987, p. 51).

Initiating Competitive Tendering

Making savings and improving efficiency meant reforming the power relations between government agencies and providers, using state power to introduce changes that by their very operation would weaken or eliminate unions and other obstacles to greater efficiency. Yet, Government initiatives, following neoliberal ideology, moved only as far and as fast as support could be marshalled. The development of Conservative policy on contracting-out follows Riddell's observation that the Thatcherites pushed forward more radical neoliberal policies out of frustration with the reception of their initial experiments. But it did this as support among critical participants in the policy process grew.

The neoliberal reform process also focused on the 'how to' in introducing competitive tendering, disarming opponents like unions and workers who lacked any ideological alternative to commercial deals. The government succeeded by engaging administrators who saw advantages and agreed with the goal, while objecting to short-term social effects of tendering or their loss of autonomy to government. While legislated reforms formalized concentration of power in a government department for the purpose of supervising the working of competitive tendering, the government initiatives succeeded by drawing support from contractors or government agents who would benefit, by organizing the energies of the opposition into the reform project and by isolating unions and workers from participation. The Government drew on these supports in creating a policy process, which operated by the practices and standards of market accountability.

The National Health Service
In the NHS, the first initiatives for contracting-out started in May 1980 with a series of circulars suggesting that the health authorities should consider contracting out and integrating independent health facilities into NHS planning, directed by Gerard Vaughan (Minister for Health). The Conservative Medical Society lobbied for contracting out at the 1978 Conservative Party Conference; in October 1979, the laundry and linen service associations did the same. Vaughan met with contract cleaning industry representatives, after issuing the circular, in order to find out if commercial marketing had led to progress in gaining contracts and if the

industry was prepared for 'wide-scale contacting out of domestic services' (Ascher, 1987, p. 27). Contractors stepped up their pursuit of work in the NHS, and were given a boost by Michael Forsyth's 1982 pamphlet, *Reservicing Health*, published by the Adam Smith Institute. Forsyth argued that savings in 'hotel services' would free up money for capital expenditures because private contractors could provide these peripheral services more cheaply than in-house providers (Ascher, 1987, p. 27).

Another initiative to explore the feasibility of contracting out in the NHS started at this time when Geoffrey Finsberg, minister for support services in the Department of Health and Social Services (DHSS), contacted his counterpart in the Ministry of Defence (MOD). Despite warnings that the MOD's experience might be irrelevant for the NHS and that small-scale trial runs at pilot hospitals were needed, the DHSS prepared a draft circular calling on authorities to compare external to in-house prices and to prepare tenders for future work (Ascher, 1987, p. 29). The leak of the draft circular aroused much hostility as 'neither the members nor the administrators of regional or district health authorities had been consulted prior to it' (Ascher, 1987, p. 29). Finally, in February 1983, Norman Fowler (Secretary of State for Social Services) published the draft circular, which proposed that NHS authorities tender for certain ancillary services. Fowler noted the NHS's failure to show an interest in private sector provision, assured authorities of the private sector's capacity to fill their needs, and highlighted the saving that would accrue.

A two-month consultation period prior to the June 1983 General Election revealed that health authorities needed convincing and would need legal coercion to get them to act. The final directive in September 1983, Circular HC (83) 18, *Competitive Tendering in the Provision of Domestic, Catering and Laundry Services*, called on health districts to subject cleaning, laundry and catering services to competitive tendering within three months. It strengthened the Ministry's determination to implement the policy. First, savings would benefit the particular authority rather than general patient care, a change aimed at gaining health authorities' support and cooperation. Second, authorities were given more independence, asked to keep the staff informed rather than having to fully consult them before deciding to write tenders. Third, timetables for implementation were required by simply permitting authorities to monitor progress and to report periodically. The document warned authorities against biasing their judgements against outside contractors. A few weeks later, the government voided the 1946 Fair Wages Resolution and permitted contractors to pay below Whitley Council rates of pay (Cousins, 1990,

p. 99). Feeling offended by the lack of adequate consultation, administrators, nevertheless, realized that the government was committed to requiring the tendering of services. The 1983 Conservative Party Manifesto made this intent clear, stating that the future government would 'ask health authorities to make the maximum possible savings by putting services like laundry, catering and hospital cleaning out to competitive tender' (Ascher, 1987, p. 30).

Despite the growing commitment of the Conservative government to contracting out in the NHS, progress was slow and pressure grew for more radical action to increase tendering. In 1984 ministers helped private contractors compete against in-house teams. Most tendering occurred in the South-east where the contractors are based and had excess capacity. By March 1985, contractors had won 52 per cent of all contracts up for tender (Ascher, 1987, p. 186). Yet, after 1985, in-house teams became more competitive and won the majority of contracts, which reflected a shift of tendering in the North of England and produced new complaints from contractors. In response, the government became more interventionist, overruling dubious decisions and issuing guidelines that benefited contractors' interests. By 1988 the DHSS reported that 96 per cent of domestic and laundry services and 76 per cent of catering services had been tendered (Cousins, 1990, p. 100). The 1989 White Paper, *Working for Patients*, which introduced the internal market into the NHS, proposed that health authorities' budgets be set by the demands of those they service, not the number and nature of the hospitals they own. It also stipulated that the authorities contract with public, private and independent hospitals in or outside their area to meet the needs of their patients (Stoker, 1990, p. 140; Weale, 1990, p. 214).

Local Government

Tendering initiatives for local government services followed much the same pattern. A weak national government initiative coincided with uneven local level take-up, followed by a renewed government request to extend the programme to a wider range of local government activities. The greatest success of contracting out through the tendering process has been in refuse collection and street cleaning, well-known for their history of poor management, inefficiency, and union domination (Ascher, 1987, p. 215).

As with the NHS, local government interest in competitive tendering grew as a result of the chaos created by unions during the 'winter of discontent' and the imperative to cut costs and make efficiency improvements during the 1980s. According to Ascher, local governments used competitive tendering to overcome unions' refusal to implement efficiency reforms (Ascher, 1987, p. 220). In 1980 Conservative controlled Southend District Council broke the hold of its DLO by tendering refuse collection and street cleaning. Conservative dominated Wandsworth, facing similar difficulties with its workforce, contracted out street cleaning the next year. After 1985, these local authorities' initiative stimulated a wide and growing interest, if not similar practice (Ascher, 1987, pp. 33–5, 220–7).

The Government drew support from these pioneering Conservative-led local government policies. A 1979 consultative document on competitive tendering became the basis of the Local Government Planning and Land Act of 1980, stipulating target rates of return on capital of 5 per cent and requiring competitive tendering for a specified proportion of work (Ascher, 1987, p. 35). Resistance from local authorities and unions gave way to Department of Environment pressure, and, according to Ascher (1987, p. 36), 'Within three years the Act had led to widespread reduction in direct labour workforces, improved efficiency among many DLOs, and the total closure of others'.

The 1980 Adam Smith Institute pamphlet by Michael Forsyth, *Reservicing Britain*, and the September 1981 consultants' report by Coopers and Lybrand into local authority service provision provided justification for improving efficiency and reducing costs (Ascher 1987, p. 37). The Treasury enthusiastically pushed for more contracting out, and the 1983 Conservative Manifesto promised greater savings from it. In early 1984, Christopher Chope organized a Ten Minute Rule Bill that provided evidence of real backbench and ministerial support for wider use of competitive tendering (Ascher, 1987, p. 40). In 1985, the result was a consultative document, which proposed a Government commitment to extend mandatory competitive tendering to a wide range of local government services. This initiative provided for more flexibility in meeting the needs of various services in implementing the reforms and gave the Secretary of State more flexible strategies for achieving compliance than previous documents. Unions and local authority associations opposed the proposals and contractors strongly supported it (Ascher, 1987, pp. 41–2). The resulting 1988 Local Government Act extended mandatory competitive tendering to refuse collection, catering, cleaning streets and buildings, maintenance of grounds and vehicles and the management of local authority sports and leisure facilities (Hartley, 1990, p. 178).

As with competitive tendering and contracting out in the NHS, central government initiatives grew more radical, covering a wider field and giving greater powers to Ministers to ensure compliance. Once experience

confirmed the success of the policy, support for reform grew among government followers and ebbed among opponents. Over time, piecemeal
policy efforts developed into a comprehensive tendering programme.
These reforms underscore the extent to which central government has set
limits on subcentral government, defining its functions, deciding the level
of its spending, reforming its financing and compelling the use of competitive tendering as a means of increasing value for money in service
provision (Stoker, 1990, p. 141).

Implementation and Policy Strategies

The separation of principal-agent or authorization-provision functions produced a shift of policy-making power. The national government had
formal but reserve direct powers, while local managers and their constituents observed the indirect controls of market decision-making.
Implementing tendering depended mostly on these indirect controls,
reflecting the triumph of New Right ideology, the fit between government
policy and the dispositions of key supporters (managers), and the utilization of these dispositions in a policy process dominated by ideas of market
accountability. The 'how to' of competitive tendering exemplified and
confirmed acceptance of the New Right valuation of private sector market
efficiency. It displaced alternative priorities and became the carrier of
control. The resulting conflicts were over procedural issues involving the
standards of service, the timing of the process, and the financial techniques
used to determine tender prices and future savings (Ascher, 1987,
pp. 158–66).

The emergence of the debate over the fairness of the competitive
tendering process meant that the government had succeeded in reorganizing the framework of decision making, denying voice to opponents of the
process and confining disputes to issues of winning or losing within the
process. Ascher points out that the procedural debate camouflages
concerns about outcomes among the unions, authorities, and contractors.
She writes:

> The only party with a genuine interest in the process itself is the
> Government. It is not primarily concerned with winners or losers, nor
> with the fairness of the current tendering mechanisms. Its primary
> concern is that the process operates smoothly and in as competitive a
> fashion as possible, so that cost-savings will be maximised and its own
> economic objectives will be met.   (1987, pp. 165–6)

In short, while applying direct controls to questionable cases as authorized by law, the central government's power to see competitive tendering implemented and successfully operating depended on engaging the energies of local authority administrators, contractors, and unions in the process.

With the DHSS acting as ultimate overseer and adjudicator of complaints, the competitive tendering process is management dominated. Contractors' vociferous complaints received responses from ministers and departments that improved their competitiveness (Ascher, 1987, p. 165). However, managers carried out most tenders. In the NHS, managers favoured in-house bids because they subjected workforces to greater discipline and efficiency standards. Yet, the managers signalled their own desire to maintain organizational stability and autonomy in the face of external political imposition (Cousins, 1990, p. 102).

Tendering placed unions in a losing situation, either overseeing a reduction in the members' pay and conditions with an in-house tender or losing members and bargaining rights with a private contractor. Union fragmentation further inhibited their ability to play the game. Once in place, competitive tendering led to more efficient use of labour through higher workloads, lower pay, and lower benefits (Cousins, 1990, pp. 104 and 106). Competitive tendering compelled unions to turn to local bargaining, away from their tradition of national bargaining, in order to respond competitively to local conditions. The reorganization of local staffs into service groups and the need to bid for contracts in different services weakened employees' collective identity and interests (Foster, 1993, p. 54). But in order to offer the lowest viable tender, potential providers or contractors had to cut costs by reducing the number of workers they employed and by shifting to a higher proportion of part-time workers (Foster, 1993, pp. 52–3). The formerly privileged DLOs had to shed workers and reduce wages and benefits in order to compete.

The implementation of competitive tendering policy accommodated managerial interests, favouring in-house deals when workers' cooperation could be realized rather than the Conservative government's preference for private contractors. Ascher (1987, pp. 245–6) points out that the outcome to government tendering policy depended on the 'political will' of the local authorities and the 'attitudes' of the unions. Political will derived from New Right ideology and from more pragmatic concerns to gain managerial control of work. Union cooperation usually led to in-house contracts, while union nonparticipation led to contracting out to private sector firms. The unions, after coming to terms with the fact that competitive tendering reduced their bargaining strength, generally concentrated on 'influencing local political opinion, the process of CCT [compulsory competitive tendering], and limiting potential "damage" to their members' (Foster, 1993, p. 59).

CONCLUSION

This chapter examined two forms of delegation or regulation involving principal-agent relations governed by market processes and criteria. First, the sale of major utilities gave rise to a new form of regulation in Britain. Rather than rules-based, it operates by informal negotiation and bargaining in which the regulator and regulated industry operate by the indirect controls of market interaction and behaviour. The DG's are favourably placed to negotiate increased efficiency and competition in their specific industries, introducing evolving systems of control that have been moving away from the initial bargains between government and industries at the time of privatization. Thus far DGs have pursued a proactive strategy, pushing open their industries to increasing competition in line with the Conservative government's policy. But the personalized character of the DG's power makes the future direction of policy somewhat uncertain.

Second, New Right ideas justified and motivated competitive tendering as the government's political strategy, intending to displace the political influence of vested interest with a process centring on commercial transactions governed by the principle of value for money. In this case, while the government could directly impose constraints on managers by cash limits, redefining tasks, or specifying the rules of the decision-making game, organizational compliance involved and depended on the informal cooperation of managers involved in applying market incentive to control principal-agent relations.

Despite political controversy arising from particular instances, the competitive tendering policy usually operated by a give and take (and sometimes breakdown in relations) among managers, contractors, and unions within defined procedures for making and operating tenders. In practice, government-initiated and legally imposed competitive tendering provided a means for breaking the power of recalcitrant union forces once sub-central government service agencies moved to improve efficiency and cut costs. The Thatcherite government's initiative drew upon the cooperation and energies of key players, namely contractors and managers, and engaged them in a procedure of private transactions from which they could gain rewarding trade-offs, but which isolated and excluded the involvement of workers and consumers. The Departments of State maintained close surveillance of tendering processes and occasionally imposed Government policy in order to ensure the benefits of the tendering procedure.

Overall, the delegation of government control through regulation exemplifies a distinctive form of indirect state power. First, the government in privatizing or tendering establishes the problem and the ends that control processes of thinking and action. It reserves the exercise of direct power and institutes the regulatory situation as the carrier of control. Second, as an independent agency, the regulator or subcentral government's management, along with the major corporate players, operates as part of a self-controlling process in which the regulator acts as the leader of the industry or producing-process rather than as external dictator. Third, a market-grounded process of regulation enables regulators and constituents to choose freely policies that facilitate their advantage in respect to what others are doing and as long as action accords with the standards (criteria of approbation) entailed in the system of controlling ideas. Breaking with the controlling ideas leads to overt conflict.

6 Deregulation and Competition as Control

The transfer of publicly owned businesses and assets to the private sector has become the main element in popular thinking about privatization. However, liberalization or the creation of alternative providers or suppliers in the marketplace, through the elimination of controls on individual action and the encouragement of new and more varied market entrants, has been consistently pursued. Liberal critics of privatization often call for more deregulation, particularly the promoting of product and service competition (Beesley, 1992, p. 15). Yet, these critics fail to appreciate the extent to which the Thatcher governments pursued liberalization and came to recognize the weakness of simply reducing barriers to entry. Instead, the government's actively provided incentives for entry into competitive markets. Thus, in addition to property ownership and regulation, competition constitutes a distinctive means of indirectly influencing the way participants coordinate their actions.

The New Right idealizes competition, heralding it as enlarging choice and the freeing of individuals from state supervision and constraint. Competition is the primary instrument defining and ensuring pure market activity. Impersonal, voluntary, and mutually advantageous exchanges among independent and self-interested agents makes each accountable and responsive to the initiatives and reactions of competing producers and consumers. Success or failure in the market is easily monitored and transparent in the connection between individual action and consequence. In liberalizing, then, the Thatcherites sought to reduce restrictions on market activity and to enlarge consumer choice among alternative providers.

The progress of the Thatcherite deregulation programme depended on its own success and support as well as a favourable opinion and predisposition among critical actors, enabling the government after the 1987 election to extend radically its commitment to increasing competition and to improving managerial performance. The government, acknowledging some management opposition to liberalization, increasingly gained the initiative. Patrick Minford, a leading monetarist and Thatcher advisor, records that the ability to deregulate grew: 'the boot is now much more on the government's foot, with privatisation a settled programme' (1991, p. 247). How did this enhanced positioning, the 'boot', effect change? And how did deregulation operate to tighten the control of interest formation and so limit representation in policy-making arenas?

This chapter examines how the Thatcherites fostered market competition in order to use economic processes to control interest representation and decision-making. It also examines how they simultaneously centralized formal direct control as one of the government's reserve powers and transferred actual control to consumers and producers involved in the informal and voluntary exchanges shaped by market competition. Such a survey must first consider the neoliberal's economic justification for competition, then the development of the liberalization programme, and finally, the way competition has been used to shape decision-making processes. An overview of bus deregulation illustrates unencumbered competition in operation, while a review of Thatcherite education reforms highlights the functioning of government-managed internal markets.

THE VIRTUES OF COMPETITION

Competition, as the rationale for reform and as a rule for projecting participation in market situations, has from the start held a high place in the New Right ideology. The Thatcherite vision of economic policy emphasized monetary control and the free market, in contrast to state intervention. Sir Keith Joseph laid out the theme that monetarism is not enough: 'Monetary contraction in a mixed economy strangles the private sector unless the state sector contracts with it and reduces its take from the national income' (cited in Jenkins, 1989, p. 62). This meant rolling back the state, reducing barriers to competition and the working of markets, and encouraging entrepreneurialism. In some arenas, these ideas were formulated as devolving control and democracy to individuals. Again, as Joseph put it: 'We are over-governed, over-spent, over-taxed, over-borrowed and over-manned'. Nicholas Ridley recalls that increasing competition was vital to Thatcher's first priority of liberating the 'wealth-creating sector' through supply-side policies (Ridley, 1991, p. 55). 'Putting markets and competition to work in the nation's interest', in the words of Geoffrey Howe (1982, p. 21), encapsulates the core ideal of the Thatcherite project. And Nigel Lawson believed that 'the recipe for economic success is the greatest practicable market freedom within an overall framework of firm financial discipline' (Lawson, 1992, p. 9). The effect was to project the competitive market as the foundation for a new politics and to justify state actions creating it.

The idealization of competition derives from the economists' belief that it effectively regulates or controls self-interested behaviour, constituting in effect a self-regulating system for production and consumption. First, market competition facilitates individual choice, yields social beneficence and harmony, and provides allocative and internal efficiency. Second, external pressures, exercised through free choices of actors maximizing their utility or profit, generate efficient resource allocation and internal rationality, that is, they minimize costs for a given level of output (Heald, 1983, pp. 85–9). This leads to competitive prices and to quantities of goods desired by society. Third, information about prices and products conveyed through consumer choices controls future behaviour, over-shadowing problems of asymmetric information (Vickers and Yarrow, 1988, ch. 2). Self-interested and sovereign agents in competition with each other comprise a mechanism of decision-making that 'is its own guardian' (Heilbroner, 1961, p. 42). Finally, as an alternative type of control to authority, markets constitute autonomous and distinctive systems of self-organizing behaviour that are self-legitimating because they involve impersonal forces and allow a depoliticization of decision-making (Taylor-Gooby and Lawson, 1993, p. 136).

From the perspective of those firms being privatized and at least par-tially liberalized, their place in the competitive private sector heightens their attempts to improve efficiency and to make profits, making economic calculation more salient as the grounds for projecting action. In the case of Cable and Wireless (C&W), privatized into a competitive sector in November 1981, the effect was to establish accountability for profits and losses on the part of the company directors as the determinant of manage-ment's attitudes and performance (Lord Sharp, in Clutterbuck, 1991, pp. 196–7). The decision to privatize C&W was part of the government's plans to liberalize telecommunications, initiated in July 1980. It focused on licensing a private sector competitor to BT, namely C&W's subsidiary MCL. The guiding idea was that competition and the need to adjust price and products to the pressures of demand in order to make profits would produce a higher quality of telecommunications services. Giving the firm its commercial freedom in a competitive market compelled managers to impose 'detailed financial controls and a reliable overview of its assets', from which they could 'forge an active financial strategy to exploit Cable and Wireless's unique position within the telecommunications world' (Clutterbuck, 1991, p. 194). The impact of commercial accountability is evident in the privatization of British Aerospace (BAe) as well. Despite its size large and profitability, BAe, having been sold off into the competitive sector, prompted it to be more proactive commercially. Privatization meant a shift toward being export-oriented, as defense contracting fell from 80 per cent to 40 per cent of its income, and as new investments in commercial aircraft were made (Clutterbuck, 1991, p. 164). While commercial accountability entails financial constraint, it just as importantly calls for and relies on internal control, with innovation and initiative shaping corporate strategies for profit-making and survival.

THE THATCHER GOVERNMENTS' PROGRAMME

From 1979 to 1985, a first phase of pro-competitive policies designed to encourage and facilitate profit-making flourished in many industries, such as telecommunications, transport, gas and electricity (Johnson, 1991, pp. 192 and 197). Foreign exchange, price, dividend, and pay controls ended, and top marginal rates of income tax dropped. Regulatory reforms affected buses and coaches, domestic air transport, financial institutions, broadcasting, the professions, and the newly privatized public utilities (Fleming and Button, 1989, pp. 86–94). In many cases this involved reducing restrictions on business activities and in other attempts to foster alternative producers (Riddell, 1989, pp. 72–3). A second phase emerged in the mid-1980s when liberalization was superseded by privatization, particularly with regard to the sales of BT, BG, BAA, and BA. These were sold as monopolies overseen by a regulator. A third and more ambitious phase developed after 1987.

The first Thatcher government gave prominence to its liberalization of the telecommunications, gas, and electricity sectors. The 1981 Telecommunications Act led to the establishment of Mercury as a competitor to BT in voice telephony and opened markets to new competitors for terminal equipment, value-added services, and mobile telecommunications. The 1982 Oil and Gas (Enterprise) Act provided for, but made little headway in, breaking into British Gas' de facto monopoly on gas supply, although in 1989 the DTI insisted that ten per cent of gas supplies from new fields come from BG competitors. The 1983 Energy Act gave statutory provision for competition in electricity generation, but had little real impact (Roberts, Elliott and Houghton, 1991, pp. 22–4).

In 1981 the liberalization of telecommunications, splitting BT from the Post Office, created a competitor in telephony, and increased competition for apparatus and alternative technologies. This shows how incremental liberalization can lead to changing interests and interactions, fostering in turn further marketization initiatives. The policy was opposed by those defending the Post Office. But the BT management allied with the telephone engineering union, the POEU, and the government to create a new deal, with new opportunities taking advantage of technological change and a growth of jobs. The commercial terms of the deal looked forward, positioning opponents as resisting and inhibiting progress.

Yet, the liberalization of telecommunications created the beginning of a new politics in the sector. Discussions between the Department of Industry and individual firms ignored the traditional channels of consultation (Moon, Richardson and Smart, 1986, p. 344). Problems about fair competition between private operators and the state-owned BT, as well as how it should be regulated, reflected profit-seeking among sector members. As conflict between BT and the government over raising capital heightened, the Minister of Trade, stepping into the fray, initiated proposals for privatizing and regulating BT. Subsequently the telecommunications industry became the leading case of regulated liberalization (see Chapter 5).

In transport, the 1980 Transport Act initiated deregulation for bus transport, leading to increased competition between a public sector incumbent and new private sector entrants. In addition to privatizing the NFC, it abolished road service licences (barriers to entry) for express services (journeys over 30 miles) and reduced regulatory barriers to competition in local buses. It placed the burden of proof for not granting licences on the Commissioners finding evidence that it would harm the public interest, relaxed controls on prices, and established trial areas for radical deregulation experiments (Vickers and Yarrow, 1988, p. 371). The 1982 Transport Act, further liberalizing the industry, privatized the state-owned National Bus Company's (NBC) express coaching and holiday tours business and the testing of heavy goods and public service vehicles. The 1983 Transport Act obligated the Passenger Transport Executives (PTEs) to prepare annually three-year rolling plans for the development of local services. This enabled the Transport Secretary to set subsidy levels, curtailing some high local property taxes (rates) and 'ultra-low' fares. In addition, the 1983 Act obliged the PTEs to tender certain services and empowered the Secretary of State to force the executives to accept what it believed to be the lowest bid (Bagwell, 1984, pp. 159–61; White, 1988, p. 19). The 1984 Act transferred control of transport policy in London from the popularly elected Greater London Council (itself abolished in 1986) to a new government appointed quango (a nondepartmental government body) of transport experts funded directly by central government and known as London Regional Transport (Bagwell, 1984, p. 162).

After the 1983 election, the Government announced in its July 1984 White Paper, *Buses*, its plan to extend deregulation of bus transport to the whole country, except for London. The White Paper, ignoring the reservations of some transport experts, justifies the proposed legislation to deregulate by citing the success of liberalizing express coach services (a 40 per cent fall in fares in real terms and 700 new services) and of the trial areas, where there was no loss of service and no increased subsidy needed in the rural areas or trial areas (Department of Transport, 1984, p. 11). The chief problem was to find a mechanism of controlling excessively rising government subsidies without reducing output (Glaister, 1991). Rather than competitive tendering, the government chose deregulation and private ownership. The market success of the previously privatized NFC indicated the need to break up public sector operators' monopoly power and then transfer ownership to the private sector (Department of Transport, 1984, pp. 16–18). The White Paper stated, 'Within the essential framework of safety regulation and provision for social needs, the obstacles to enterprise, initiative and efficiency must be removed' (1984, p. 3).

The subsequent 1985 Transport Act aimed to complete the replacement of political and bureaucratic processes by unregulated market decision-making. The government believed that local bus services could operate on a viable commercial basis if competition could be introduced in place of political decision-making. More pointedly, it 'felt that the planning bodies initially established under the 1968 Transport Act, and reorganised under subsequent legislation, had essentially been "captured" and revenue support in the major urban areas was not being utilised effectively' (Button, 1988, pp. 74–5). To achieve full deregulation, the Act introduced further competition for inter-city passenger business, with the remaining public transport authorities functioning to authorize the expenditure while private sector companies supplied the services.

The 1985 Transport Act, the culminating step toward a deregulated bus industry, extended competition in local bus services (outside London). The Act first abolished road service licensing, permitting any party wishing to run a service to notify the Traffic Commissioners (who now oversaw bus safety). It reduced the standard for express services from 30 to 15 miles. Second, services deemed socially necessary but not commercially viable would be tendered to the lowest bidder by the county council. It eliminated local government duties for coordinating services (Vickers and Yarrow, 1988, p. 376; Bell and Cloke, 1990a, pp. 43–5). Third, quality licensing remained and was reinforced. Fourth, Transport Secretary Nicholas Ridley ensured the break-up of NBC into numerous small businesses, despite the opposition of the NBC itself, the Labour Party, bus manufacturers and unions (Ridley, 1991, pp. 61–2). Yet, support came from the desire of its constituent bus companies to be independent operators (Foster, 1992, p. 121). The NBC was split into 72 constituent companies (52 separate local bus companies, six coach operating companies, eight engineering companies, National Express, National Holiday, National Travelworld, and the Coach Station subsidiary) and sold off to the private sector with revenues of over £300 million (less than if sold off as a single unit). This ended cross-subsidization. About two-thirds of the businesses were sold as management buy-outs to consortia of managers and banks and one as an Employee Share Ownership Plan (Graham and Prosser, 1991, p. 130). PTEs and municipal bus operations were transformed into companies separate from their parent bodies (Bell and Cloke, 1990a, pp. 44–5; Vickers and Yarrow, 1988, p. 382). Initial registration of commercial services started in February 1986, with final additions by deregulation day in October 1986. After operating for three months without change, full deregulation started on 16 January 1987. Any changes thereafter were restricted only by a 42 day notice (Bell and Cloke, 1990, pp. 43–5).

Other areas of liberalization included domestic air transport, financial institutions, broadcasting, the professions, and privatized industries. In the 1980s, the CAA made it easier for small domestic airlines to take over routes BA gave up, and for larger airlines to compete out of Heathrow, to set routes, and to lower fares (Fleming and Button, 1989, p. 87). A combination of pressures made for radical changes in the British financial system, as recent legal changes deregulating the industry led to efforts to establish mechanisms of self-regulation (Fleming and Button, 1989, p. 88). Measures aimed to widen competition between types of financial institutions and to provide better consumer protection. In other fields, the 1981 Broadcasting Act established 'Channel Four' and the 1984 Cable and Broadcasting Act set up a cable licensing system and permitted the development of satellite broadcasting. Further, the professions faced limited deregulation, with monopoly control in dispensing spectacles ending for opticians and for conveyancing ending for solicitors. Laws eased restrictions on fees and advertizing in order to encourage competition for many professions (Fleming and Button, 1989, p. 91).

After 1987, a third phase with greater emphasis on liberalization is apparent in the structural breakup of the water and electricity industries during privatization, in the intensification of regulated liberalization in telecommunications and gas, and in efforts to marketize choice processes in the welfare state. Vickers reports:

> It has been argued that in all four areas – structure, entry, pricing, and quality and investment – policy has become more vigorous over time,

notably in the last few years. The trend is evident both within industries such as telecommunications and gas, and from the fact that the government has given much more attention to structural and regulatory matters in later privatizations, such as electricity, than in some previous ones. (1991, p. 28)

In contrast to the United States where deregulation encouraged renewed competition only to lead over time to a greater industry concentration, British liberalization policy became the main instrument for breaking up vested interests that gained from quasi-corporatist forms of policy-making and for subjecting the way decisions are made to economic criterion. Gerry Stoker's captures this shift in his characterization of the Thatcher governments' policy toward local government and the welfare state in the late 1980s:

The aim is to fragment public sector institutions and stimulate private and voluntary sector alternatives in order to create a market place of service providers. The production and allocation of state-supported provision will be increasingly conditioned by market or quasi-market systems as opposed to the established political, bureaucratic and professional forms of mediation. Who produces what and who gets what will become less a matter of political, professional or bureaucratic judgement and will depend more on the operation of quasi-market mechanisms. (1990, p. 133)

Increasingly the sale of public assets was paralleled by processes of liberalization – increasing competitors in particular markets – as the radical commitment to make decision-making turn on calculations of cost opportunities gained force. With popular support for New Right thought, the government moved into reforming many aspects of the welfare state by liberalizing delivery and creating 'a market place of service providers'. This affected a wide range of sub-national government agencies, such as health, education, local government, housing and community care (Stoker, 1990, 132–40).

The Thatcherites took a lead in breaking the barriers to competition and in generating structures or incentives leading to a multiplicity of producers of goods and services. Thatcherite policy-makers seemed to realize that while competition can transform the behaviour of companies without a change of ownership, the 'legal possibility of entry is not enough to guarantee effective competition' (Vickers and Yarrow, 1988, pp. 382–3). Efforts to level the playing field, before and after liberalization, are necessary (Thompson, 1987). Second, regulation varies with market segmentation. A minimum of regulation is required where operations are strictly commercial and structurally competitive. Liberalization and privatization in the bus sector, for example, produced no regulator. Where social needs demand subsidized services, for example, rural bus routes, competitive tendering facilitated 'a closer tying of efficiency and distributional goals' (Fleming and Button, 1989, p. 87).

Finally, a by-product of liberalization in one industry is greater competitive pressures in another industry. Lower express coach fares led British Rail (BR) to lower its fares and attempt to attract customers of coaches. The privatization and liberalization of the ESI has led to the use of gas fired power stations and undermined the price of coal, contributing to the destabilizing of the industry.

To recap, the early Thatcherite enthusiasm for liberalization dissipated as little progress was made and attention turned to the large-scale privatization programme. After 1987, Thatcherites show a renewed radical commitment to competition in a much wider range of policy areas. Drawing on the New Right ideas, Thatcherites took initiatives in the face of varying amounts of opposition and achieved varying degrees of success. At each successive stage of policy initiative, the government built on the previous measures, trying to overcome its failings, and gained momentum.

BIFURCATING POLICY-MAKING PROCESSES

The government's initiatives in introducing competition engaged key players in market-led decision processes and marginalized a diminishing opposition, but not by directly imposing its will. If the making of law required an exercise of direct state power, implementing reforms relied on government-defined parties initiating and negotiating for favourable terms, though within government-approved guidelines sanctioned by the threat of state intrusion. In introducing and maintaining market competition, the government strategy of marketizing decision-making narrowed the policy process to a private commercial bargain involving those who had real or potential interest in its success, relying on ideology to make opponents appear to be Luddite and visionless.

By displacing decision-making into competitive practices, authorities devolved actual control to the working of an economic framework of decision-making, relying on the economic processes of choice and competition to carry controls. Decision processes involved private transactions among privileged or specialized business operators responding to market conditions, while marginalizing and eliminating alternative noncommercial interests. The result was a mode of neoliberal policy-making in which the state's direct involvement is even more limited than in the case of depoliticized quasi-governmental regulators, particularly in the situations where the potential for direct involvement depended on private sector actors deciding to redress grievances through competition laws. In practice, the underlying economic ideas inspired a form of activity that obliged participants to comply with market practices. In effect, Government instituted processes of competition between purchasers and providers constitute an indirect mode of control involving a complex interplay of actors in which expectations about the behaviour of other participants condition commercial outcomes.

The bifurcating of government control, dispersing continuous operational controls to competitive markets while concentrating in the government reserve formal powers for occasional application, occurred in both the private and the public sectors. Policy-making in the busing sector illustrates competitive choice mechanisms, while the marketizing of education highlights the operations of managed markets.

Liberalizing Express Coach and Local Bus Transport

The deregulation and sell-off of the publicly owned bus industry represents the boldest attempt by Thatcherites to fulfil the New Right ideal of setting the market free. Using liberalization to create multiple and competing providers of services, market trade-offs between purchasers and providers determine public service outcomes. The sell-off of NBC reinforced the policy of using competition as a means of decision-making in the bus industry (Harrison, 1988, p. 132). While still in flux, changes in the bus transport sector provide the main instance of a shift from a highly regulated and politicized public sector regime to an industry responding to the choices of consumers and producers, subject only to British competition laws that prohibit unfair restrictive practices.

The 1930 Road Traffic Act, following the free competitive era of the 1920s, initiated fifty years of regulating quality and quantity of bus services. While the system of quality regulation has not been changed, the market-based reforms since 1980 have substantially changed the way transport policy is made. Prior to 1980, Traffic Commissioners determined vehicle safety standards which had to be met in order to obtain a certificate of fitness. Quantity controls amounted to a corporatist pattern of a stable, limited and closed policy-making group. Traffic Commissioners granted operator licences for running services in particular areas, setting fares and arranging timetables. Also obligated to protect the public interest, the Commissioners protected incumbents from new entrants since incumbents cross-subsidized loss-making but socially desirable services with revenue from more profitable ones. According to Button (1988, p. 72), 'operators tended to be granted licences for profitable routes, with protection from subsequent competition, if they also ran unprofitable services deemed necessary for the wider transport needs of the area'. As a result, operators were under no pressure to increase productive or allocative efficiency (Vickers and Yarrow, 1988, p. 368). Public funding became increasingly necessary with the rise of car ownership, higher fares, and fewer passengers. Authorities specified their transport needs and met cost of the public sector operators – these being the NBC, local government PTEs, municipal operators, the Scottish Bus Group, and London Regional Transport (Vickers and Yarrow, 1988, pp. 368 and 370).

The effect of express coach deregulation, resulting from the 1980 legislation noted above, was a period of intense competition. A major new entrant, British Coachways, set fares at about half those charged previously by National Express, the NBC subsidiary, while providing for new services, such as refreshments and entertainment. National Express quickly matched the new low prices. Services changed to 'frequent, rapid, and direct services with fewer stopping points on the main truck routes', by-passing the smaller towns. The number of passengers increased in response to lower fares, more frequent services between major population centres (though many small towns lost express services) and luxury services. Some users switched from travel on British Rail, which in turn responded with lower fares. Within months, however, the competition subsided, National Express maintained the dominant position and British Coachways withdrew from the market (Davis, 1986, pp. 147–61). Once National Express lowered its fares, it gained the advantage through its nationwide network, customer awareness and trust, and access to major terminals, such as Victoria Coach Station in London (Vickers and Yarrow, 1988, p. 373). Competition on price alone failed. Other entrants were able to survive by cooperating with National Express or finding particular market niches (Bell and Cloke, 1990a, p. 39). Fares on trunk routes have fallen on the average, though not fares on minor or cross-country routes without competitors. Moreover, services are more responsive to consumer demands, though some customers have lost out. Competition between coaches and rail have meant lower fares for inter-city travel (Kilvington and Cross, 1986, p. 130). The deregulation of express coaching shows both public and private sector firms responding to the opportunities and risks of competition, even though the uneven character of the initial playing field disadvantaged new entrants, despite the removal of barriers to competition (Vickers and Yarrow, 1988, p. 375; Bell and Cloke, 1990a, p. 40). The deregulation of express coaching started a process in which market accountability directed the initiation of a restructuring of the industry.

The 1985 Transport Act put managers in charge. As the White Paper promised, 'The managers of bus operations will have more freedom to manage and compete within a clear structure of responsibility' (Department of Transport, 1984, p. 25). According to Wayne Talley, 'In the UK market forces rather than the public transit firm (as in the US) determine the extent of competition in the provision of local bus services' (1988, p. 182). The government's role depends on the initiative of aggrieved operators, who under the 1976 Restrictive Trade Practices Act can file a compliant with the Office of Fair Trading when they feel that their commercial freedom has been inhibited by other bus operators (Talley, 1988, p. 180; Pickup *et al.*, 1991, pp. 106–9). John Hibbs, a neoliberal transport economist, pictures the emerging market-driven process: '...the consequences of bus deregulation, and its concomitant, privatisation (or, better, re-structuring), are working through to the benefit of the consumer by way of the increased freedom of managers to take bottom-line decisions independent of political or administrative edict, and the pressure of the market to see that these decisions are product-related' (1990, p. 186).

Given their competitive context, private sector operators have followed three main managerial strategies, 'on the road' (deregulation), 'off the road' (competitive tendering), and 'boardroom' competition. Their combined effect is reshaping the industry. Yet, unleashing profit-seeking processes has not produced a plethora of new entrants, passengers, and services or even lower fares. Bell and Cloke (1990c, p. 200) state, 'In Britain the particular mix of privatisation, deregulation and contracting out seems to have permitted managers to adjust their networks of provision, but has largely failed to stimulate the promotion of new competitive ventures'. Outer rural areas, like rural Wales, studied by Bell and Cloke (1990b), have seen little impact on the levels of service provided. Pre-deregulation networks are much the same and new competition nil. In the outer Metropolitan areas, Peter Stanley (1990) finds only two cases of sustained new competition between bus operators in South-East England. Other cases of actual or potential competition met with the successful efforts of the incumbent to drive the new entrant out of the market or to buy-out the smaller firm.

Finally, in the Metropolitan areas, the three strategies are clearly seen (Pickup *et al.*, 1991, ch. 6). With higher population density an initial burst of new competitors has given way to fewer larger operators appearing to run most commercial services, while smaller independents confine themselves to tendered work. The effect of deregulation has varied, with the most competitive markets developing in Manchester, Strathclyde, South Yorkshire, and Oxford (Bell and Cloke, 1990c, p. 201; Banister and Pickup, 1990; Pickup *et al.*, 1991, p. 65 and 79; Harrison, 1988, p. 131).

Market-led transport provision tended to go in unexpected directions. 'On the road' competition developed in the first two years after the Act came into effect; in the third year, it shifted toward takeovers of the smaller and weaker firms. At first, independent operations stimulated most of the competition rather than the privatized NBC or PTE companies, which carried on much as before deregulation and countered new entrants. Moreover, most new competitors, whether large independents or small operators have been careful not to be too aggressive or to provoke an aggressive counter by the incumbent. Competition tends to be about service levels and not fare levels, with the use of minibuses introducing a new element of service. Lastly, independents compete more successful for tendered services, such as schools and socially necessary work rather than for commercial services (Pickup *et al.*, 1991, ch. 6). Increased competition between existing operators and a small but steady influx of new entrants has meant that service levels have increased and fares have gone up, while patronage has fallen slightly (Banister and Pickup, 1990, pp. 72–6).

The success of 'off the road' competition in London, where competitive tendering is used and services are contracted out by the quango London Regional Transport. Competitive regulation has permitted the coordination of fares and ticketing and a full network of services. It has resulted in a 10 per cent cost reduction compared to 20 per cent for all Metropolitan areas (Banister and Pickup, 1990, pp. 79–81). These bus markets, in short, have become more contestable than opponents of the 1985 Transport Act argued, yet significant barriers to entry and incumbent advantages so far have inhibited the operation of fuller contestability.

Despite the unencumbered play of market forces in busing transport so far, the government retains the authority to intervene if it is deemed necessary. In fact, the government retains the reserve capacity to regulate the private sector market in terms of the distribution of shareholdings, anti-competitive activity, and mergers. Competition law in Britain gives broad discretionary power to the government, thereby encouraging companies to negotiate with public officials when conflicts arise in order to prevent formal referral to the MMC (Graham and Prosser, 1991, p. 201). Yet, openness and accountability to third parties is formally unnecessary. Reports by the Director General of the Office of Fair Trading are unpublished; no reasons are stated in cases where the report does not result in the Secretary of State referring a case to the MMC. Further, the MMC has broad discretion in deciding its procedures. This is evidenced, for example, in the criticism that the MMC was biased in its procedures toward BA in its bid to takeover BCal, in which the MMC appeared to negotiate with BA over its bid, while other parties' comments were ignored (Graham and Prosser, 1991, p. 208). Moreover, in most cases, once the MMC makes its recommendations, the Secretary of State can issue an order for the Director General of the Office of Fair Trading to negotiate undertakings with the affected firms. Negotiation between key interested parties then takes place at all stages of the process (Graham and Prosser, 1991, p. 203).

The government retains the ability to use competition policy to affect the composition of shareholdings in a private firm. In the case of BP, the Kuwait Investment Office (KIO) took a 21.6 per cent stake in the company after the collapse of the stock market in autumn 1987, thereby becoming the largest shareholder. The Secretary of State referred the matter to the MMC, which reported that 'the holding was a merger situation against the public interest because of possible future pressure on the Company by Kuwait and the effect on its US activities' (Graham and Prosser, 1991, p. 162). The Secretary of State then implemented its recommendation that the KIO shareholding be reduced to not more than 9.9 per cent, and BP agreed to buy back the relevant shares. In sum, unchecked by the courts and involving closed bargaining, the government can regulate ownership structure, essentially controlling 'the working of the "market for corporate control"' (Graham and Prosser, 1991, p. 164).

Managed Markets in Education

Education reform illustrates how deregulation or competition operating as indirect control has been combined with and circumscribed by direct power relationships to reorganize decision-making control in the welfare state, centralizing some direct and reserve powers in the government and dispersing resource allocation decisions to consumer choices. Peter Taylor-Gooby summarizes recent changes as involving the 'central control of curriculum and examinations, with resources allocated through a managed market, a substantial enhancement of immediate consumer choice and a reduction in the influence of local government and professional teachers...' (Taylor-Gooby, 1993, p. 105).

A shift to managed competition in resource allocation occurred because the Thatcherites were able to draw on and redirect the cooperation of key

actors, not because they imposed reforms. The 1944 Education Act established a partnership between local authorities, teachers and their unions,
churches, and central government to provide education. This pattern lasted
until the Thatcher era (McVicar, 1990, p. 131). Central and local government shared administrative control. The centre passed legislation,
inspected schools, and offered advice; the local education authorities
(LEAs) set budgets and managed operations; and professional educators,
including teachers devised the curriculum. J.R.G. Tomlinson characterizes
the system as 'deriving from broad legislative objectives, convention, and
consensus' (1989, p. 185).

In the 1970s, a growing debate, encouraged by the government-initiated
'Great Debate' on education, developed about the effectiveness of the educational system in meeting demands for job training, preparation and
motivation for work, and individual opportunity (Taylor-Gooby, 1993,
pp. 104–5). This debate, started by Prime Minister Callaghan in 1976,
reflected a collapse of the postwar consensus. It unleashed a political call
for change that enhanced professional discussions about the future of education. Education was being increasingly linked to the changing world of
work in the context of a more individualistic social structure. New forms
of knowledge seemed to require different motivations for success at school
and a shift to more 'active learning'. By the early 1980s, then, criticism of
secondary education led to demands for education for competence in
living and working for all rather than 'education' for the few and 'training'
for the many, education for opportunity, new styles of teaching, and
greater economy in operation (Tomlinson, 1989, pp. 187–9). Education, in
short, needed to be more practical, open, and efficient.

The Education Acts of 1980 and 1986 drew on these debates and
demands for change, pushing the bipartisan demand for educational
reform incrementally in a neoliberal direction. In shifting to methods of
contracting and using managerial techniques, the Thatcher government
'eroded the vitality and self-confidence of the system in many essential
aspects–the morale of the teachers, the place of the teachers' unions, and
the authority of the LEAs' (Tomlinson, 1989, p. 186). These early policies
used public money to support private sector provision of education and
training, blurring distinctions between public and private sectors (Whitty
and Menter, 1989, p. 45). The Acts introduced spending cuts, curtailed the
power of LEAs, increased vocationalism (through training programmes
and technical education), enlarged parental choice as against teachers' and
administrators' interests, weakened the bargaining power of teachers
(replacing the collectivist negotiation system, the Burnham Committee, by
imposing a new set of conditions and pay), and developed governing

boards and other tools of parental power in order to displace teacher and local authority influence (Robins, 1994, p. 177). By 1986 the possibility for a radical education programme emerged.

The government was able to take a bold initiative to redirect educational policy-making by drawing upon and modifying still further changing ideas, defining the ends and methods of educational policy, isolating opposition intellectually and morally and drawing support from new enthusiasts. Core Thatcherites took the initiative for radical reform. The Prime Minister wanted greater parental choice. She gained support from Chancellor Lawson who wanted to take schools out of local control altogether and from Nicholas Ridley who proposed the compromise of providing for parents' choosing to opt-out of local control. Though claiming to support parental choice, the Minister of Education, Kenneth Baker initially took the DES line and opposed radical changes (Baker, 1993; Ridley, 1991, pp. 92–3). Nigel Lawson (1992, pp. 609–10) relates how the policy, following his own personal initiative, emerged from a cabinet subcommittee on educational reform: 'The process would start by Margaret putting forward various ideas – in addition to the Anson paper [initiated by Lawson] she had the Number 10 Policy Group heavily involved in the subject and its then head, Brian Griffiths, was engaged in little else at this time – and there would then be a general discussion, to which I would contribute my four pennyworth. At the end of it, Margaret would sum up and give Kenneth his marching orders'. Baker would return with proposals reflecting the views of DES officials, only to receive a 'handbagging' from Thatcher, thereby coming back next time with proposals corresponding to her ideas. The resulting policy went into the 1987 Conservative manifesto and subsequently became the 1988 Education Reform Bill.

Success in carrying radical reform through depended on the way neoliberal leaders used their ideas and market decision-making to take advantage of circumstances. Despite vocal opposition from political and professional groups, the consultation period for the legislation was short and the Bill little changed. Opposition parties, unions, LEAs, churches, academics, educationalists, and Association of County Councils had no impact in the House of Commons, although the Church of England and the University lobby had some impact in the Lords (Whitty and Menter, 1989, p. 56). Introducing competition and choice had helped to marginalize the teachers and the LEAs and to enhance the role of parents, industry and boards of governors while simultaneously binding them into market processes of decision-making in which market accountability functioned as the criterion for choice. McVicar (1990, p. 138) points out that the LEAs and the unions were much weakened by 1988, while Baker was in a strong position to carry the DES and to carry through the reforms, given his desire to upgrade his standing among Thatcherites. Geoff Whitty, placing the 1988 Education Reform Act (ERA) in the context of the New Right state power and strategy, writes that the market oriented and curriculum provisions 'can also be seen as part of a broader attempt to atomise educational decision-making within a clear legislative framework, using central government powers to remove or dissipate the influence of intervening power such as LEAs, trade unions and entrenched professional interest groups' (1990, pp. 308–9). Yet, reforms succeeded because circumstances facilitated the Conservative strategy of engaging key interests and marginalizing opponents through using commercial practices.

The ERA completed the task of replacing the postwar policy-making community with a comprehensive and irreversible reform of the public education system. The Act introduced a centrally imposed curriculum and a managed market for the distribution of educational resources. Self-contradictory in reflecting different strands of Conservative thinking, the Act combined neoliberal themes for controlling resource allocation and traditionalist Conservative ideas about the content of education. It introduced a new national curriculum, ten subjects with a core of English, mathematics and science plus attainment examinations at 7, 11, 14 and 16 years of age, and established an education market place driven by consumer choice.

These reforms, ending the old politics of partnership between local councils, teachers' unions, and the Department of Education and Science (DES), recast the processes by which resources are allocated as the outcome of market choices in which 'separate providers compete for the custom of service users' (Taylor-Gooby, 1993, p. 114). Economical trade-offs became the basis of choice for parents in choosing a school for their child and for school managements in deciding how to operate most efficiently. The new Thatcherite formula for enhancing efficiency centred on using competition between a variety of education providers in order to make them accountable to consumers (parents and industry), all under the watch of a Minister of State at the DES (after 1992 the Department for Education) concerned to promote the internal market.

With the content of education directly controlled by the centre, decisions about resources depended on the operation of the internal market. The publication of information on school performance further strengthened parental ability to make choices, exercised through open enrolment. Governing bodies controlled their school's finances, including the hiring of teachers, maintenance of facilities, and purchasing of books and other equipment. LEAs, and those opting out of LEA control in favour of 'grant-maintained' status, increasingly depended on government finances that in turn depend on the number of students matriculating. Provisions facilitate governing boards' responsiveness to consumer choice by permitting parents to vote for their school to opt-out of local control and to choose 'grant maintained schools' status. This meant that a governing body, made up of parents and DES appointees, ran the school and central government financing depended on attracting students. For those schools staying under LEA control, headteachers gained greater control over their budgets and the management of school affairs (McVicar, 1990, pp. 138–42). These opt-out provisions and the abolition of ILEA (Inner London Education Authority) diminished permanently the power of LEAs; a 1993 Education Act further reduced LEA functions and encouraged opting-out (Raab, 1993, p. 234). Parents' choices about where to send their children determined in effect a school's resources.

While it may be too soon to reach definitive conclusions about the effects of the ERA, its operation so far reveals some consequences of mar- ketization. First, teachers are under cost-cutting pressures, leading to the use of unqualified persons and to pressures in which teachers are evaluated in terms of their ability to raise funds (Robins, 1994, p. 178). Second, the move to grant-maintained status has gathered pace because of their being given large capital spending grants. By 1993 about one quarter of eligible secondary schools had opted out of control by local education authorities or were seeking to (Taylor-Gooby, 1993, p. 111). Others sought to opt-out as a way to prevent closure due to decreasing enrolment, although the gov- ernment intends to prevent this (Robins, 1994, p. 179–80). The 1993 Education Act provided further incentives to opt-out, set up Funding Agencies for Schools with grant-maintained status, and authorized special treatment for the most ineffective schools (McVicar and Robins, 1994, p. 207–8). Third, the operation of the internal market encourages a stratification among schools. League tables encourage selectivity, with top students competing for the top schools and low-achieving students choosing less demanding and less attractive schools (Robins, 1994, pp. 181–12; Taylor-Gooby, 1993, pp. 114–15). This appears to differ from neoliberal expectations that market competition would raise the standards of achievement for all. Finally, recent changes and concessions in the implementation of the national curriculum show that the government's direct power depends on the cooperation of teachers and school adminis- trators. The internal market processes for allocating resources may in time influence the substantive content of education.

In sum, both the reform process and the post-reform implementation phase relied on indirect control to achieve results. The Thatcherites drew

on the support and involvement of the parents and the business community, the segment of the educational establishment which felt they would
benefit (such as headteachers and Polytechnic directors), rightwing backbenchers and some elements at the DES. In commenting on the new politics of education, Whitty suggests that under the new regime teachers and
LEAs serve as agents of central government within a context of dispersed
pluralism and aiming for an 'atomised market' (1990, p. 316). The government mobilized new participants, the parents and industry, into a market-
led process of policy-making, a state supervised regime in which providers
(public and private) vie for the custom of parents. Whitty notes, 'It may
well be that a more open pluralist model of decision-making will apply at
that [implementation] level, but it cannot be seen independently of the
strengthened role of central government in determining who are legitimate
parties in that decision-making process and the context in which it is
carried out' (1990, p. 317). While maintaining direct control over the
content of the curriculum and direct but reserve power over the internal
market, the latter functions to facilitate the government's intention to
shape interest formation and representation.

CONCLUSION

The neoliberal Thatcherites effort to open up markets to competition grew
out of an ideological belief that pure market exchange relationships exemplify free choice. During the 1980s, the Conservative governments' initiatives, moreover, covered a wide range of activities and met with more
success than most commentators acknowledge. They always depended on
the self-propelling disposition of new market entrants. Reform itself, thus,
depended on changing the direction of individual experience and action,
setting in motion responses that in turn modified the character of interests
and the manner of their representation. Finally, the emergent decision-
making process diverged between concentrating reserve formal power in
the government and decentralizing effective control to the tutelage of
economic ideas and gamesmanship.

    While the state retains a potential for intervention, deregulation relies
on a conception that private sector exchange generates public accountability in the provision of services. Rupert Murdoch, the media tycoon,
captured the essence of this idea of decision-making when he stated that
'My own view is that anybody who, within the law of the land, provides a
service which the public wants at a price it can afford is providing a public
service' (*Financial Times*, November, 13–14, 1993, p. 1). Free choice

among competing providers precludes consideration of nonmarket values and legitimates only those initiatives optimizing self-interest. In fact, debate about whether choice among competitors fosters material betterment for all or widens the gap between the haves and the have-nots obscures the tendency of competitive market exchanges to exact compliance with processes that prefigure the ends of efficiency and economy.

7 Commercializing Association: the Reform of Union Power

During the 1960s and 1970s weakening trade union power became a special concern for British governments. Legal restrictions, direct assaults, and negotiations in the context of collectivist pluralism failed to deflate their strength. Leaders of major unions shifted to the left, militancy flourished, and union membership grew. By the mid-1970s the 'social contract' and incomes policies further politicized industrial relations and fostered ideological factionalism. During the 1978–79 'Winter of Discontent', uncoordinated militancy gained the upper hand. The 1979 election of the Thatcher government signalled the public's mood for abandoning the collectivist framework and the unions' privileged position within it.

In the 1980s, the Conservative governments turned to the indirect controls of individualized market participation to undermine workers' ability to engage in working-class collective action. Inspired by Hayek's neoliberalism, the Thatcherite programme incrementally deregulated the labour market and unions' role in it. As a result, the association of employees in unions increasingly became a matter of market transactions, determined by returns on costs. As a medium of indirect control, markets excluded traditional working-class solidarity, interest in justice and equality, and mass control of union policy. Instead union officials and member-consumers came to make decisions on the basis of the price of benefits received.

Making economic transactions primary in driving union organization and policy-making involved three developments. First, Thatcherites changed the ideological framework or justification for trade unionism. They shifted from accepting unions as basic to working-class representation to rejecting them as destructive of free labour market transactions. Second, they pursued a programme that took the initiative away from unions as organizers of working-class opposition and turned them into market players. Third, deprived of external and internal support, union leaders adopted business-oriented or commercial strategies in relation to employees and employers. Individualizing and commercializing workers' association made the indirect control of market transactions primary. This narrowed internal democracy and the representation of working-class interests without relying on a continuous expenditure of direct power or force.

THE NEOLIBERAL FRAMEWORK: PRIVATIZING ASSOCIATION

The motivations for Thatcherite trade union reforms were historical, pragmatic, and ideological. The legacy of the 1926 General Strike, the trade unions' disregard for the 1971 Industrial Relations Act, and the miners' victories against the Conservative government in 1972 and 1974 ignited a determination to tame a difficult enemy. Changing social and economic circumstances made union reform necessary and workable. And the writings of Friedrich von Hayek gave neoliberals a vision for diminishing union power that fit with the cultural trends toward individualism. As a result, neoliberals viewed unions with antipathy, as repugnant organizations which abuse the freedoms of individuals and need to be made accountable to their individual members.

The Thatcherite programme broke with the industrial relations framework that encouraged the corporatist bias and the post-WWII collectivist consensus. From the late 1960s governments had been intent on curtailing the power of trade unions, but they accepted the right of workers to organize and act in their class interests. While the Conservative Government of 1970–1974 and the Labour Governments of 1974–1979 introduced elements of neoliberalism, they sought to check union power through legal restrictions or quasi-corporatist strategies, such as, incomes policies, planning, and tripartite negotiations (Crouch, 1979, chs 3 and 4). Immunities and 1970s legislation legalizing new forms of picketing and strikes had given unions the ability to push successfully for wage raises.

During these years, a number of independent economic and social trends eroded union power. These included the world recession of the early 1980s; the long-term decline in the British economy; intensified racial and ethnic tension; a new culture of individualism that challenged class solidarities; new technologies and forms of work organization adopted by international corporations and driven by international competition; the shift toward service, part-time, and female employment; and the rise of mass unemployment (Longstreth, 1988, p. 425; Rubery, 1986, p. 76; Crouch, 1986, pp. 5–17).

The Thatcher Government took advantage of these social developments with an overarching neoliberal strategy that explicitly aimed to restore the ability of managers to manage labour more efficiently and to emancipate the individual union member. Reforming the labour market and reducing union power went hand-in-hand with, and depended on, economic policy and changes in labour law (Davies and Freedland, 1993, p. 435; Mayhew, 1991; Lawson, 1992, p. 437). For example, Thatcher rejected incomes policies, abandoned the collectivist commitment to full employment, and removed unions from a politicized public sector context by selling state assets. These policies combined with legal reforms that made industrial action difficult and potentially very costly.

Thatcherites have consistently justified their trade union measures as fighting the abuse of individual freedom. The reformers claim that unions are able to extract a surplus benefit because of their ability to coerce individuals. In 1983, then Employment Secretary Norman Tebbit stated: 'By 1979, the trade unions enjoyed a highly privileged position in society but they had also come increasingly to exploit that position irresponsibly. In so doing, they harmed the economy, the community and individuals within the community' (1983, p. 4). Therefore Thatcherite reforms aimed 'to end abuses, to protect individuals and the community... to restore a sensible balance in our industrial relations' (Tebbit, 1993, p. 5). In 1994, Employment Secretary David Hunt characterized the 1993 Trade Union Reform and Employment Rights Act (TURERA) as carrying forward the government's commitment to 'protection for trade union members against the abuse of union power' (Morris, 1995, p. 126). Purportedly unwarranted organizational leverage gave unions direct control over their members and enabled them to obtain job guarantees and wages that were inefficient and wasteful for the overall economy. Accordingly, unions' nonmarket privileges, such as statutory immunities, caused inflation and unemployment (Lewis, 1991, p. 62). Neoliberal Shirley Letwin confirms, 'The union is thus a contrivance of an organized minority to pursue its self-interest at the expense of the rest of the community, which pays the bill both in monopoly prices and disorder' (1992, p. 142).

Inspiring this vision of a union-free labour market is the political philosophy of Friedrich von Hayek. Targeting unions as especially obnoxious institutions, picturing them as coercive and exploitative actors, and displacing them with unencumbered labour markets are persistent Hayekite themes. In advancing this interpretation, Lord Wedderburn suggests that 'Hayek did not of course write the "step-by-step" programme of labour law for 1980–88; but one would need to be juridically tone deaf not to pick up the echoes of his philosophy in recent policies and pronouncements' (1989, p. 15). In this view, 'individualist market-capitalism is the real and only "democracy"' (Wedderburn, 1989, p. 14). Only markets provide uncoerced interaction or freedom and must therefore be protected by law.

For neoliberals, unions have no right to represent working-class interests. In Hayek's view: 'The employee's freedom depends on choice between "a great number and variety of employers," and that can be achieved only in a competitive market. The pressures of organised groups such as trade unions on that market create distortions and must therefore be ended' (Wedderburn, 1989, p. 9). The White Paper setting out the proposals for the 1993 TURERA agrees, claiming that the government's role is 'to create a framework within which individual choice and opportunity can flourish' (Departments of Employment, Scotland and Wales, 1992, p. 70). The government, it contends, achieved 'the opening up of individual choice and opportunity in the 1980s, ...[showing] how the growing importance of the role of the individual has been mirrored by a decline in the coverage of collective bargaining and in trade union membership' (Departments of Employment, Scotland and Wales, 1992, p. 69).

The neoliberal vision proposes that freedom can be achieved by making unions, like all economic actors, accountable to the choices of individuals in free labour markets. Labour market deregulation, increased managerial prerogative, and giving individual workers choices would achieve greater freedom. The government used 'rights, freedoms, and protections' as the legal means for 'removing barriers to the efficient working of the labour market' (Department of Employment, 1989, pp. 1 and 3). Indeed, the government claims substantial progress toward giving workers market freedoms. The 1991 Green Paper, *Industrial Relations in the 1980s: The Achievement of Reform,* announced a wide acceptance of the legislation that enabled workers and union members 'to decide for themselves whether or not to join a trade union... to vote in a secret ballot to elect their leaders... [and] to decide for themselves whether or not to go on strike' (Department of Employment, 1991, p. 4).

Arguing that trade union leaders were 'socialist politicians' who preferred monopolistic and protected markets, Thatcher believed that giving greater influence to the rank and file would produce more modern and cooperative union behaviour. The former Prime Minister writes, 'In due course, we must liberate them [rank and file members] by breaking down the closed shop and by ensuring genuine democracy within the unions; then they themselves would bring the extremists and union *apparatchiks* into line' (Thatcher, 1993, pp. 100–1). The market provides a self-regulating guide for uncoerced behaviour: 'Once the state had intervened to set the new rules then it should leave the regulation of industrial relations to employers, individual and residual trade unions' (McIlroy, 1991, p. 11). Thus, the indirect control of competitive labour markets will shape individual participation, overseen by a legal framework that becomes involved only when a conflict between participants goes beyond the usual play of economic practices.

In short, the neoliberals shifted the ideological foundations for industrial relations, replacing the longstanding pluralist vision that accepted group and class consciousness of injustices as the legitimate motive for unionization. Drawing on the thought of Hayek, neoliberals instead viewed unions a exploitative and abusive. They aimed to free employees by exposing unions to workers' choices in a deregulated labour market. Individual 'pure' market exchanges epitomized freedom and democracy.

REFORMING THE UNIONS: COMMERCIALIZING INDIVIDUAL CHOICE

Since neoliberals equate democracy with markets, they believed that voluntary groups would better represent membership interests if they operated as any other private sector firm, producing services in response to members' demands. To commercialize associational processes, Thatcherites pursued an incremental and multifaceted programme to individualize and marketize the choices workers make about unions. Rather than weakening unions by imposing overt and external restrictions, Thatcherite's devised a complex array of government decisions, legislation, and economic policies that diminished or withdrew government and employer institutional support for unions and increased employee and union exposure to market forces. This deregulated context changed the expectations and behaviour of union leaders. Choices about membership, leadership, industrial action, political funds and the like increasingly reflected individual choices about advantageous trade-offs. Unions, in turn, targeted the services they could offer to employees and to employers.

This programme of trade union reform relied on direct and indirect forms of power. The use of direct force is most evident in the government's showcase attacks on unions at the Government Communications Headquarters (GCHQ) at Cheltenham in 1984, the National Union of Mineworkers (NUM) in 1984–85, the printing unions in 1986, the seafarers' union (NUS) in 1988 and the dockers in 1989. While important in demoralizing unions, more important was the strategy of utilizing the indirect force of self-interested individuals. Legislation set the new rules of behaviour, empowering employers and union members to use the law to redefine and test the limits of what was to be acceptable as union activities (Howell, forthcoming, p. 15). The government facilitated change, avoiding direct confrontation with unions in general. It empowered employers and workers to take legal action for financial compensation for injury and undercut class solidarity by formalizing workers' individual rights to decide on their union membership and on industrial action. Also, the resurgence of managerial prerogative drove economic changes that helped redirect unions and workers away from the organizational politics that go with union and class consciousness toward a logic of collective action dependent on the choices of economizing individuals. While the government did engage in tests of direct power, then, reforming trade union power mainly involved redirecting actors' behaviour rather than imposing restrictions and harms on them.

Government policy of privatizing association comprised three main strategies for getting the workers to anticipate and make their choices about unionization and industrial action in terms of their expectations about returns on cost and about other actors' calculations. First, government policies aimed to weaken unions' capacity to use its control of labour to bargain successfully for scarce resources. To make unions more responsive to the interests of employers and the government meant reducing or ending the support they received from participation in policy formation and implementation and making it more costly for them to use industrial action to extract benefits from employers. By limiting the variety, decisiveness and duration of possible industrial action, legislation weakened the unions' ability to enhance their future interests (McIlroy, 1991, p. 16).

Government decisions removing political and institutional support for unions redirected them into having to pay their own way through their achievements or earnings. The elimination of incomes policies, the reduction in contacts between government and union leaders, an absence of influence on labour legislation (except for the dropping of the contracting out proposal in the 1984 Trade Union Act), and the exclusion from policymaking and implementation (e.g., the youth employment policy) – these underscore the precipitous decline in the political role of unions (Marsh, 1992, ch. 5; King, 1993). John Purcell states, 'If this [institutional] support is withdrawn by the state and or by employers the strength of trade unions recedes and the secondary institutions of collective bargaining wither' (1993, p. 7). By denying unions external support and assistance, the government removed important conditions facilitating their development.

A related strategy aimed to weaken unions' internal organizational privileges and resources by increasing the cost of industrial action, constraining and making vulnerable their capacity to use direct power to achieve their ends. Initiatives removed the legal immunities of unions on employers' losses incurred during a strike. In Marsh's words, this meant the loss of 'immunity for action in tort,' where 'tort is the breach of a duty imposed by law, and when the breach occurs some person...acquires the right of action for damages' (1992, pp. 2 and 3). Immunity applied so long as unions and unionists confined their action to a legally defined trade dispute. The blanket immunity for unions ended with the Employment Act 1982, which narrowed the definition of a legitimate trade dispute and reduced the immunities of individual unionists for secondary action, action without a prior secret ballot, action in support of selectively dismissed workers, and secondary and mass picketing (Marsh, 1992, pp. 74–81). The 1990 Employment Act requires unions to repudiate unofficial industrial action or to use a ballot procedure to make it official. The Act also permits the dismissal of workers engaged in unofficial strikes, permits workers to take legal action against unions when leaders are not elected by secret ballot, and allows a closed shop only if 85 per cent of the union members vote for it. The 1993 TURERA broadened the right to engage in legal challenges to unlawful union actions to include the public at large (Howell, forthcoming, p. 16). Thus, removing immunities and making them more conditional by narrowing strike limitations, hemming in strike action with complicated legal procedures and making their resources vulnerable if procedures are violated diminishes unions' ability to take industrial action (MacInnes, 1987, pp. 54–6; Auerbach, 1993).

The Thatcher union legislation reinforced the trend toward the legal regulation of industrial relations dating from the 1960s by allowing the government to make increased use of the law to interrupt or halt industrial action. By narrowing the definition of a legitimate trade dispute, legislation during the 1980s made it more likely that courts would grant employers interlocutory injunctions, effectively ending strikes. Over 90 per cent of requests for injunctions between 1980 and 1988 were granted (Marsh, 1992, pp. 85–7). While injunctions were the most frequently used legal device, the overall number was small and was concentrated in printing, shipping, and the public sector (Marsh, 1992, pp. 88–9). Injunctions against strike action were likely to be granted for a range of remedies provided in the law, such as being in breach of contract, violating restraints on picketing, political strikes, and failing to hold a secret ballot. If a union did not abide by an injunction, then it was in contempt of court and could be fined or have its assets sequestrated. The most notable cases involved the 1984–85 Miners' strike, the 1986 Wapping dispute involving printing unions (SOGAT) and Rupert Murdoch's News International, and the 1988 shipping disputes between the National Union of Seafarers (NUS) and the employers Sealink and P&O (McIlroy, 1991, p. 41). Besides the use of injunctions, the law of contract was applied in several cases to limit industrial action (for example, the NUM's failure to ballot for strike action and their use of union funds in violation of union rules) or to dismiss employees (for example, Murdoch) (Marsh, 1992, pp. 96–101).

Finally, the specialization of police and criminal law further reduced the likelihood that industrial action would be effective. A National Reporting Centre was set up after the 1972 Miners' strike to coordinate police forces. Following the inner-city riots at Toxteth and Brixton in 1981, the police were restructured, and given riot training and increased resources (Marsh, 1992, pp. 101–4). This enabled the police to impose order in accord with what they determined as necessary during the Miners' strike. Citing the Miners' strike, the government then passed legislation 'to *formalize* and *legitimise* some of the power that the police had arrogated to themselves during the mining strike' (McIlroy, 1991, p. 103). This Public Order Act 1986 gave new power to the police, 'powers to *impose conditions on the location, duration and size of certain public assemblies and demonstrations* – which would include *mass pickets*' (McIlroy, 1991, pp. 103–4). The police would henceforth be able to inhibit public assemblies, with violations penalized by imprisonment or fines.

A second way Thatcherites aimed to reduce the unions' capacity to organize labour, and from their perspective, to impose artificial scarcity in labour markets, was through internal union reforms. Mancur Olson (1982) points out that the free rider problem (benefiting from public goods without having paid for them) makes the organization of a mass membership very difficult without selective incentives or costs. From this perspective, government reforms can be interpreted as aiming to make collective organization and action, such as workers' votes for union recognition, leaders, political funds, and strikes, depend on the their economic benefits by limiting the ability of unions to impose costs on all workers. One effort to reduce the coercive hold of unions on their members created rights to disassociation, to be free of compulsory union membership (Lewis, 1991, p. 68). This gave workers the ability to refuse union membership by ending the closed shop and by making union recognition more difficult. The Employment Acts of 1980, 1982, and 1988 created the right to disassociate without being dismissed or discriminated against, in other words, abolishing legal protection for post-entry closed shops. The 1990 Employment Act ended pre-entry or de facto closed shop agreements between unions and employers, giving a legal right of redress if non-membership or union approval results in being refused a job (Lewis, 1991, p. 68). Freedom from employer-related harms for nonmembership was complemented in the 1988 Employment Act by the workers' right not to be disciplined by a union for not participating in an official strike or other activity. This provision undercuts union organizational solidarity or membership control (Lewis, 1991, p. 69). The 1993 TURERA outlaws union practices of excluding some workers from membership, gives individuals the right to join any union that might be preferred, and protects individuals who prefer individual contracts in the place of union representation (Howell, forthcoming, p. 17)

Another initiative formalized exchange relationships between union leaders and members, purporting to increase union democracy. Forcing unions to use secret ballots in elections aimed to moderate union behaviour. An increased voice for a purportedly more conservative rank and file would prevail over radical leaders and activists (McIlroy, 1991, p. 80). While the 1980 Employment Act made public funds available for secret elections, the 1984 Trade Union Act legislated internal reforms, giving members the right to elect all voting members of the union executive, to decide on industrial action, and to approve the collection of political funds. The 1988 Employment Act introduced postal balloting for all strikes and union elections. The 1993 TURERA strengthened regulations for elections and ballots, stipulating that the scrutiner have all the names of members and investigate complaints about the register and that political fund and merger ballots must be postal (Morris, 1995, p. 126). The Act also requires that union members give written authorization every three-years for dues check-off arrangements (employer deduction of union dues) and that union give detailed financial information to the Certification Officer and all members each year (Morris, 1995, p. 127). These provisions redesigned the traditional and solidaristic modes of union decision-making and contributed further to narrowing union action to local disputes. For example, it precluded secondary strikes that might result from or foster class sympathies. These provisions furthered the de-collectivization of union power relations, enhancing the consciousness and expression of individual and non-workplace interests as against workers' solidaristic interests. By extending these rights to individuals, this legislation gave members the right to cast votes for particular results. What can be presented as the giving of rights is more accurately diagnosed as a forfeiting of democracy.

A third major force for change was management's drive to enhance its ability to control labour efficiently, backed by the government's strategy of facilitating market forces. As the economy changed, the government put similar pressures on the public sector to redirect union leadership and workers away from collectivist politics toward a logic of self-regarding choices. Thatcherite macro-economic policy, focusing on limiting public expenditure, forsaking pay policies, encouraging profit-related pay schemes and a variety of public sector counter-inflationary policies, made businesses operate in more competitive product markets and necessitated a more efficient utilization of labour. With private sector manufacturing competing more openly against international rivals, product market uncertainty led to a dramatic rise in unemployment (Rubery, 1986, pp. 76–8; Beaumont, 1987; Turnbull, 1986, pp. 193–206). Thus, the 1980s witnessed a significant deregulation of the labour market, as seen by 'the development of the firm-specific labour market and organization-based employment systems in contrast to the traditional reliance on the external labour market for labour supply, and on industry-wide wage-fixing institutions for the determination of basic terms and conditions of employment' (Purcell, 1991, pp. 33–4).

The programme of deregulating the labour market also enhanced managerial control by encouraging labour mobility and job uptake. The programme weakened unions' control of the pay and conditions of those workers who were either weakly organized or unorganized. It included the abolition of procedures for establishing trade union recognition and enforcing collective bargaining agreements in nonunion firms, the prohibition of union-labour-only contracts, and the limiting of rights to unfair dismissal claims and maternity leave (Rubery, 1986, pp. 76–80). Other initiatives aimed to induce individuals to take jobs at lower wage levels, to reduce social security benefits available to strikers, to lower protective standards for working youths and women, to eliminate minimum wages (by abolition of the Wages Councils), and other miscellaneous measures. Taken together such measures weakened the capacity of the labour movement to resist the Thatcher government's initiatives in 'freeing up' management's use of labour at work.

The selling-off and deregulation of nationalized industries and contracting out local government services also facilitated managerial control by eliminating or reducing public sector labour problems (Lawson, 1992, p. 437; Moran, 1988, p. 288; Sheaff, 1988). Selling-off national assets makes property rights primary in managerial decision-making and so facilitates managerial prerogative. Deregulating increases competitiveness in product markets and flexibility in the use of labour, contracting out particular functions breaks public sector union influence on wages and conditions and lower costs, and charging for services shifts responsibilities from public authorities to consumers. Even initiatives challenging the status and role of unions, such as attacks against powerful public sector unions and banning unions at the government's national security headquarters in Cheltenham, aimed to promote economic rationality and the sanctity of the law (Saville, 1986).

These developments heightened managerial prerogative in three ways. First, deregulation enabled employers increasingly to link wage increases to firm performance. The movement away from national level collective bargaining toward company and firm bargaining facilitated employer adjustments by disaggregating bargaining issues, producing more formalized plant relations and enhancing employer autonomy. Second, the competitive context facilitated employers in dividing workers within the firm between a core of full-time and better-paid workers benefiting from job flexibility and training (functional flexibility) and a peripheral group of temporary or part-time employees (numerical flexibility). This encouraged the growth of part-time employment, self-employment, sub-contracting, the expansion of company-specific training, and the adoption of incentive pay schemes related to company performance (Brown, 1986, pp. 161–2). It also encouraged the introduction of Japanese-style module or team production systems in which team goals shape worker motivation (Turnbull, 1986, p. 199). Third, market conditions allowed employers to respond to the need to improve productivity and increase flexibility in the use of labour by introducing 'organizational based employment systems' (Purcell, 1991, p. 39).

In short, the government offensive individualized the labour market and eliminated nonmarket external and internal sources of associational activity, gaining reinforcement from the employers' own autonomous offensive to restore its ability to manage. In contrast to the United States where there has been an emphasis on union derecognition, in Britain the programme to deregulate and individualize the labour market circumvents unions. In Britain, Purcell writes, the 'preference has been for reducing the disadvantages of unionism by getting collective bargaining linked strongly to firm-specific issues while simultaneously reducing the dependency on collective bargaining as the medium for the management of change, and on trade unions as the main link with the work force' (1991, p. 37). Government policy and managerial initiatives linked, in Purcell's words, 'industrial relations with the needs of the business and away from external market structures'. Such circumstances advantaged corporate strategies in reshaping work and labour forces for the purpose of improving performance targets. The effect was real wage gains in return for greater flexibility and work intensification for many of those working; a major regressive shift in income, wealth, and influence for workers; substantial interference in the internal processes of the unions; and the exclusion of unions from decisions involved in restructuring working practices in the larger enterprises (McIlroy, 1988, p. 224).

DECISION-MAKING: MARKETING SERVICES AND INCREASING
EFFICIENCY

Unable to rely on external assistance and internal institutional assets that
bolster membership and bargaining influence, unions turned to positive
incentives to secure their future as intermediary organizations. This meant
working with employees and employers rather representing one against
the other, offering a harmonious combination of 'voice and co-operation'
(Metcalf, 1991, p. 28). Leaders promised employers improved use of the
workforce and offered employees special benefits. The characteristics of
the employee and employer markets besides any non-economic criteria
figure into the mix of particular union packages (Willman, Morris and
Aston, 1993). Enhanced discretion in the deployment and control of
resources enabled official to make internal processes more efficient
in recruiting and serving members and responsive to their external
dependency on employers.

Internal Control of Resources

In response to government initiatives and changes in the economic
context, unions acted to make their own internal structures and finances
more efficient and initiated programmes that appeal to individuals as
potential recruits. First, union leaders adapted commercial standards and
procedures to organizational operations. Competition for members encouraged efficient financial management for the Banking, Insurance, and
Finance Union (BIFU) and the Electricians (EETPU). Expansion into low
income groups prompted economizing in the General Municipal and
Boilermakers Union (GMB), whereas financial crisis compelled similar
measures in the AEU and the NUM (Willman, Morris and Aston, 1993,
p. 198). The EETPU attracted members by offering the efficient provision
of services, reducing its ability to cross-subsidize loss-making subunits
and making it important to organize the employers market with mergers
and single-union deals (Willman, Morris and Aston, 1993, p. 214–15).
During the 1980s the trend toward the centralizing financial control
occurred in rightwing and leftwing unions of diverse organizational
structure, even when the formal organizational structure gave power, as in
the NUM or the AEU, to decentralized components.

Another important effort to economize involved union mergers. In
1990, twenty TUC affiliates were considering mergers, while the number
of unions fell from 586 in 1968 to 314 in 1988 (Metcalf, 1991, p. 24). The
1993 merger of white-collar local government (NALGO), manual public

sector (NUPE), and health service (COHSE) workers created in UNISON the largest union with 1.6 members, larger than the TGWU with 1.2 million. Five other important recent mergers added to a trend toward 'superunions'. These included the rightwing electricians (EETPU) and engineers (AEU) uniting in 1992 in the Amalgamated Engineering and Electrical Union (AEEU); the railwaymen (NUR) and seamen (NUS) creating the RMT; the large general union GMB and the while-collar APEX combining in a new GMB (1991); white-collar professional TASS and ASTMS joining into a 'general technical' Manufacturing, Scientific and Finance Union (MSF) in 1989; and printers SOGAT and NGA uniting in the GPMU union (Howell, forthcoming, p. 52–3). More recently, the NCU and UCW merged to create the CWU (Communications Workers' Union). Mergers are, according to Metcalf (1991, p. 24), 'a cost effective mechanism for increasing membership in an individual union,' a way to maintain or increase 'market share' for a particular union. Pressures from employers to restructure work, from other unions for members, and for the need to provide a wider range of services make mergers a means to greater efficiencies that strengthen organization (Edwards, *et al.,* 1992, p. 37). As a result, unions have become general unions, organizing many occupations and industries and being opportunistic in their approach (Edwards, *et al.,* 1992, pp. 38 and 47). However, Willman and Cave (1994) question the administrative benefits and underscore the representational damage done by mergers. The effect of incorporating new groups and offering them policy-making independence leads to sectionalization by increasing organizational diversification but weakening collective identity.

Second, as unions amended their structures of internal government to accommodate the sectionalization influences of mergers and the enhanced role of individual choice, leaders enhanced their decision-making autonomy. While policy among unions such as the Miners and Electricians diverged, three writers conclude from their study of union finances that 'unions have become more commercially aware in the management of their own affairs and that this awareness has affected decision making within unions...' (Willman, Morris and Aston, 1993, p. 213). They write that commercial management coincided with a centralization of control: 'The installation of automated payment methods, subscription indexation, centralised accounting, and asset management systems, the disappearance of rule book provisions on investment and the emergence of a group of appointed finance officers in the larger union controlled by the General Secretary or Executive Committee all support the proposition that the exercise of managerial discretion supports both the centralization and depoliticisation of union financial management' (Willman, Morris and Aston, 1993, p. 205). In sum, commercialization of union business furthered elitist internal politics.

The introduction of postal ballots for electing principal executive committee members and officers as stipulated by the Trade Union Act 1984 and the Employment Act 1988 prompted unions to reshape their constitutions in ways that helped concentrate power. Postal ballots, producing lower participation and potential unpredictability, appears to encourage electoral bossdom by emphasizing an individualist and populist type of union democracy (Edwards, *et al.,* 1992, p. 43). The EETPU is the best example of 'elective dictatorship', with postal balloting of the executive and General Secretary and retaliation against leftwing opposition (McIlroy, 1988, p. 140). Through the 1990 merger of textile workers, APEX, and the National Union of Tailor and Garment Workers with the GMB, the GMB moved toward a centralization of power among top executives by introducing postal ballots at the expense of the regions (Smith, *et al.,* 1993, p. 374). The introduction of postal ballots also helped concentrate power in the construction workers' union (UCATT).

The AUEW–Engineering Section, now a component of Britain's third largest union, placed stewards under strict control of district committees. It streamlined the organization by restructuring branches around employment location. New industrial relations practices; declining labour and product markets; co-ordinated industrial relations strategies in multi-plant firms; postal balloting for union officials, Trades Union Congress delegates, and Labour Party delegations and a restructuring of the national executive facilitated this consolidation of official decision-making (Undy and Martin, 1984). As a result, the rightwing captured the AUEW–E leadership. Its merger, as part of the AEU, with the rightwing EETPU reinforced a shift of formal authority away from districts to the centre (Smith, *et al.,* 1993, p. 376).

Elitism, however, has not benefited moderate or rightwing factions exclusively (McIlroy, 1988, p. 140; Smith, *et al.,* 1993, p. 378 and 380). A 'broad Left' faction continues to dominate TASS, which organizes draughtsmen and is now part of the larger MSF union. It has changed its system of elections, maintained lifetime appointments for its full-time officials, and undermined its opponents (McIlroy, 1988, p. 131). Even the left-leaning TGWU, which had undergone a process of devolving power to workplace activists in the 1970s and 1980s and turned balloting as required by the 1984 legislation over to workplace units, became more centralized as postal ballots ended voting by union branches and eliminated the political role of shop stewards. Ballots for the general secretary, the deputy general secretary and executive officers gave them a new and powerful source of legitimacy, but diminished that of the General Executive Council, trade groups, and factions (Smith, *et al.* 1993, p. 372).

Third, efforts to recruit membership by offering individual services encouraged populist elitism. Officials treated employees 'as discerning and calculating consumers who must be attracted to the union fold' (Heery and Kelly, 1994, p. 7). Recruitment consequently focused on appealing 'to prospective members on the basis of individual services: advice and representation in the case of individual problems at work, but also discounts for banking, insurance, pensions and other personal expenditure' (Edwards, *et al.,* 1992, p. 43). The TUC's special review supported such methods in recruitment, citing 'the need for more targeted recruitment methods, encouraging increased attention in membership campaigns and in bargaining priorities to vulnerable groups with distinctive needs, such as women, young workers, and ethnic minorities' (Edwards, *et al.,* 1992, p. 44). Similarly, Willman, Morris and Aston report that many important unions (NUM, GMB, AEU, BIFU, and EETPU) offered reduced-priced services as the selective incentives attracting members (1993, p. 210–11). In March 1994, the TUC reorganized itself in order to focus more on servicing its members, from offering a wide array of benefits programmes to skills training, partnerships with employers and a less partisan approach to the Conservatives and Liberal Democrats (*Economist*, March 5, 1994, p. 65; *Financial Times*, September 6, 1993, p. 10).

The growing use of selective benefits to attract members reflects the loss of collective bargaining strength and a decline in its relevance to many workers, despite overall public popularity for trade unions (Metcalf, 1991, p. 28). Edwards and his co-authors contend that 'the persistent tendency for pay increases to outstrip increases in productivity – there was no year in the 1980s in which the growth in average earnings in manufacturing was less than 7 per cent – suggests there is considerable continuity' (1992, p. 30). Yet, it is dubious that wage increases result only from union bargaining strength. As Moran points out, skills shortages and performance of strategic social functions now give more bargaining leverage than collective bargaining (1988, pp. 285–6). Moreover, real wage increases went mainly to 'insiders' while the ranks of the 'outsiders' swell as unemployment grows. Insiders' gains are a productivity reward for the benefits they bring to particular establishments (Metcalf, 1993, p. 260). Given the lack of labour market competitiveness for some skills and within some firms, higher and higher levels of unemployment may be needed to control inflation.

Further, there has been a trend toward significantly reducing the wage differential between union and non-union workers. Metcalf reports that 'In the vast majority of establishments facing competitive product market conditions, unions are unable to achieve wage levels above those paid elsewhere to comparable non-union workers...[nor can they] create differential over non-union pay in establishments that operate primarily in international markets – foreign competition restrains union influence' (1993, p. 262). While unions can gain added benefits for workers in comparison to non-union workers in firms with market power, this applies only where union density is over 95 per cent of the workplace, where multiple unions are present and bargain separately, though not when they bargain in single-table fashion (Metcalf, 1993, p. 262). With more firms facing product market competition, fewer closed shops, and unemployment at record postwar levels, fewer workers join unions because the benefit they receive from membership is less than substantial.

As unions shift toward treating members and potential members as if they were consumers, unions have become more business-like in their internal operations. In response to declining membership, the 'union bureaucracy must become more managerial in its functioning, researching and monitoring employee needs, designing and promoting union services to match and planning the organisation, training and deployment of its own human resources to support service delivery' (Heery and Kelly, 1994, p. 7). This strategy entails making membership easier and more desirable, specializing officer functions, monitoring performance, and relying more on union officials. Managerial unionism, as Heery and Kelly name it, implies 'that negotiators and organisers will increasingly be responsible for implementing policies and campaigns designed by specialists' (1994, p. 10).

Finally, the experiences of the NUM show the effects of failing to accommodate to the emerging market-based rules of the trade unionism. The 1984–85 Miners' strike exemplified a radical conservatism of self-regarding and sectionalized motives for action in which mining jobs and communities became nonnegotiable ends-in-themselves (Samuel, *et al.*, 1986). Influenced by decentralized pay mechanisms and different employment prospects in different coalfields, the Miners' federal structure proved unable to contain diverging practices of internal democracy and a split in the NUM. Participation in the militant areas, such as Yorkshire, South Wales, and Scotland, which faced imminent closures and redundancies was driven by the radical defense of workers' communities and jobs. In Nottinghamshire, Derbyshire and others areas anticipating a secure employment future, material self-interest resulted in refusing to strike, despite the NUM's impassioned and sometimes coercive strike call (Hyman, 1986, pp. 346–7). One result of the different motivations and conflicting actions was the refusal of the NUM's Executive to call a national ballot on the strike, itself a result of the collapsing working class solidarity in the coalfields (Hyman, 1986, p. 345). The Executive's inaction stemmed from contradictory pressures: fears of losing a ballot because the government's identification of those pits which were to be closed undercut an already weakened solidarity (Chris Howell, personal communication) and fears that key areas, such as moderate Nottinghamshire and militant Yorkshire, would go their own way in any case (Benn, 1994, p. 341). The lack of a national ballot further divided miners and enabled the government to use its new legal rights to sequester NUM funds. In the end, these conflicts led, in the moderate areas, to the formation of a breakaway union, the Union of Democratic Mineworkers, which took a conciliatory approach to bargaining with British Coal. Faced with a hostile government favouring confrontation, disfavour among the public and an absence of sympathetic support from other unions, the strike ended in defeat and division for the union. Its rightwing gained strength from the belief that the 'new realism' was the only feasible strategy for unions in an openly anti-union environment (Saville, 1987, pp. 308–13).

Adapting to Employers

The primacy of economic criteria in union decision-making also encouraged pragmatism, voice and cooperation in dealings with employers. The latter benefit through union services facilitating economic performance. For unions, cooperation from employers helps make them attractive to employees. It enables unions to provide workers with wage increases and jobs-related services more efficiently. The leading example of these changes is the EETPU, having been characterized as pursuing a 'market-based trade unionism' (Bassett, 1987, p. 174). Moreover, most unions are adopting the EETPU's concern with job training, flexibility, and structural change (Metcalf, 1991, p. 28). Harmonious and cooperative relationships with employers enables unions to participate in changes and to benefit their members. Yet, in doing this, they dispense with traditional working-class issues of justice and equality.

The marginalization of unions contributed to their accommodating to employers' interests. Membership fell from 13.3 million in 1979 to just under 9 million at the end of 1992 (Howell, forthcoming, p. 6; Morris, 1995, p. 124). In 1979 TUC membership was 12 million; in 1994 it was only 7.5 million (*Economist*, March 5, 1994, p. 65). Membership density fell from 58 per cent in 1984 to 48 per cent in 1990 for all industries and a corresponding 42 per cent to 35 per cent for the private sector (Millward, Stevens, Smart and Hawes [hereafter MSSH], 1992, pp. 60 and 64). A 1991 household survey found union density at 37.5 per cent, reflecting the use of different data (Purcell, 1993, p. 19). By 1993, density dropped to 31 per cent. Two-thirds of public sector workers are union members, as compared to only one in three private sector workers (Metcalf, 1991, pp. 19–22). While some sectors like medical and social services in the public sector and banking and insurance in the private sector grew, these were the exceptions. Unemployment contributed significantly to the loss of union membership in the early 1980s. However, in the second half of the decade, 'the explanations for the continuing decline are more likely to be weakening support for unionism among employees, various government measures constraining it and antipathy amongst a growing number of employers' (MSSH, 1992, p. 102). Moreover, union recognition and the proportion of union employees covered by collective bargaining declined. Collective bargaining coverage fell from 71 to 54 per cent of the work-force in firms of 25 or more employees; in private sector from 65 to 51 per cent manufacturing and from 41 to 33 per cent in services (Brown, 1993, p. 192; Kessler, 1993, p. 216; Gilbert, 1993).

The authors of the third workplace industrial relations survey (WIRS3) underscore the growing marginalization and struggle for survival as free market trade-offs become more prominent in shaping trade unionism. They point to three trends during the 1980s.

> Perhaps the most important of these were the decline in the representa-
> tion of workers by trade unions and the decline in the coverage of
> collective bargaining, particularly in the private sector. Indeed, so great
> were the changes that it is not unreasonable to conclude that the
> traditional, distinctive 'system' of British industrial relations no
> longer characterized the economy as a whole. But, secondly, in work-
> places where trade union representation and collective bargaining
> persisted, surprisingly little altered...Thirdly, no new pattern of
> employee representation emerged to replace trade union representation.
> (MSSH, 1992, p. 350)

The decline in union representation, then, occurred because of the sizeable decline in firms where the traditional industrial relations had existed and because of the absence of union growth in new sectors. Yet, even in work-places recognizing unions, there was still a decline in the proportion of employees included in the negotiations. By 1990, just over half of the employees in the WIRS3 survey were covered by collective bargaining and was under half for the whole economy (MSSH, 1992, p. 352).

The rise of strategic management contributed to the decentralization of workplace bargaining and organization (Purcell, 1991; Brown, 1986, pp. 161–7; Brown, 1987). The spread of single-employer agreements in the private sector promoted widespread decentralizing and formalizing of bargaining, use of job evaluation techniques, and introduction of more individualized wage systems. The move to plant and company bargaining also led to greater reliance on lay officials (shop stewards) capable of dealing with local problems. These ranks grew rapidly during the 1970s and into the 1980s but diminished in the late 1980s, when falling membership resulted in a decrease in lay representatives and a greater reliance on full-time union officials. The recession of the early 1980s resulted in a decline in the number of full-time shop stewards, especially in the hardest hit sectors of engineering, metal manufacturing and shipbuilding. The recession of the early 1980s, however, only marginally diminished the overall power of the bureaucratic hierarchy of stewards' committees (Terry, 1986). During the late 1980s, however, the number of lay representatives declined, particularly in smaller workplaces and in those with low levels of union membership. In the few workplaces where such representatives traditionally had been strong, their number continued unchanged (MSSH, 1992, pp. 142–3). At the workplace, paid officials became more involved as the numbers of lay representatives and members declined and as lay representatives demanded their assistance (MSSH, 1992, p. 130).

The decentralization of bargaining to companies and plants accentuated employee and union concerns about jobs in particular businesses, differentiating interests among workers and binding them to the enterprise. Unions have to appeal to workers who, identifying with their firms' emphasis on performance, profit, and productivity, are fragmented by interests, experiences, and deals. According to the current TUC General Secretary, John Monks, 'Solidarity across plants is difficult to develop; workers in different plants have different experiences and different agreements' (1993, p. 231). The individuation of interests among workers goes along with identifying with one's employer. Philip Bassett reports that, as companies decentralize their operations, workers focus more on their employer as the source of their jobs and the unions centre more on local issues. He continues: 'That kind of development will reinforce the new unionism, the overt rejection of the idea of the employer as an enemy, the replacement of the class struggle with the struggle for markets' (1987, pp. 173–4).

As management asserted its prerogative to control labour and as it bypassed traditional shop stewards who became less willing and involved in managing change, unions reformulated their strategy toward employers. Since workers are more likely to join a union if the employer's policy accepts and assists unionization, unions offered orderly industrial relations, the flexible use of labour, and other services that assist restructuring and competitiveness in return for recognition. Metcalf reports, 'In the absence of statutory recognition procedures, and in the face of laws which make industrial action to enforce recognition difficult, unions have tended to adopt the carrot rather than the stick in the 1980s' (1991, p. 25). Despite this effort, recognition declined during the late 1980s, in part because new companies were simply not inclined to recognize unions (MSSH, 1992, p. 73).

This turn toward cooperation and pragmatism gained momentum as union leaders realized that the assertion of managerial prerogative went hand-in-hand with shifting from institutional and corporatist decision-making to bottom-line performance and financial economies through decentralization of decisions to divisional profit centres (Purcell, 1991, p. 39). Managements, facing union resistance, tried different strategies for asserting their control. Dunn (1993) develops this point, citing representative instances. In one case of a tire company undergoing restructuring, management's decision to reduce manpower by half while maintaining the same production level without prior talks with stewards led to restructuring relationships between them. Ultimately, the stewards accepted and then reestablished relationships on narrower grounds in which they negotiated terms and conditions but not working practices. In another case, management of an engineering company had little hope of working with the entrenched union and looked to greenfield (new operations outside inner cities) sites with optimism. In a third case involving a food and drink company, a mid-1980s restructuring led to the re-education of management and workers alike in total quality management and decentralized bargaining (Dunn, 1993, pp. 179–81). In many cases, then, stewards and paid officials increasingly cooperated with management, taking a defensive or protective role but guarding against complete exclusion. Employers asserted their right to manage by incentives and persuasion more than by imposition. Edwards writes, '[Managements] have not ridden roughshod over workers interests but have tried to persuade workers of the benefits of accepting and co-operating with the logic of the market as it is interpreted by management' (cited in Marsh, 1992, p. 201; see also pp. 193–4).

In the 1980s, stewards identified their interests increasingly with the success of their employers and less with the issue of job control, because of fears of the unemployed or concerns of the union (Brown, 1986, p. 165). One manifestation of this approach is productivity bargaining (money for flexibility), which yielded increases in workers' real earnings during the 1980s, probably reflecting employers' longer-term interests in trading increased flexibility and loyalty for wage raises rather than short-term interests in lower wages (Brown, 1986; Metcalf, 1991, p. 27; Kelly, 1987). Productivity bargaining works as long as the firm's competitive position permits, and then gives way to alternative strategies for getting around unions.

In the 1980s, union cooperation with employers also emerged in the form of joint consultation committees without bargaining power. These committees discuss corporate investment decisions, new product development, productivity and competitiveness. While enlisting workers' loyalty, consultation reaffirms management's right to make decisions (Terry, 1983, pp. 54–7). Their permanence has been questioned (MacInnes, 1987, p. 105). WIRS3 reports a fall in the proportion of workplaces with joint consultative committees as a result of the changing composition of workplaces and employers, who use a wider range of methods of communication with employees (MSSH, 1992, p. 157).

Accommodating to the new legal regulations and pitfalls furthered the pragmatic orientation of minimizing costs by cooperating with employers. The array of new laws operated to change the rules of interaction: enveloping union leaders in a network of legal channels that limited and delayed their actions and made their organizations vulnerable to costly penalties if they stepped outside the rules. David Marsh sums up:

> In fact, the major role the legislation passed since 1979 has played has been indirect…Unions, union leaders and unionists are now much more conscious of the consequences of stepping outside the increasingly restricted protection of the 'golden formula' and this affects the strategic judgements they make in the pursuit of a trade dispute particularly, and in the conduct of, industrial relations generally. At the very least, union leaders have to prepare the ground very carefully before they take industrial action and this delays action and weakens their bargaining position.   (1992, p. 109)

The main effect of restrictive and coercive laws was indirect, redirecting the play of the industrial relations game that in itself provided for the control of behaviour.

In this adverse environment, strikes become cumbersome and costly and are in decline along with other types of industrial action. Though turning to other types of more 'cost effective' action, industrial action of all types is much reduced (MSSH, 1992, p. 309; Edwards *et al.*, 1992, p. 58). 'The overall extent of industrial action among either manual or non-manual employees fell by half between the 1984 and 1990 surveys from a quarter to 12 per cent of workplaces' (MSSH, 1992, p. 278). Non-strike activity, diminishing even more than strike action, did not replace striking. While strike action was higher in the public than private sector, some public sector areas, such as central government and schools, experienced fewer strikes (MSSH, 1992, p. 282). By 1990, strikes were mainly about pay. In the 1990s, the number of strikes and days lost dropped to record lows (Howell, forthcoming, p. 8).

Derecognition remains a potential threat. Overt moves to derecognize unions took place in printing and publishing, coastal shipping, the docks, engineering, and vehicles, the latter two owing to a collapse of industry-wide negotiating procedures (MSSH, 1992, p. 72 and 74; Marsh, 1992, p. 195). Evidence indicates that derecognition is most likely when companies are restructuring, where organization is weak, or where a company is determined to have a single union deal (Marsh, 1992, pp. 194–5). According to Metcalf, 'Clearly unions must maintain a co-operative but robust presence where they are recognized; if density decays or is confined to a limited group the union may face derecognition' (1991, p. 26). In short, strong organization and cooperation with employers helps reduce the risk of derecognition.

The 'strike free' pacts and single-union agreements initiated by the EETPU reflect the boldest manifestation of the unions' accommodation to a more commercial environment, with an instrumental orientation inspiring the pragmatic strategies and populist internal politics. Eschewing the longstanding political vision of trade unionism that links politics to disputes with employers (since it sees government policy shaping employers' behaviour), advocates of the strike free approach envision a nonpolitical, conciliatory unionism which will be advantageous to their organizations, to the employers, and to their members. Faced with the Thatcher government's measures, labour leaders fell back on protecting employment and benefits in particular firms and sectors. The EETPU leadership, which initiated this approach, sought to provide services to both employers and employees. According to Philip Bassett, the EETPU in part aimed 'its bid for members at *employers* rather than their employees: the more responsibly it can conduct itself, the theory goes, the greater distance it can put between itself and other unions, the more employers will be attracted towards it' (1987, p. 67). But the 'enlightened self-interest' strategy applies equally to employees. Leading EETPU strategist Roy Sanderson, forsaking any ideals or emotions about working-class struggle, calculated that strikes hurt his workers' self-interests in improved pay more than they helped them: 'We took the view that if strikes are failing to win members what it is they might deserve, then we should be looking for some alternative to strikes as a means of doing it' (cited in Bassett, 1987, p. 85).

Though as yet limited in impact, the 'strike free' or single-union package is an important indicator of recent trade union efforts to merge the self-interest of the employer with that of the employee. The EETPU's 'strike free' package, was first agreed to by workers in Japanese electronic and car companies and Eddie Shah's *Today* newspaper. By 1989 the electricians had negotiated about 40 single-union contracts (*Economist*, May 20, 1989, Survey p. 10). Marsh reports 76 single-union agreements by that time, involving the EETPU, TGWU, AEU and GMB (1992, p. 200). These contracts aimed to overcome British industrial relations problems by fostering Japanese-style stability and co-operation through single-unionism, single status for all employees, a participative corporate culture involving workers directly (in addition to union involvement) in corporate affairs, functional flexibility and training, pendulum arbitration (that is, the arbitrator choosing either in favour of the employer or the union), and no strike provisions.

Similar trends toward cost cutting and decentralized management, driven by restructuring, budget constraints and sub-contracting, are found in the public sector, though industrial relations institutions have changed less than in the private sector (Marsh, 1992, p. 218). Nationalized industries (British Coal, British Rail) experienced dramatic labour reductions and changes in working processes, in some cases preceded by industrial disputes, as did former nationalized industries preceding negotiations and the sell-off (BT, BL, British Steel, BA, Electricity, Post Office, NFC, British Shipbuilders). While institutions persist, more aggressive managers and significant working practice changes prevail (Marsh, 1992, p. 221). Further, work measurement and incentive pay systems, and local and industry specific bargaining, constituted a move away from the traditional practice of centralized collective bargaining that made unionization easier. In 1987, teachers lost negotiating rights in a major move to decentralize bargaining, while management is being devolved in health and other public sector areas. Most significantly, the tacit alliance between unions and management in the nationalized industries and local governments ended as the Thatcherite policies subjected unions to commercial pressures. As a result, unions increasingly developed pragmatic responses consistent with the criterion of value for money (Marsh, 1992, pp. 218–26).

Finally, despite the union leaders' best efforts to strengthen their organization, for example, through mergers, membership has declined because of the loss of institutional support by the government, a decline in support among workers, and economic restructuring. Their own strategic manoeuvres having little effect on reversing the decline of membership, leaders recognized that their future, then, depends largely on gaining external backing, especially through the acceptance of the European Union's (EU) Social Charter or a return of a Labour government (Metcalf, 1991). Yet, with increasing calls for labour market deregulation across Europe as an antidote for unemployment, it is not clear how far a Labour government would go to support unionization or how long the EU will pursue policies that assist the labour movement.

CONCLUSION

British trade unions have clearly lost power. The growth of market-based unionism is itself an expression of this loss of power and an adaptation to it. Unions have been unable to define the objectives or grounds of action in class terms, to influence government and employer decision-making in ways that favour workers' class interests, or to organize themselves or the industrial relations system to the advantage of the working class. The role of mass participation and solidarity along with the influence of ideological leaders has declined.

Undermining unions as representatives of working-class aspirations involved shifting the ideological foundations of industrial relations, a policy programme deregulating the industrial relations environment, and the adaptive response of union leaders to a more competitive labour market. First, from the early 1980s, Conservative governments promoted a new ideological foundation for industrial relations. They favoured a labour market centering on free and voluntary trade-offs between employers and employees. This vision drew on the political philosophy of Hayek. Decisively breaking with the tradition of collectivist pluralism, this identified individual choice with freedom and denigrated labour organizations as coercive. Moreover, Conservative governments incrementally and systematically pursued a programme that undermined the external and internal factors facilitating the representation of working-class interests. Neoliberal policies changed unions by changing the objective circumstances in which they operated. Policies individualized and deregulated relations between employers and employees. These circumstances directed the participation of the key players of the industrial relations game – union leaders, members, and employers – into processes governed by market pricing rather than political or institutional criteria.

Thus, market transactions increasingly operated as a mode of indirect control. Individual, self-interested choices based on trade-offs between costs and benefits have become the primary determinant of unionization and union behaviour. Employees expect gains from membership, and employers demand commercial advantages. Lacking political and institutional support, union leaders in turn need members in order to influence employers and employer recognition in order to attract employees. They therefore market benefits packages to individuals and offer services to employers. Finally, unions adopt a business-like internal organization in order to enhance their capacity to engage in advantageous, competitive, and cost-effective trade-offs with employers and potential members.

8 The Privatization of Democracy

What is the overall picture of democracy suggested by this study of privatization in Britain since 1979? The concept of privatized democracy, developed in this chapter, provides an answer. This depicts how neoliberal changes in policy-making recast the nature of democracy by changing its operative forms of power relations. Examining the different ways the elements of power combine brings out the contrast between collectivist pluralism and privatized democracy. More specifically, privatized democracy involves government officials redesigning the state; while retaining formal power of authorization, supervision, and coercion, core state officials introduce indirect control through market-led policy-making processes. Privatized democracy, moreover, changes the structure of power. It diminishes individual and group freedom on which democracy depends. The market decision-making processes enable the state to disengage from and sidestep direct involvement and, at the same time, to institute a method of control that is more efficient and autonomous than administrative edict or political bargaining. Paradoxically, the freedom of choice offered by markets diminishes the self-controls associated with democratic ideals.

The chapter also summarizes the scope of privatized democracy. Four main patterns distinguish subtypes of privatized democracy, that is, major variations in the privatized patterns of policy-making, and bring out the way different patterns of market control have been applied to different problems. This clarifies the adaptability and complexity of privatized decision-making. Finally, the chapter points to the possible limits of neoliberal modes of political control and, in light of this discussion, considers the future of democracy in Britain.

PRIVATIZING BRITISH DEMOCRACY

Conceptions of pluralist democracy focus on the responsiveness of political decisions to societal values and pressures. Representation, with individuals and groups acting to redress grievances or to improve benefits, is uninhibited by state organization or policy. Issues arise in response to

171

societal concerns, reflecting its character and operations; issue groups set the agenda; and the political decision-making process involves inclusiveness and compromise, responsiveness and negotiation, accommodation and sharing out. In studies of British democracy, the important works of Samuel Beer (1969, 1982), Keith Middlemas (1979), and a host of policy community analysts (Rhodes, 1992; Budge and McKay, 1993; Jordan and Richardson, 1987) moved the analysis of British politics beyond a focus on cabinet government, with its controversy over collegial or prime ministerial rule and with the party as the ultimate aggregator of interests and determinant of policy. These studies made clear that democracy in Britain also required the careful study of interest groups. Middlemas emphasized the importance of quasi-corporatist practices that Beer had earlier characterized as the 'new group politics'. As we posited in Chapter 2, post-WWII collectivist pluralism in Britain entailed an inclusiveness of representation, the fullest consultation among those to be affected and a consensus on the policy to be implemented. At the same time, the social democratic era fuelled a diffusion of prosperity and inspired a movement toward the unleashing of individualism. Postwar collectivism, then, was representative and consensual, inclusive of a wide range of values, and for the most part group-dominated.

By the 1960s, the peculiar pluralistic practices of social democratic collectivism threatened the state's power to manage the political economy. As the old formula's failure became increasingly apparent, the democratic virtues it embodied became destructive. The 1970s witnessed corporatist attempts to recapture control, as efforts were made to contain interest group demands by offering public status and participation in policy-making in exchange for group enforcement of limits on members' demands. Using public status to create obligations and responsibility through cooptative relationships between the state and producer groups implied a limiting of issue representation. Yet, a corporatist strategy proved unable to regain a hold on the public order, and ideological ferment ensued, as the left became increasingly statist and the right increasingly neoliberal.

Despite a continuity in Westminster institutions and politics during the 1980s, Britain underwent a dramatic change in democratic practice. Instead of the collectivism that reached its zenith in the 1960s and early 1970s, market-based processes of making policy are dominant. The state created alternatives to the collectivist patterns by privatizing in different ways the nationalized industries, local governments, and welfare services. Central-government agencies became supervisors of privatized decision-making and service provision, with public activities shifting to the private

sector and public funding being subjected to market criteria. Desmond
S. King pinpoints recent changes and defines their direction:

> Privatization of council housing, reforms to the trades unions, the intro-
> duction of market practices into local government, the restructuring of the
> civil service under the Next Steps programme, the reform of the NHS and
> the integration of unemployment and welfare policy, collectively represent
> a fundamental rightward redefinition of British politics and institutions.
> While pragmatic calculations have informed the choices between policy
> options, most of these options have themselves belonged to a neoliberal
> framework. That is their significance.   (King, 1994, pp. 490–1)

Jeremy Moon offers a more general summary: 'The overwhelming conclu-
sion here is that by any yardstick from modern peace-time democracy, the
Thatcher decade was dramatic in public policy terms' (1993, p. 120; cf.
Douglas, 1989).

How should these changes be characterized? The neoliberal Cento
Veljanovski (1987) pictures a new consensus on a 'protective state', while
the marxist Andrew Gamble (1988) depicts Thatcherism as a caricature of
its own image: a strong state imposing a free market. Students of public
policy refer to the 'enabling state'; authors of a recent overview of policy
trends, for example, write that Thatcherism changed the state into a 'facili-
tator/enabler' rather than a 'front-line provider' (Atkinson and Savage,
1994, p. 11). One American scholar captures these trends in the phrase
'government by proxy' (Kettl, 1988). In a broad-ranging review of developments in subcentral and local government in Britain, Desmond King
distinguishes formal from informal local government. He writes: 'since
1979 the Conservatives have striven to weaken local government, to
impose private sector performance measures upon local authorities, and
to establish organisations administering public programmes previously
administered by local authorities' (1993, p. 214). These new organizations
comprise what he calls '*informal* local government and result in a
sub-national governmental network' (King, 1993b, p. 205).

In concluding their study of recent changes in the delivery of welfare
provision, Peter Taylor-Gooby and Robyn Lawson (1993) see power
moving both upward toward the core state and downward toward the
individual consumer. The decentralization of management and the use of
internal markets to allocate resources enables the core state to control provision and the periphery to adjust provision to local circumstances. Key
features that emerge include 'the use of contractual rather than bureaucratic and professional mechanisms to achieve policy goals, the evaluation

of quality by consumers rather than experts located within the service and, crucially, the separation of purchasing and providing agencies within a state-financed service' (Taylor-Gooby and Lawson, 1993, p. 134). One important effect is to minimize intermediary actors like local governments, trade unions and community groups.

While accurately capturing the divergence in policy-making between the center and new agencies of decentralized policy-making, these descriptions stop short of characterizing emerging power relations. They assume a model of direct power in which the core state effectively manages to implement and use market tools and resources to enforce its grip on peripheral units. This posits that political actors in all their variety are sovereign agents, contesting interests and imposing their will. Marxists, such as Gamble, interpret Thatcherism as evidencing an authoritarian state expanding market freedoms, which involve sovereign individuals voluntarily engaging in mutually advantageous exchanges. Pluralists, such as Budge and McKay (1993), see privatization contributing to a differentiated polity, one in which diverse groups and organizations subvert the ability of the core state to implement its will. Economic liberals, such as Veljanovski (1987), picture privatization as increasing individual freedom and democracy.

This study, however, shows that the neoliberal programme involved fundamental changes in the type and form of the power relations comprising the processes of democratic policy-making. Bifurcating policy processes involves changes in the balance between direct and indirect types of power and in the form of power. While the formal, collective, and direct power of the state has become more concentrated – though generally held in reserve and utilized occasionally – the informal, individual, and indirect controls effected through market or commercial practices have been expanded into a wide range of public policy-making spheres.

THE POWER STRUCTURE OF PRIVATIZED DEMOCRACY

In shifting from the direct controls of collectivist pluralism to the indirect methods of privatized democracy, Thatcherites increased state control. Rather than directly rejecting societal claims or imposing a state-centric institutional agenda, government leaders found in commercial processes a means for redefining and curbing societal claims. The government used market processes to restrain group demands and assert its own autonomy. By privatizing decision-making, government leaders provided a totalizing basis of activity, gave advantage to those with economic interests and skills, and established the criterion for concluding trade-offs. Increased external freedom of markets paradoxically reduces genuine freedom and self-control.

By contrast, the neoliberals' rhetoric about markets and power links individual choice, competition, and efficiency to greater democracy, freedom, and liberty. Consumers choose among alternative services or products; producers compete for customers. Market norms locate the grounds of collective action in the autonomy of individual human actors, agency relationships in voluntary and mutually beneficial initiatives and exchanges within objective exchange situations, and decision and action in accordance with the criterion of optimization. Individual energy and initiative within the 'rational' systems of commercial practices means that each agent is free to search for and participate in trade-offs yielding optimal returns. Market freedom, then, removes the imposition of bureaucratic and statist direction and offers individuals greater objective or external choices.

However, market situations constitute the structure of power by internal or ideational control. The neoliberal focus on the external obfuscates the internal side of human action, particularly the role of economic ideas and norms in defining situations and activity that preclude the freedom to develop a wide range of goals in response to their various consequences. Displacing direct state controls with the internal and self-motivated controls of economic transactions enhances political control. Economic logic provides a complex and effective yoke.

As a tool of reform and as a post-reform institution of policy-making, privatized decision-making operates through individual participation in an activity itself. A market regime acts as a medium structuring behaviour, yet is itself an effect constituted by the voluntary and spontaneous choices of individuals, motivated by ideas about participation in commercial logistics. Economic discourse and business practices establish a self-legitimating framework of activity that moves in accord with its own norms. Sustained through participants' own interests and initiatives, decision-making processes take on the self-enforcing and regenerative traits of markets. Participation in economic activity, then, becomes the carrier of control for decision-making.

The Thatcherite reform process grew deeper and wider over time and now amounts to a new post-collectivist political settlement. Privatization gained its own momentum as enthusiasm grew and the objective and internal conditions became more favourable to market reform. Shifting the balance of power in decision-making coincided with aims of improving efficiency and gaining political support (Feigenbaum and Henig, 1994).

The government's ability to institute and utilize market styles of choice grew out of the Thatcherites' ability to change the expectations governing the way individuals participated in the processes of decision-making. In part, the shift involved a 'flank movement', redirecting participants' individualism and self-interest into realizable goals that led, in turn, to changed patterns of working or habits. Involving agents in business transaction processes rather than acts of imposition or offers of pots of gold reshaped expectations and behaviour. The pace and scope of the programme, then, depended on the degree to which the Thatcherite proposals were able to gain support from key participants and to engage those already predisposed and skilled at private commercial transactions.

In prescribing an indirect mode of control, neoliberalism enhances state power, the ability to organize and order a complex array of interests and energies into a limited variety of purposive activities. It provides a strategy for separating individual interests from group bonds, giving individual subjective preferences priority, and making optimization the test of rational decision-making. In practice, privatization processes transforms political questions into matters of optimal trade-offs and, in turn, become self-governing regimens directing the necessary steps in decision-making. Thus, privatizing decision-making increases state power and narrows democracy because it constricts and fixes the political agenda, enables leaders to shape the political debate in ways that advantage their ability to govern, and institutes a self-operating method of final decision-making.

First, the norms and processes of private commercial transactions afford government an indirect way to limit representation to economic players, deflect noneconomic values, and assimilate new events or challenges. Market ideas and practices increase the amount of information that can be organized, yet require a closure of experimentation and self-control. Closure derives from the way market ideas provide the foundations of activity and exclude noneconomic values. The world of economic agents and trade-offs is reified, and actors behave as if choices were given by nature. In so doing, privatizing decision-making establishes individual preference maximization as the primary value. To realize this value requires organizing the energy of individuals into coordinated and productive processes of commercial exchanges in which rational actors take advantage of differences in efficiency, the ratio of costs to rewards. These activities require and generate economic expectations as participants impute economic motives to others and use market-beliefs to guide their own actions. In effect, market processes become an autonomous medium of indirect control.

Neoliberalism, thus, provides a totalizing logic. Commercial standards and practices are seen to constitute a self-renewing and self-organizing system of control. Proponents posit that all behaviour is or can be driven by economic interests, choices and rationality. The overall effect is to expand without limit the realm of market behaviour, by redefining situations as involving the self-interested behaviour of externally free agents. The separation of individual from society frees agents from group bonds and obligations. Objective self-rewarding trade-offs mediate between persons to the exclusion of all other social relationships and values. This means that people discount non-economic bonds of social solidarity in favour of individual self-interest. Economic actors objectify one another and calculate how exchanges can bring favourable returns. Social relations become instrumental opportunities for self-aggrandizement.

Second, privatizing policy-making shapes the public agenda in ways that benefit state interests. One source of advantage is that market processes mobilize the energies, initiatives, and resources of private sector actors. Market skills and resources, which are not equitably distributed, facilitate involvement and raise the probability of economic success. Markets, further, reward individual initiative and rationality by penalizing collaboration and frustrating non-economic interests. Since making choices involves weighing the efficiency of trade-offs in terms of personal resources and preferences, it appears natural for economic exchanges to produce differential outcomes. Still another advantage is that market processes mobilize individual self-interest into a governing process. It engulfs and rewards the accomplished players, the insiders, and excludes those with other concerns or who cannot play effectively. Another advantage for government is the depoliticization that accompanies market-based decision-making. Bifurcating and privatizing policy-making transforms public controversies into private commercial exchanges. This reduces the scope for political conflict, redirects claims for benefits away from the core state, and engages individuals in an order enforcing enterprise. Finally, government interest in retrenchment benefit because objective economic choices require actors to adjust their rewards to external constraints and opportunities, indirectly generating efficiency.

Third, the optimization criterion guiding economic transactions enables political leaders to control the character of decisions. Maximizing self-interest becomes the operational guideline or principle connecting subjective preferences and external opportunities. Instituting utility maximization as the primary and universal criterion of judgement makes efficiency standardized and self-enforcing. As a result, policy-making adapts to an environment of scarce resources by economizing and improving efficiency. Political leaders gain because the operating principle ensures that decisions are made correctly by self-governing actors who automatically discount noneconomic issues. Economic rationality optimizes the return on a given effort or minimizes the cost for a given output. By thus separating means from ends, optimization denies the relevance of substantive values and standardizes the judgement of each participant. This transforms the question of who makes final decisions into how well choices accord with the fixed criterion. Thus, optimization indirectly shapes the administration of decision-making and enhances government control.

Contrary to neoliberal ideology, then, market mechanisms of competition and choice involve players in routines that entail a loss of freedom, autonomy and equality. Market-based decision-making does not provide for an enhancement of democracy but rather its limitation. Individuals surrender internal control to the tutelage of economic ideas. The separation of the subjective and the objective dislocates the ability of agents to control their relation to their environment by alternative strategies. In consequence, the givens of market processes define interests, shape options for the interplay of initiative and response, and determine 'rational' decisions or choices. Genuine power of individuals to shape their own ends, to take their own unfettered initiatives, and to relate substantive ends to means is prevented.

In contrast to a pluralist system of inclusive societal interests, group initiatives, and government accommodation, then, privatized democracy changes the structure of power. It involves the government in initiating and participating in processes of market-led decision-making as a player and referee. Rather than having state decisions imposed on them, societal actors control themselves as they engage in market interactions. Democracy centres on market-defined transactions, not on pressure group politics, electoral contests, or interactions between citizens and representatives.

THE VARIATION AND ADAPTABILITY OF PRIVATIZED DECISION-MAKING

The Conservative's neoliberal programme increasingly bifurcated policy-making between the government functioning as a steward of market-based processes of choice and private sector participants operating under the tutelage of commercial mechanisms. Despite a common tendency to limit freedom, privatizing policy-making took a variety of patterns. The challenge of establishing control in different policy arenas meant using different economic processes. Categorizing varieties of privatizing decision-making refines the picture of controlling through markets and emphasizes the adaptability of the neoliberal programme.

Variation in the neoliberal programme depends on the ways the optimizing principle connects and organizes the relations between subjective preferences and external opportunities. This depends on the *arenas* of activity which provide the context for economic activity. The main arenas are capital, service, producer, and resource markets. Different contexts call for different *strategies* for utilizing market participation. The main strategies identified in this study are divestment, delegation, displacement, and charging. Each, in turn, identifies methods of structuring decision-making. These can be analyzed as *separations* between public and private ownership, authorizing and delivering services, alternative producers competing for consumers, and prices signalling demand for supply. (See Tables 8.1 and 8.2.)

The first strategy focuses on the sell-offs of state-owned assets. This shifts control to capital markets and shareholders through divestment from state ownership. The bases of action are the maintenance and development of property. The sell-offs remove political, bureaucratic, and noneconomic questions from the decision-making process. The ability, next, to set the agenda favours the shareholders over consumers and social interests. Decision-making, then, turns on striving to maximize profits through expanding the capacity to accumulate the rewards of capital accruing to property holders. Finally, this is a transitional mode relying on processes of commercial selling to achieve the desired end. In this process, property holders gain, particularly large institutional investors, although share ownership has become more common among the population at large.

The second pattern involves control through using market relations to structure principal-agent obligations. This concerns regulatory politics and applies to the new regulatory authorities overseeing the public utilities and to the central and subcentral governments contracting out of basic services. In this instance, the basis of action is the use of material incentives to motivate economically efficient behaviour. Initiatives come from the authorities, such as the regulations increasing competition or prescribing competitive tendering, and from the market players taking up opportunities offered. Decisions, therefore, turn on increasing efficiency and competition without injuring the incumbent or entering producers. Finally, the effects favour entrepreneurs, those with skills and the social and financial resources, because they are more efficient organizationally or technologically.

The third pattern involves opening product markets to competition and letting consumer decisions about purchases determine the policy product or outcome. The notion of competition is paramount in economic thinking because it fosters internal and allocative efficiency. Competition among producers for consumers' business corresponds to the ideal notion of pure exchange relations. It is so fundamental to liberal economics that it often is taken as the essence of economic relations and lead to calls for its enhancement. Competition in practice, although firmly grounded in economic logic, is difficult to introduce or maintain. The first government initiatives to open markets produced little change, with the exception of busing. This revealed the power of market incumbents to take action to protect their market shares. Over time, as the neoliberal programme gained force, policies displaced monopolies by breaking up producers or creating opportunities for new producers. Restructuring for enhanced competition created separate and alternative producers from which purchasers could choose. Displacement of economic activities precludes collaborative arrangements that distort pure market exchanges. In theory, the effects of competition favour consumers, who benefit from wide choices and low prices.

The fourth pattern applies to the way individuals choose to use their resources and how the subsequent demand affects the provision of collective goods. According to economic theory, exchange involves individuals making mutually advantageous choices. Prices depend on demand and supply and enable people to choose. Moreover, prices or charges for commodities give the initiative to the consumers. Their willingness to pay a particular price or to bargain for a lower price enables them to signal preferences that determine what producers will supply. Finally, pricing goods favours those with plentiful resources in contrast to those who have little or no resources. It also makes pooling of resources difficult, unless selective incentives can be mobilized by leaders. In short, pricing undercuts free riding and makes voluntary organizations pay their way.

By establishing, regulating and occasionally reshaping these systems, the state frames complex regimens of economic behaviour which indirectly control interest formation, expression, and decision-making. Requiring less direct state control, this self-operating system is a more efficient and effective method of control. Privatization limits the claims typical of pluralism, while preventing forms of collaboration and inclusiveness through organizational connections typical of corporatism. It establishes the framework in which the relationship between costs and rewards are transparent and primary, encouraging actors to adapt by

Table 8.1   Varieties of market decision-making

Arenas	Strategies	Separations
Capital Markets	Divestment	Private vs Public Ownership
Service Markets	Delegation	Authorization vs Provision
Producer Markets	Displacement	Producers vs Consumers
Resource Markets	Pricing	Demand vs Supply

Table 8.2   Effects of market processes

Arenas	Effects	Rewards	Penalizes
Capital Markets	Property Primacy	Property	Consumers/No Property
Service Markets	No Self-Administration/ Principal gets more from agent	Efficiency	Noneconomic Values
Producer Markets	No collusion No monopoly/ Creates Competitors	Competitive Advantages	Competitive Disadvantages
Resource Markets	No Free-Riders No Subsidies/ Groups provide services in exchange for members' payment	Wealth/Skills	No resources

orienting themselves toward providing saleable services or goods and then accumulating or pyramiding the returns (Wolfe, 1989, pp. 161–8). The wide diffusion of privatized decision-making signals a significant restructuring of British democracy.

CHALLENGING PRIVATIZED DEMOCRACY

The privatization programme in Britain heralds a new, more effective form of state power. The application of market accountability to decision-making fundamentally alters the nature of state power and democracy. Privatization shifts the operation of power away from direct state imposition toward indirect control. Depoliticized, depersonalized, individualized, and ultimately opaque market transactions displace state intervention, centralized administration, and the extension of public status to private groups. While new right ideologists hail these developments as an increase in freedom, I argue the opposite.

By reorganizing power relations in Britain over a wide range of policy making arenas, choice and competition function as a medium of indirect control that diminishes representation and restricts the criteria for decision-making. Key political elites introduced economic accountability to redesign the internal controls regulating collective decision-making, thereby enhancing state autonomy while limiting representation of social interests. Once set in motion economic situations shape the course of interaction and in the process take on and fulfil political purposes. Actors' choices are manipulated from above and then reproduced from within. Merging political and economic spheres, privatization recasts what values count, what sorts of interests and actors take the lead, and what criterion applies when actors make choices. In so doing, privatization succeeds by drawing upon the involvement and resources of the participants themselves. The privatization strategy enables the government to lure key economic actors into operating new forms of decision-making.

This picture of the changing character of democracy in Britain suggests that privatized power is more efficient and effective than the inclusive push and pull of collectivist pluralism. Privatizing power depoliticized formerly controversial state activities, limited material demands, and excluded non-economic or social values. Most importantly, the state, using economic activity as decision-making, enhanced its own power. To focus on privatization as a solution to the problems of economic revitalization ignores how privatization in Britain strengthened the state by overcoming problems of ungovernability.

The future direction of democracy in Britain depends on the extent to which governability again becomes problematic. The manifestation of ungovernability varied under collectivist pluralism, as did the ability of government authorities to respond with indirect controls. Taking place within formally complex representative systems, different mixes of direct and indirect power produce differences in effectiveness of control. From this viewpoint, institutional procedures and traditions represent a formalized medium through which political actors work out their solutions to problems of governability.

Constitutional and policy style differences among states affect the process of privatizing decision-making (Moran and Prosser, 1994). The move toward deregulation in the United States in the late 1970s reflected a growing concern about the effectiveness of regulatory controls. There, with a long tradition of public utility regulation, very little public sector ownership and a federal system with a legalistic approach to administering policies, it was in the area of regulation that signs of stagnation and inefficiency emerged (McKie, 1989; Graham and Prosser, 1991, ch. 7). In France, by contrast, the sell-off of state industry developed in response to a decline in the effectiveness of traditional French state interventionist controls. Constitutional limits on privatizing public services and pricing provisions were laid out by the *Conseil Constitutionnel* (Graham and Prosser, 1991, chs 3 and 8). In short, national differences matter in privatizing because national differences involve differences in the problem of governability and responsiveness to it.

If institutional differences do not impede the shift toward the development of the neoliberal framework of bifurcated and indirect power relations, it is possible that the emergence of new issues will generate problems of state control. New issues facing Britain – the ethnic and nationalistic movements and the constitutional questions about the monarchy, the electoral system, and the union with Scotland and Northern Ireland – may be not be assimilated by the preclusiveness that characterizes market styles of activity. Indeed, David Beetham (1993) suggests just this – that the totalizing logic of the market has been superseded by issues of nationalist and ethnic rights to representation and self-government. However, the solidaristic ties of ethnic identity and other constitutional issues so far emergent challenge the sovereignty of the state center. While prefiguring a restructuring of the state, accommodations to cultural politics do not necessarily entail wider popular participation and influence in decision-making, nor are such changes likely to undo the tightening of control resulting from the privatization of decision-making.

A further contention is that market-driven decision-making may well have its own limits, thereby generating weak government. The diminishment of democratic consensus in favour of individualistic self-interest may have opened up new debates about consummatory values and lessened the prospect of applying alternative policy instruments to meet future economic, political, and constitutional issues of the 1990s (Dunleavy, 1993, pp. 13–15). Rod Rhodes (1994) writes that privatization has led to the 'hollowing out of the state'. Marketizing and bifurcating administration, he suggests, reduces representation, fragments and duplicates implementation, eliminates centralized coordination, distorts communication, and thereby creates a possible threat to governing capacity. Looking at developments similar to those surveyed in this study, Rhodes comes to the opposite conclusion. His thinking appears to assume that the strong state is the large, bureaucratic state of collectivist pluralism. To the contrary, despite questions about a permanent reversal of long-term economic decline and about the place of Britain in the EU, there can be no doubt that the British state has gained a relative preeminence over the groups that once threatened its viability.

Each of these purported challenges offers little prospect for diminishing the enhanced power of a neoliberal government or for generating a fuller democracy because they ignore the fundamental change in the type and form of power that has occurred. The older notion of power gives primacy to sovereign agents or to objective structures by separating state from society and state from market. Even recent discussions of the 'end of ideology' picture power in terms of the economic model of power. In this utilitarian model, sovereign agents interact as direct forces through exchange relations. The conventional view of power presupposes a model of physical force acting between external objects. The resulting image is one of overt causation: the use of direct force to protect oneself or to subjugate others.

The possible challenges to privatized democracy obfuscate the shift of state power to a more specific and efficient indirect mode. The power of privatized democracy arises from organizing participation in the work of society. This transmutes individual energy into organized and productive activity. Drawing on internal control, this self-acting collective force achieves a degree of order and work that direct state imposition could never match. Yet, participation in marketized decision-making undermines individual and group autonomy. It forecloses the ability to question conditions and their consequences. Freedom, individual and collective, narrows.

Challenging privatized democracy, then, must come from exposing and addressing the sources of its power, from the way market capitalism operates as an indirect mode of state control. The important question is whether the methods of organizing energies for collective ends can be controlled in a way that refurbishes or even advances popular control. Market-based democracy, in constricting the influence of non-economic interests in policy-making, ultimately challenges citizens to control the future of democracy themselves.

Once we see that human association depends on the way ideas shape activities, power can be thought of as not only direct force but as purposive organized energy. Power reflects and realizes the ways in which collective control and coordination generate effects. Through intelligent control, power can improve the possibilities of life. Language and ideas convey meanings, the positing of connections between events, that permit the assessment of activities. Ideas or meanings are tools for indicating what is happening and what may happen, thereby making possible the intelligent control of consequences. Optimistically, a pragmatist perspective encourages the intelligent control of power in order to solve public problems and enlarge individual autonomy.

Bibliography

Abromeit, Heidrun (1988) 'British Privatisation Policy', *Parliamentary Affairs* 41:1 (January), pp. 68–85.

Almond, Gabriel (1991) 'Capitalism and Democracy', *PS: Political Science and Politics* 24 (September), pp. 467–74.

Ascher, Kate (1987) *The Politics of Privatisation: Contracting Out Public Services* (New York: St Martin's Press).

Atkinson, Rob (1990) 'Government During the Thatcher Years', in S.P. Savage and L. Robins (eds) *Public Policy Under Thatcher* (New York: St Martin's Press), pp. 8–22.

Atkinson, Rob and Savage, S.P. (1994) 'The Conservatives and Public Policy', in S.P. Savage, R. Atkinson, and Lynton Robins (eds) *Public Policy in Britain* (New York: St Martin's Press), pp. 3–14.

Atkinson, Rodney (1984) *The Moral Basis of Monetarism* (Tyne and Wear: Compuprint Publishing).

Auerbach, Simon (1993) 'Mrs Thatcher's Labour Laws: Slouching Towards Utopia?', *The Political Quarterly* 64:1, pp. 37–48.

Bagwell, Philip S. (1984) *End Of The Line?* (London: Verso).

Baker, Kenneth (1993) *The Turbulent Years: My Life in Politics* (London: Faber and Faber).

Banister, David and Pickup, Laurie (1990) 'Bus Transport in the Metropolitan Areas and London', in P. Bell and P. Cloke (eds) *Deregulation and Transport: Market Forces in the Modern World* (London: David Fulton), pp. 67–83.

Barry, Norman (1990) 'Ideology', in P. Dunleavy, A. Gamble and G. Peele (eds) *Developments in British Politics 3* (New York: St Martin's Press), pp. 17–41.

Bassett, Philip (1987) *Strike Free: New Industrial Relations in Britain* (London: Papermac).

Bealey, Frank (1976) *The Post Office Engineering Union: The History of the Post Office Engineers 1870–1970* (London: Bachman and Turner).

Beaumont, P.B. (1987) *The Decline of Trade Union Organisation* (London: Croom Helm).

Beer, Samuel H. (1969) *British Politics in the Collectivist Age* (New York: Alfred A. Knopf).

Beer, Samuel H. (1982) *Britain Against Itself* (New York: Norton).

Beesley, Michael (1981) *Liberalisation of the Use of the British Telecommunications Network* (London: HMSO).

Beesley, Michael (1992) *Privatization, Regulation and Deregulation* (London: Routledge).

Beesley, Michael (ed.) (1993) *Major Issues in Regulation* (London: IEA).

Beesley, Michael and Littlechild, Stephen (1983) 'Privatization: Principles, Problems, and Priorities', *Lloyds Bank Review* (July), pp. 1–20.

Beesley, Michael and Littlechild, Stephen (1991) 'The Regulation of Privatized Monopolies in the United Kingdom', in C. Veljanovski (ed.) *Regulators and The Market* (London: IEA), pp. 29–58.

Beetham, David (1993) 'Political Theory and British Politics', in P. Dunleavy, A. Gamble, I. Holliday, and G. Peele (eds) *Developments in British Politics 4* (New York: St Martin's Press), pp. 353–70.

Bell, Philip and Cloke, Paul (1990a) 'Regulation and Control of Transport in Britain', in *idem* (eds) *Deregulation and Transport: Market Forces in the Modern World* (London: David Fulton), pp. 28–52.

Bell, Philip and Cloke, Paul (1990b) 'Bus Deregulation in Rural Localities: An Example from Wales', in *idem* (eds) *Deregulation and Transport: Market Forces in the Modern World* (London: David Fulton), pp. 100–21.

Bell, Philip and Cloke, Paul (1990c) 'Deregulation: Problems, Warnings and a Continuing Case for Regulation', in *idem* (eds) *Deregulation and Transport: Market Forces in the Modern World* (London: David Fulton), pp. 194–206.

Benn, Tony (1994) *The End of an Era: 1980–90* (London: Arrow).

Bishop, Matthew and Kay, John (1989) 'Privatization in the United Kingdom: Lessons from Experience', *World Development* 17:5, pp. 643–57.

Bleaney, Michael (1983) 'Conservative Economic Strategy', in S. Hall and M. Jacques (eds) *The Politics of Thatcherism* (London: Lawrence and Wishart), pp. 132–47.

Bös, Dieter (1991) *Privatization: A Theoretical Treatment* (Oxford: Clarendon Press).

British Telecommunications Unions Committee (1984) *The Battle for British Telecom* (London).

Brittan, Samuel (1984) 'The Politics and Economics of Privatisation', *The Political Quarterly* 55:2 (April–June), pp. 109–128.

Brittan, Samuel (1987) *The Role and Limits of Government: Essays in Political Economy* (Aldershot: Wildwood House).

Brooke, Rodney (1991) 'The Enabling Authority', *Public Administration* 69 (Winter), pp. 525–32.

Brown, William (1986) 'The Changing Role of Trade Unions in the Management of Labour', *British Journal of Industrial Relations* 24:2, pp. 161–68.

Brown, William (1987) 'Pay Determination: British Workplace Industrial Relations 1980–84, Chapter 9', *British Journal of Industrial Relations* 25:2 (July), pp. 291–4.

Brown, William (1993) 'The Contraction of Collective Bargaining in Britain', *British Journal of Industrial Relations* 31:2, pp. 189–200.

Bruce-Gardyne, Jock (1984) *Mrs Thatcher's First Administration: The Prophets Confounded* (London: Macmillan).

Buckland, Roger and Davis, Edward W. (1984) 'Privatisation Techniques and the PSBR', *Fiscal Studies* 5:3, pp. 44–53.

Budge, Ian and McKay, David (1993) *The Developing British Political System: The 1990s*, 3rd edition (New York: Longman).

Bulford, Chris (1983) 'British Telecom', in S. Hastings and H. Levie (eds) *Privatisation?* (London: Spokesman), pp. 130–7.

Bulpitt, Jim (1986) 'The Discipline of the New Democracy: Mrs Thatcher's Domestic Statecraft', *Political Studies* 34:1, pp. 19–39.

Button, Kenneth (1988) 'Contestability in the UK Bus Industry, Experience Goods and Economies of Experience', in J.S. Dodgson and N. Topham (eds) *Bus*

Deregulation and Privatisation: An International Perspective (Aldershot: Avebury), pp. 69–96.

Carsberg, Bryan (1988) 'OFTEL in an Evolving Environment'. Address to the 21st Telephone Managers Association Conference, November.

Carsberg, Bryan (1991) 'OFTEL: Competition and the Duopoly Review', in C. Veljanovski (ed.) *Regulators and The Market* (London: IEA), pp. 98–106.

Carsberg, Bryan (1993) 'Promoting Entry into Regulated Industries', in M. Beesley (ed.) *Major Issues in Regulation* (London: IEA), pp. 89–98.

Clegg, Stewart R. (1989) *Frameworks of Power* (London: Sage).

Clutterbuck, D. (1991) *Going Private: Privatisations Around the World* (London: Mercury).

Cousins, Christine (1990) 'The Contracting-out of Ancillary Services in the NHS', in G. Jenkins and M. Poole (eds) *New Forms of Ownership: Management and Employment* (London: Routledge), pp. 97–111.

Crewe, Ivor and Searing, Donald (1988) 'Ideological Change in the British Conservative Party', *American Political Science Review* 82:2, pp. 361–84.

Crewe, Ivor (1988) 'Has the Electorate Become Thatcherite?', in Skidelsky (ed.) *Thatcherism* (London: Chatto and Windus), pp. 25–50.

Crouch, Colin (1979) *The Politics of Industrial Relations* (London: Fontana).

Crouch, Colin (1986) 'The Future Prospects For Trade Unions in Western Europe', *The Political Quarterly* 57:1 (January–March), pp. 5–17.

Dahl, Robert A. (1984) *Modern Political Analysis*, 4th edition (Englewood Cliffs, NJ: Prentice-Hall).

Davies, Paul and Freedland, Mark (1993) *Labour Legislation and Public Policy* (Oxford: Clarendon).

Davis, Evan (1986) 'Express Coaching Since 1980: Liberalisation in Practice', in J. Kay, C. Mayer, and D. Thompson (eds) *Privatisation and Regulation* (Oxford: Clarendon Press), pp. 147–61.

Department of Employment (1989) *Removing Barriers to Employment: Proposals for Further Reform of Industrial Relations and Trade Union Law* Cm 655 (London: HMSO).

Department of Employment (1991) *Industrial Relations in the 1980s: The Achievement of Reform* Cm 1602 (London: HMSO).

Departments of Employment, Scotland and Wales (1992) *People, Jobs, and Opportunity* Cm 1810 (London: HMSO).

Department of Industry (1982) *The Future of Telecommunications in Britain* (London: HMSO), Cmnd 8610.

Department of Transport (1984) *Buses* (London: HMSO).

Dewey, John (1903) *Studies in Logical Theory*. Reprinted in *Essays on Logical Theory 1902–1903: The Middle Works of John Dewey 1899–1924*, Volume 2 (Carbondale: Southern Illinois University Press, 1983).

Dewey, John (1916a) *Democracy and Education*. Reprinted in *Democracy and Education 1916: The Middle Works of John Dewey 1899*, Volume 9 (Carbondale: Southern Illinois University Press, 1985).

Dewey, John (1916b) 'Force, Violence and Law'. Reprinted in *Essays on Philosophy and Education 1916–1917: The Middle Works of John Dewey 1899–1924*, Volume 10 (Carbondale: Southern Illinois University Press, 1985), pp. 211–15.

Dewey, John (1916c) 'Force and Coercion'. Reprinted in *Essays on Philosophy and Education 1916–1917: The Middle Works of John Dewey 1899–1924*, Volume 10 (Carbondale: Southern Illinois University Press, 1985), pp. 244–51.

Dewey, John (1917) 'The Need for a Recovery of Philosophy'. Reprinted in *Essays on Philosophy and Education 1916–1917: The Middle Works of John Dewey 1899–1924*, Volume 10 (Carbondale: Southern Illinois University Press, 1985), pp. 3–48.

Dewey, John (1922) *Human Nature and Conduct*. Reprinted in *Human Nature and Conduct 1922: The Middle Works of John Dewey 1899–1924*, Volume 14 (Carbondale: Southern Illinois University Press, 1988).

Dewey, John (1938) *Experience and Education*. Reprinted in *John Dewey: The Later Works, 1925–1953*, Volume 13 (Carbondale: Southern Illinois University Press, 1988), pp. 1–62.

Dobek, Mariusz Mark (1993a) 'Privatization as a Political Priority: the British Experience', *Political Studies* 41:1 (March), pp. 24–40.

Dobek, Mariusz Mark (1993b) *The Political Logic of Privatization: Lessons from Great Britain and Poland* (Westport, CT: Praeger).

Dorey, Peter (1993) 'One Step at a Time: The Conservative Government's Approach to the Reform of Industrial Relations Since 1979', *The Political Quarterly* 64:1, pp. 24–36.

Douglas, James (1989) 'Review Article: The Changing Tide – Some Recent Studies of Thatcherism', *British Journal of Political Science* 19:3, pp. 399–424.

Dunleavy, Patrick (1986) 'Explaining the Privatization Boom: Public Choice Versus Radical Approaches', *Public Administration* 64 (Spring), pp. 13–34.

Dunleavy, Patrick (1989) 'The Architecture of the British Central State. Part II: Empirical Findings', *Public Administration* 67 (Winter), pp. 391–433.

Dunleavy, Patrick (1991) *Democracy, Bureaucracy and Public Choice* (London: Harvester Wheatsheaf).

Dunleavy, Patrick (1993) 'Introduction: Stability, Crisis or Decline?', in P. Dunleavy, A. Gamble, I. Holliday, and G. Peele (eds) *Developments in British Politics 4* (New York: St Martin's Press), pp. 1–16.

Dunn, Mike and Smith, Sandy (1990) 'Economic Policy and Privatization', in S.P. Savage and L. Robins (eds) *Public Policy Under Thatcher* (New York: St Martin's Press), pp. 23–44.

Dunn, Stephen (1993) 'From Donovan to ... Wherever', *British Journal of Industrial Relations* 31:2, pp. 169–87.

Economist (May 20, 1989) 'Survey: Business in Britain'.

Economist (August 12, 1993) 'The Privatisation Fashion', pp. 18–20.

Economist (October 5, 1991) 'Telecommunications Survey'.

Edwards, P.; Hall, M.; Hyman, R.; Marginson, P.; Sisson, K.; Waddington, J.; and Winchester, D. (1992) 'Great Britain: Still Muddling Through', in A. Ferner and R. Hyman (eds) *Industrial Relation in the New Europe* (Oxford: Blackwell), pp. 1–68.

Ernst, John (1994) *Whose Utility? The Social Impact of Public Utility Privatization and Regulation in Britain* (Buckingham: Open University Press).

Feigenbaum, Harvey and Henig, Jeffrey (1994) 'The Political Underpinnings of Privatization: A Typology', *World Politics* 46 (January), pp. 185–208.

Financial Times, October 7, 1991, 'World Telecommunications Survey'.

Financial Times, October 7, 1992, 'World Telecommunications Survey'.

Fleming, Michael and Button, Kenneth (1989) 'Regulatory Reform in the UK', in K. Button and D. Swann (eds) *The Age of Regulatory Reform* (Oxford: Oxford University Press), pp. 79–103.

Foreman-Peck, James and Manning, Dorothy (1988) 'How Well is BT Performing? An International Comparison of Telecommunications Total Factor Productivity', *Fiscal Studies* 9, pp. 54–67.

Foster, Deborah (1993) 'Industrial Relations in Local Government: The Impact of Privatisation', *The Political Quarterly* 64:1, pp. 49–59.

Foster, C.D. (1992) *Privatization, Public Ownership and the Regulation of Natural Monopoly* (Oxford: Blackwell).

Foucault, Michel (1979) *Discipline and Punish: the Birth of the Prison* (New York: Vintage).

Fry, Geoffrey K. (1988) 'Inside Whitehall', in H. Drucker, P. Dunleavy, A. Gamble, and G. Peele (eds) *Developments in British Politics 2*, revised edition (New York: St Martin's Press), pp. 88–106.

Gamble, Andrew (1983) 'Thatcherism and Conservative Politics', in S. Hall and M. Jacques (eds) *The Politics of Thatcherism* (London: Lawrence and Wishart), pp. 109–31.

Gamble, Andrew (1985) 'Smashing the State: Thatcher's Radical Crusade', *Marxism Today* (June), pp. 21–6.

Gamble, Andrew (1988) *The Free Economy and the Strong State* (London: Macmillan).

Gamble, Andrew (1989) 'Privatization, Thatcherism, and the British State', *Journal of Law and Society* 19:1, pp. 1–20.

Gilbert, Robbie (1993) 'Workplace Industrial Relations 25 Years After Donovan', *British Journal of Industrial Relations* 31:2, pp. 235–53.

Glaister, Stephen (1991) 'UK Bus Deregulation: The Reasons and the Experience', *Investigaciones Economicas* 15:2 (May), pp. 285–308.

Graham, Cosmo and Prosser, Tony (1991) *Privatizing Public Enterprises* (Oxford: Clarendon Press).

Grant, Wyn (1989) 'The Erosion of Intermediary Institutions', *The Political Quarterly* 60:1, pp. 10–21.

Grimstone, Gerry (1990) 'The British Privatization Programme', in J.J. Richardson (ed.) *Privatisation and Deregulation in Canada and Britain* (Aldershot: Dartmouth), pp. 3–13.

Hall, Peter (1986) *Governing the Economy: The Politics of State Intervention in Britain and France* (New York: Oxford University Press).

Hall, Stuart (1983) 'The Great Moving Right Show', in S. Hall and M. Jacques (eds) *The Politics of Thatcherism* (London: Lawrence and Wishart), pp. 19–39.

Hall, Stuart and Jacques, Martin (eds) (1983) *The Politics of Thatcherism* (London: Lawrence and Wishart).

Hallett, Richard (1990) 'Privatization and the Restructuring of a Public Utility: A Case Study of British Telecom's Corporate Strategy and Structure', in G. Jenkins and M. Poole (eds) *New Forms of Ownership: Management and Employment* (London: Routledge), pp. 112–33.

Harrison, Anthony (1988) 'Deregulating Bus Services', in C. Whitehead (ed.) *Reshaping the Nationalised Industries* (Hermitage, UK: Policy Journals), pp. 122–37.

Hartley, Keith (1990) 'Contracting-out in Britain: Achievements and Problems', in J.J. Richardson (ed.) *Privatisation and Deregulation in Canada and Britain* (Aldershot: Dartmouth), pp. 177–98.

Hartley, Nicholas and Culham, Peter (1988) 'Telecommunications Prices under Monopoly and Competition', *Oxford Review of Economic Policy* 4:2 (Summer), pp. 1–19.

Haywood, Peter (1987) 'Trying to Put a Great Past Behind Us: The NCU and Change in British Telecom', unpublished draft.

Heald, David (1983) *Public Expenditure: Its Defence and Reform* (Oxford: Martin Robertson).

Heald, David (1985) 'Will the Privatization of Public Enterprises Solve the Problem of Control?', *Public Administration* 63, pp. 7–22.

Heald, David (1989) 'The United Kingdom: Privatisation and its Political Context', in J. Vickers and V. Wright (eds) *The Politics of Privatisation in Western Europe* (London: Frank Cass), pp. 31–48.

Heald, D.A. and Steel, D.R. (1982) 'Privatising Public Enterprises: An Analysis of the Government's Case', *The Political Quarterly* 53:3, pp. 333–49.

Heald, David and Thomas, David (1985) 'Privatization as Theology', Paper presented at University of York, September 2–4.

Heery, Edmund and Kelly, John (1994) 'Professional, Participative and Managerial Unionism: An Interpretation of Change in Trade Unions', *Work, Employment & Society* 8:1 (March), pp. 1–22.

Heilbroner, Robert (1961) *The Worldly Philosophers* (New York: Simon and Schuster).

Helm, Dieter (1994) 'British Utility Regulation: Theory, Practice, and Reform', *Oxford Review of Economic Policy* 10:3, pp. 17–39.

Helm, Dieter and Yarrow, George (1988) 'The Assessment: The Regulation of Utilities', *Oxford Review of Economic Policy* 4:2 (Summer), pp. i–xxxi.

Hibbs, John (1990) 'Deregulation: Prospects, Possibilities and the Way Ahead', in P. Bell and P. Cloke (eds) *Deregulation and Transport: Market Forces in the Modern World* (London: David Fulton), pp. 183–93.

Hills, Jill (1986) *Deregulating Telecoms: Competition and Control in the United States, Japan, and Britain* (Westport, CT: Quorum).

Hills, Jill (1992) *Residential Users and BT's Network* (London: Director General of Telecommunications).

Holmes, Martin (1985) *The First Thatcher Government, 1979–1983: Contemporary Conservatism and Economic Change* (Brighton: Wheatsheaf Books).

Hoover, Kenneth and Plant, Raymond (1989) *Conservative Capitalism in Britain and the United States: a Critical Appraisal* (London: Routledge).

Horton, Sylvia (1990) 'Local Government 1979–89: A Decade of Change', in S.P. Savage and L. Robins (eds) *Public Policy Under Thatcher* (New York: St Martin's Press), pp. 172–86.

Howe, Rt. Hon. Geoffrey (1982) *Conservatism in the Eighties* (London: Conservative Political Centre).

Howell, Chris (forthcoming). 'Unforgiven: British Trade Unionism in Crisis', Oberlin College, pp. 1–118.

Hyman, Richard (1986) 'Reflections on the Mining Strike', in R. Miliband, J. Saville, M. Liebman, and L. Panitch (eds) *Socialist Register 1985/86* (London: Merlin Press), pp. 330–54.

Jacques, Martin (1983) 'Thatcherism – Breaking Out of the Impasse', in S. Hall and M. Jacques (eds) *The Politics of Thatcherism* (London: Lawrence and Wishart), pp. 40–62.

Jenkins, Peter (1989) *Mrs Thatcher's Revolution: The Ending of the Socialist Era* (London: Pan Books).

Jessop, Bob; Bonnett, Kevin; Bromley, Simon; and Ling, Tom (1988) *Thatcherism: A Tale of Two Nations* (Cambridge: Polity Press).

Johnson, Christopher (1991) *The Economy Under Mrs Thatcher 1979–1990* (Harmondsworth: Penguin).

Jones, G.W. (1989) 'A Revolution in Whitehall? Changes in British Central Government Since 1979', *West European Politics* 12:3, pp. 238–61.

Jordan, A.G. and Richandson, J.J.(1987) *Government and Pressure Groups in Britain* (Oxford: Clarendon Press).

Kavanagh, Dennis (1990) *Thatcherism and British Politics: The End of Consensus?*, 2nd edition (Oxford: Oxford University Press).

Kavanagh, Dennis (1994) 'A Major Agenda?', in D. Kavanagh and A. Seldon (eds) *The Major Effect* (London: Macmillan), pp. 3–17.

Kay, John (1984) 'The Privatization of British Telecommunications' in D. Steel and D. Heald (eds) *Privatizing Public Enterprises* (London: RIPA), pp. 77–85.

Kay, John and Thompson, D.J. (1986) 'Privatisation: A Policy in Search of a Rationale', *The Economic Journal* 96 (March), pp. 18–32.

Kay, John and Vickers, John (1988) 'Regulatory Reform in Britain', *Economic Policy* 7, pp. 286–351.

Kay, J.A.; Mayer, C.; and Thompson, D. (eds) (1986) *Privatisation and Regulation: The UK Experience* (Oxford: Oxford University Press).

Keegan, William (1984) *Mrs Thatcher's Economic Experiment* (Harmondsworth: Penguin).

Kelly, John (1987) 'Trade Unions Through the Recession, 1980–1984', *British Journal of Industrial Relations* 25 (July), pp. 278–82.

Kessler, Sid (1993) 'Procedures and Third Parties', *British Journal of Industrial Relations* 31:2, pp. 211–25.

Kettl, Donald F. (1988) 'Government by Proxy and the Public Service', *International Review of Administrative Sciences* 54:4 (December), pp. 501–15.

Kilvington, Russell and Cross, A.K. (1986) *Deregulation of Express Coach Services in Britain* (Aldershot: Gower).

King, Desmond S. (1987) *The New Right: Politics, Markets and Citizenship* (London: Macmillan).

King, Desmond S. (1989) 'Political Centralization and State Interests in Britain: the 1986 Abolition of the GLC and MCCs', *Comparative Political Studies* 21:4, pp. 486–91.

King, Desmond S. (1993a) 'The Conservatives and Training Policy 1979–1992: From a Tripartite to a Neoliberal Regime', *Political Studies* 41:2 (June), pp. 214–35.

King, Desmond S. (1993b) 'Government beyond Whitehall', in P. Dunleavy, A. Gamble, I. Holliday, and G. Peele (eds) *Developments in British Politics 4* (New York: St Martin's Press), pp. 194–218.

King, Desmond S. (1994) 'The New Right and Public Policy', *Political Studies* 42, pp. 486–91.

Krieger, Joel (1986) *Reagan, Thatcher and the Politics of Decline* (New York: Oxford University Press).
Kuhn, Thomas S. (1970) *The Structure of Scientific Revolutions*, 2nd edition (Chicago: University of Chicago Press).
Lawson, Nigel (1992) *The View from No. 11: Memoirs of a Tory Radical* (London: Bantam Press).
Lee, Geoff (1994) 'Privatisation', in B. Jones (ed.) *Political Issues in Britian Today*, 4th edition (Manchester: Manchester University Press), pp. 243–87.
Le Grand, Julian (1982) *The Strategy of Equality: Redistribution and the Social Services* (London: George Allen and Unwin).
Letwin, Oliver (1988) *Privatising the World* (London: Cassell).
Letwin, Shirley (1992) *The Anatomy of Thatcherism* (London: Fontana).
Lewis, Norman and Harden, Ian (1983) 'Privatisation, De-regulation and Constitutionality: Some Anglo-American Comparisons', *Northern Ireland Legal Quarterly* 34:3 (Autumn), pp 207–29.
Lewis, Roy (1991) 'Reforming Industrial Relations: Law, Politics, and Power', *Oxford Review of Economic Policy* 7:1, pp. 60–75.
Lilley, Peter (1989) Speech of 5 September 1989. Draft at OFTEL Library.
Littlechild, Stephen (1988) 'Economic Regulation of Privatised Water Authorities and Some Further Reflections', *Oxford Review of Economic Policy* 4:2 (Summer), pp. 40–67.
Longstreth, Frank (1988) 'From Corporatism to Dualism?': Thatcherism and the Climacteric of British Trade Unions in the 1980s', *Political Studies* 36:3, pp. 413–32.
Lukes, Steven (1974) *Power: A Radical View* (London: Macmillan).
McAllister, Ian and Studlar, Donley (1989) 'Popular Versus Elite Views of Privatization: The Case of Britain', *Journal of Public Policy* 9:2, pp. 157–78.
McIlroy, John (1988) *Trade Unions in Britain Today* (Manchester: Manchester University Press).
McIlroy, John (1991) *The Permanent Revolution? Conservative Law and the Trade Unions* (Nottingham: Spokesman).
MacInnes, J. (1987) *Thatcherism At Work* (Milton Keynes: Open University Press).
McKie, James W. (1989) 'US Regulatory Policy', in K. Button and D. Swann (eds) *The Age of Regulatory Reform* (Oxford: Oxford University Press), pp. 27–48.
McVicar, Malcolm (1990) 'Education Policy: Education as a Business?', in S.P. Savage and L. Robins (eds) *Public Policy Under Thatcher* (New York: St Martin's Press), pp. 131–44.
McVicar, Malcolm and Robins, Lynton (1994) 'Education Policy: Market Forces or Market Failure?', in S.P. Savage, R. Atkinson, and Lynton Robins (eds) *Public Policy in Britain* (New York: St Martin's Press), pp. 203–20.
Maloney, William and Richardson, J.J. (1992) 'Post-Privatisation Regulation in Britain', *Politics* 12:2 (October), pp. 14–20.
Marquand, David (1988) *The Unprincipled Society: New Demands and Old Politics* (London: Fontana).
Marsh, David (1991) 'Privatization Under Mrs. Thatcher: A Review of the Literature', *Public Administration* 69 (Winter), pp. 459–80.

Marsh, David (1992) *The New Politics of British Trade Unionism: Union Power and the Thatcher Legacy* (Basingstoke: Macmillan).

Marsh, David and Rhodes, R.A.W. (1992a) 'Implementing Thatcherism: Policy Change in the 1980s', *Parliamentary Affairs* 45:1 (January), pp. 33–49.

Marsh, David and Rhodes, R.A.W. (eds) (1992b) *Implementing Thatcherite Policies: Audit of an Era* (Buckingham: Open University Press).

Marwick, Arthur (1968) *Britain in the Century of Total War: War, Peace and Social Change 1900–1967* (Harmondsworth: Penguin Books).

Mayhew, Ken (1991) 'The Assessment: the UK Labour Market in the 1980s', *Oxford Review of Economic Policy* 7:1, pp. 1–17.

Metcalf, David (1991) 'British Unions: Dissolution or Resurgence?', *Oxford Review of Economic Policy* 7:1, pp. 18–32.

Metcalf, David (1993) 'Industrial Relations and Economic Performance', *British Journal of Industrial Relations* 31:2, pp. 255–83.

Middlemas, Keith (1979) *Politics in Industrial Society* (London: André Deutsch).

Millward, Neil; Stevens, Mark; Smart, David; and Hawes, W.R. [MSSH] (1992) *Workplace Industrial Relations in Transition: The ED/ESRC/PSI/ACAS Surveys* (Aldershot: Dartmouth).

Minford, Patrick (1988) 'Mrs Thatchers's Economic Reform Programme', in Skidelsky (ed.) *Thatcherism* (London: Chatto and Windus), pp. 93–106.

Minford, Patrick (1991) *The Supply Side Revolution in Britain* (London: Edward Elgar/IEA).

Mitchell, Timothy (1991) 'The Limits of the State: Beyond Statist Approaches and Their Critics', *American Political Science Review* 85:1, pp. 77–96.

Monks, John (1993) 'A Trade Union View of WIRS3', *British Journal of Industrial Relations* 31:2, pp. 227–33.

Moon, Jeremy (1993) *Innovative Leadership in Democracy: Policy Change Under Thatcher* (Aldershot: Dartmouth).

Moon, Jeremy; Richardson, J.J.; and Smart, Paul (1986) 'The Privatisation of British Telecom: A Case Study of the Extended Process of Legislation', *European Journal of Political Research* 14:1, pp. 339–55.

Moore, John (1983) 'Why Privatise?'. Speech given on 1 November, Treasury Press Release 190/83.

Moore, John (1984) 'A People's Capital Market'. Speech given on 5 December.

Moran, Michael (1988) 'Industrial Relations', in H. Drucker, P. Dunleavy, A. Gamble, and G. Peele (eds) *Developments in British Politics 2*, revised edition (New York: St Martin's Press), pp. 279–94.

Moran, Michael and Prosser, Tony (eds) (1994) *Privatization and Regulatory Change in Europe* (Buckingham: Open University Press).

Morgan, Austin (1992) *Harold Wilson* (London: Pluto Press).

Morgan, Kenneth (1988) 'The Twentieth Century (1914–1987)', in *idem* (ed) *The Oxford History of Britain* (Oxford: Oxford University Press), pp. 582–661.

Morris, Tim (1995) 'Annual Review Article 1994', *British Journal of Industrial Relations* 33:1 (March), pp. 117–35.

Newman, Karin (1986) *The Selling of British Telecom* (New York: St Martin's Press).

Norton, Philip (1991) *The British Polity*, 2nd edition (New York: Longman).

O'Gorman, Frank (1986) *British Conservatism: Conservative Thought from Burke to Thatcher* (New York: Longman).

Olson, Mancur (1982) *The Rise and Decline of Nations: Economic Growth, Stagflation and Social Rigidities* (New Haven: Yale University Press).

Peacock, Alan (1984) 'Privatisation in Perspective', *Three Banks Review* 144 (December), pp. 3–25.

Peacock, Alan (1991) 'Enter the Regulators', in C. Veljanvoski (ed.) *The Regulators and the Market* (London: IEA), pp. 79–84.

Peele, Gillian (1988) 'State and Civil Liberties', in H. Drucker, P. Dunleavy, A. Gamble, and G. Peele (eds) *Developments in British Politics 2*, revised edition (London: Macmillan), pp. 144–75.

Pickup, Laurie; Stokes, G.; Meadowcroft, S.; Goodwin, P.; Tyson, B.; and Kenny, F. (1991) *Bus Deregulation in the Metropolitian Areas* (Aldershot: Avebury).

Pint, Ellen (1990) 'Nationalization and Privatization: A Rational-Choice Perspective on Efficiency', *Journal of Public Policy* 10:3, pp. 267–98.

Pirie, Madsen (1988a) *Micropolitics* (Aldershot: Wildwood House).

Pirie, Madsen (1988b) *Privatization: Threory, Practice and Choice* (Aldershot: Wildwood House).

Pirie, Madsen (1988c) 'Principles of Privatization', in M.A. Walker (ed.) *Privatization: Tactics and Techniques* (Vancouver, B.C.: The Fraser Institute), pp. 3–15.

Pitt, Douglas (1990) 'An Essentially Contestable Organisation: British Telecom and the Privatisation Debate', in J.J. Richardson (ed.) *Privatisation and Deregulation in Canada and Britain* (Aldershot: Dartmouth), pp. 55–76.

Plant, Raymond (1988) 'Ideology', in H. Drucker, P. Dunleavy, A. Gamble, and G. Peele (eds) *Developments in British Politics 2*, revised edition (New York: St Martin's Press), pp.8–33.

Pollard, Sidney (1969) *The Development of the British Economy 1914–1967*, 2nd edition (London: Edward Arnold).

Post Office Engineering Union (1984) *Making the Future Work: The Broad Strategy* (London).

Punnett, R.M. (1988) *British Government and Politics*, 5th edition (Chicago: Dorsey).

Purcell, John (1991) 'The Rediscovery of the Management Prerogative: The Management of Labour Relations in the 1980s', *Oxford Review of Economic Policy* 7:1, pp. 33–43.

Purcell, John (1993) 'The End of Institutional Industrial Relations', *The Political Quarterly* 64:1, pp. 6–23.

Pym, Francis (1984) *The Politics of Consent.* (London: Hamish Hamilton).

Raab, Charles (1993) 'Education and the Impact of the New Right', in G. Jordan and N. Ashford (eds) *Public Policy and the Impact of the New Right* (London: Pinter), pp. 230–50.

Reed, Peter (1984) 'Taking Regulation Out of Politics: The Case of the Civil Aviation Authority', *Public Money* 5:2 (September), pp. 27–30.

Rees, Ray (1986) 'Is There an Economic Case for Privatisation?', *Public Money* 5:4 (March), pp. 19–26.

Rhodes, R.A.W. (1992) 'Local Government Finance', in D. Marsh and R.A.W. Rhodes (eds) *Implementing Thatcherite Policies* (Buckingham: Open University Press), pp. 50–64.

Rhodes, R.A.W. (1994) 'The Hollowing Out of the State: the Changing Nature of the Public Service in Britain', *The Political Quarterly* 65:2, pp. 138–51.

Richardson, Jeremy J.; Maloney, W.A.; and Rudig, W. (1992) 'The Dynamics of Policy Change: Lobbying and Water Privatization', *Public Administration* 70 (Summer), pp. 157–75.

Richardson, Jeremy J. (1994) 'The Politics and Practice of Privatization in Britain', in V. Wright (ed.) *Privatization in Western Europe: Pressures, Problems and Paradoxes* (London: Pinter), pp. 57–82.

Riddell, Peter (1985) *The Thatcher Government* (Oxford: Basil Blackwell).

Riddell, Peter (1989) *The Thatcher Decade* (Oxford: Basil Blackwell).

Ridley, Nicholas (1991) *'My Style of Government': The Thatcher Years* (London: Hutchinson).

Roberts, Jane; Elliott, David; and Houghton, Trevor (1991) *Privatising Electricity: The Politics of Power* (London: Belhaven Press).

Robins, Lynton (1994) 'The Education Issue: The Search for Radical Solutions to Raise Standards', in B. Jones (ed.) *Political Issues in Britain Today* (Manchester: Manchester University Press), pp. 170–82.

Rubery, Jill (1986) 'Trade Unions in the 1980s: The Case of the United Kingdom', in R. Edwards, P. Garonna, and F. Toedtling (eds) *Unions in Crisis and Beyond* (Dover, MA: Auburn House), pp. 61–113.

Samuel, Raphael, *et al.* (1986) *The Enemy Within: Pit Villages and the Miners' Strike of 1984–5* (London: Routledge and Kegan Paul).

Sarlvik, Bo and Crewe, Ivor (1983) *Decade of Dealignment: The Conservative Victory of 1979 and Electoral Trends in the 1970s* (Cambridge: Cambridge University Press).

Saunders, Peter (1995) 'Privatization, Share Ownership and Voting', *British Journal of Political Science* 25, pp. 131–37.

Savage, Stephen and Robins, Lynton (1990) 'Introduction', in S.P. Savage and L. Robins (eds) *Public Policy Under Thatcher* (New York: St Martin's Press), pp. 1–7.

Saville, John (1986) 'An Open Conspiracy: Conservative Politics and the Miners' Strike 1984–5', in R. Miliband, J. Saville, M. Liebman, and L. Panitch (eds) *Socialist Register 1985/86* (London: Merlin Press), pp. 295–329.

Self, Peter (1990) 'What's Wrong With Government? The Problem of Public Choice', *The Political Quarterly* 61, pp. 23–35.

Sheaff, Mike (1988) 'NHS Ancillary Services and Competitive Tendering', *Industrial Relations Journal* 19 (Summer), pp. 93–105.

Shibutani, Tamotsu (1961) *Society and Personality: An Interactionist Approach to Social Psychology* (Englewood Cliffs, NJ: Prentice-Hall).

Skidelsky, Robert (1988) 'Introduction', in *idem* (ed.) *Thatcherism* (London: Chatto and Windus), pp. 1–23.

Smith, David (1987) *The Rise and Fall of Monetarism* (Harmondsworth: Penguin Books).

Smith, Paul; Fosh, Patricia; Martin, Roderick; Morris, Huw; and Undy, Roger (1993) 'Ballots and Union Government in the 1980s', *British Journal of Industrial Relations* 31:3, pp. 365–82.

Society of Telecom Executives (1983) *Liberalisation, Privatisation & Regulation: What future for British Telecom?* (London: STE), July.

Stanley, Peter (1990) 'Deregulation in the Outer Metropolitan Area', in P. Bell and P. Cloke (eds) *Deregulation and Transport: Market Forces in the Modern World* (London: David Fulton), pp. 84–99.

Steel, David (1984) 'Government and the New Hybrids', in D. Steel and D. Heald (eds) *Privatizing Public Enterprises* (London, RIPA), pp. 101–12.

Steel, David and Heald, David (1985) 'The Privatization of Public Enterprises, 1979–83', in P. Jackson (ed.) *Implementing Government Policy Initiatives: the Thatcher Administration 1979–83* (London, RIPA), pp. 69–91.

Stelzer, Irwin M. (1991) 'Regulatory Methods: A Case for "Hands Across the Atlantic"', in C. Veljanovski (ed.) *Regulators and the Market* (London: IEA), pp. 59–75.

Stewart, Michael (1978) *Politics and Economic Policy in the UK Since 1964: The Jekyll and Hyde Years* (Oxford: Pergamon Press).

Stoker, Gerry (1990) 'Government Beyond Whitehall', in P. Dunleavy, A. Gamble and G. Peele (eds) *Developments in British Politics 3* (New York: St Martin's Press), pp. 126–49.

Survey of Current Affairs (1990) 'Telecommunications' (London: Foreign and Commonwealth Office), pp. 432–4.

Survey of Current Affairs (1991) 'Telecommunications' (London: Foreign and Commonwealth Office), pp. 108–9.

Survey of Current Affairs (1991) 'Telecommunications Licences' (London: Foreign and Commonwealth Office, 1991), pp. 347–8.

Talley, Wayne (1988) 'Competition in the Provision of US and UK Urban Bus Services: Privatisation vs Deregulation', in J.S. Dodgson and N. Topham (eds) *Bus Deregulation and Privatisation: An International Perspective* (Aldershot: Avebury), pp. 171–84.

Talley, Wayne (1989) 'Regulatory Reform of the US and UK Inter-city Bus Industries', in K. Button and D. Swann (eds) *The Age of Regulatory Reform* (Oxford: Oxford University Press), pp. 257–78.

Taylor, Robert (1983) 'Thatcher's Public Putsch', *Management Today* (May), pp. 54–9 and 144.

Taylor-Gooby, Peter (1993) 'The New Educational Settlement: National Curriculum and Local Management', in P. Taylor-Gooby and R. Lawson (eds) *Markets and Managers: New Issues in the Delivery of Welfare* (Buckingham: Open University Press), pp. 102–16.

Taylor-Gooby, Peter and Lawson, Robyn (1993) 'Where We Go From Here: The New Order in Welfare', in *idem* (eds) *Markets and Managers: New Issues in the Delivery of Welfare* (Buckingham: Open University Press), pp. 132–49.

Tebbit, Norman (1983) 'Industrial Relations in the Next Two Decades: Government Objectives', *Employee Relations* 5:1, pp. 3–6.

Terry, Michael (1983) 'Shop Stewards Through Expansion and Recession', *Industrial Relations Journal* 14:3 (Autumn), pp. 49–58.

Terry, Michael (1986) 'How Do We Know If Shop Stewards Are Getting Weaker?', *British Journal of Industrial Relations* 24:2 (July), pp. 169–79.

Thatcher, Margaret (1993) *The Downing Street Years* (New York: HarperCollins).

Thomas, Ceri (1988) 'Contracting-Out: Managerial Strategy or Political Dogma?', in V.V. Ramanadham (ed.) *Privatisation in the UK* (London: Routledge), pp. 153–70.

Thomas, David (1984) 'The Union Response to Denationalization', in D. Steel and D. Heald (eds) *Privatizing Public Enterprises* (London: RIPA), pp. 59–75.

Thompson, D.J. (1987) 'Privatisation in the UK', *European Economic Review* 31, pp. 368–74.

Tomlinson, J.R.G. (1989) 'The Schools', in D. Kavanagh and A. Seldon (eds) *The Thatcher Effect* (Oxford: Clarendon Press), pp. 183–97.

Turnbull, Peter J. (1986) 'The "Japanisation" of Production and Industrial Relations at Lucas Electrical', *Industrial Relations Journal* 17 (Autumn), pp. 193–206.

Undy, Roger and Martin, Roderick (1984) *Ballots and Trade Union Democracy* (Oxford: Basil Blackwell).

Veljanovski, Cento (1987) *Selling the State: Privatisation in Britain* (London: Weidenfeld and Nicolson).

Veljanovski, Cento (ed) (1991) *Regulators and the Market: An Assessment of the Growth of Regulation in the UK* (London: IEA).

Vickers, John (1991) 'Government Regulatory Policy', *Oxford Review of Economic Policy* 7:3, pp. 13–30.

Vickers, John and Wright, Vincent (1989) 'The Politics of Industrial Privatisation in Western Europe: An Overview', in *idem* (eds) *The Politics of Privatisation in Western Europe* (London: Frank Cass), pp. 1–30.

Vickers, John and Yarrow, George (1988) *Privatization: An Economic Analysis* (Cambridge, MA: MIT Press).

Vickers, John and Yarrow, George (1991) 'Reform of the Electricity Supply Industry in Britain', *European Economic Review* 35 (April), pp. 485–95.

Vickers, John and Yarrow, George (1991) 'The British Electricity Experiment', *Economic Policy* 12 (April), pp. 187–232.

Walker, David (1990) 'Enter the Regulators', *Parliamentary Affairs* 43:2 (April), pp. 149–58.

Weale, Albert (1990) 'Social Policy', in P. Dunleavy, A. Gamble and G. Peele (eds) *Developments in British Politics 3* (New York: St Martin's Press), pp. 197–220.

Wedderburn, Lord (1989) 'Freedom of Association and Philosophies of Labour Law', *Industrial Labour Journal* 18:1 (March), pp. 1–38.

White, Peter (1988) 'British Experience with Deregulation of Local Bus Services', in J.S. Dodgson and N. Topham (eds) *Bus Deregulation and Privatisation: An International Perspective* (Aldershot: Avebury), pp. 13–44.

Whitty, Geoff (1990) 'The Politics of the 1988 Education Reform Act', in P. Dunleavy, A. Gamble and G. Peele (eds) *Developments in British Politics 3* (New York: St Martin's Press), pp. 305–17.

Whitty, Geoff and Menter, Ian (1989) 'Lessons of Thatcherism: Education Policy in England and Wales 1979–88', *Journal of Law and Society* 16:1, pp. 42–64.

Willetts, David (1992) *Modern Conservatism* (Harmondsworth: Penguin).

Willman, Paul and Cave, Alan (1994) 'The Union of the Future: Super-Unions or Joint Ventures?', *British Journal of Industrial Relations* 32:3, pp. 395–412.

Willman, Paul; Morris, Timothy; and Aston, Beverly (1993) *Union Business: Trade Union Organisation and Financial Reform in the Thatcher Years* (Cambridge: Cambridge University Press).

Wiltshire, Kenneth (1987) *Privatisation: The British Experience* (Melbourne: Longman Cheshire).

Wolfe, Joel D. (1989a) 'Reorganizing Interest Representation: A Political Analysis of Privatization in Britain', in R.E. Foglesong and J.D. Wolfe (eds) *The Politics of Economic Adjustment: Pluralism, Corporatism, and Privatization* (New York: Greenwood), pp. 9–25.

Wolfe, Joel D. (1989b) 'Democracy and Economic Adjustment: A Comparative Analysis of Political Change', in R.E. Foglesong and J.D. Wolfe (eds) *The Politics of Economic Adjustment: Pluralism, Corporatism, and Privatization* (New York: Greenwood), pp. 153–76.

Wolfe, Joel (1991) 'State Power and Ideology in Britain: Mrs Thatcher's Privatization Programme', *Political Studies* 39:2, pp. 237–52.

Young, Hugo (1990) *One of Us: A Biography of Margaret Thatcher* (London: Pan).

Young, Stephen (1986) 'The Nature of Privatisation in Britain, 1979–85', *West European Politics* 9:2, pp. 235–52.

Index